MOBILIZING AGAINST INEQUALITY

Frank W. Pierce Memorial Lectureship and Conference Series
Number 15

This book is published with an accompanying website that will provide
case studies, updates, and links to additional information:

http://www.mobilizing-against-inequality.info

MOBILIZING AGAINST INEQUALITY

Unions, Immigrant Workers, and
the Crisis of Capitalism

**Edited by Lee H. Adler,
Maite Tapia, and Lowell Turner
Foreword by Ana Avendaño**

ILR PRESS

AN IMPRINT OF

CORNELL UNIVERSITY PRESS   ITHACA AND LONDON

First published 2014 by Cornell University Press
First printing, Cornell Paperbacks, 2014
Printed in the United States of America

Library of Congress Cataloging-in-Publication Data

Mobilizing against inequality : unions, immigrant workers, and the crisis of
capitalism / edited by Lee H. Adler, Maite Tapia, and Lowell Turner.
        pages cm
    Includes bibliographical references and index.
    ISBN 978-0-8014-5279-6 (cloth : alk. paper)
    ISBN 978-0-8014-7933-5 (pbk. : alk. paper)
    1. Foreign workers—Labor unions—Organizing—Case studies. 2. Minority
labor union members—Case studies. 3. Labor movement—Case studies.
I. Adler, Lee H., editor of compilation. II. Tapia, Maite, 1981– editor of
compilation. III. Turner, Lowell, editor of compilation. IV. Tapia, Maite,
1981– Union campaigns as countermovements. Contains (work):
    HD6490.R2M63   2014
    331.87'32086912—dc23   2013045579

Cornell University Press strives to use environmentally responsible suppliers and
materials to the fullest extent possible in the publishing of its books. Such materials
include vegetable-based, low-VOC inks and acid-free papers that are recycled,
totally chlorine-free, or partly composed of nonwood fibers. For further information, visit our website at www.cornellpress.cornell.edu.

Cloth printing   10 9 8 7 6 5 4 3 2 1
Paperback printing   10 9 8 7 6 5 4 3 2 1

Contents

Foreword

Ana Avendaño

The case studies collected in *Mobilizing against Inequality* expertly explore what is increasingly apparent to scholars, labor activists, and workers: traditional models of worker representation that have allowed workers to win a greater share of productivity and a political voice are failing to adapt to a changing economic and political environment. In recent decades, corporate-funded politicians have pushed trade liberalization, privatization, and austerity. Employers have shifted traditional employment relationships and informalized workers through "subcontracting, privatization, or some other form of intermediary contracting arrangement in order to reduce labor costs and avoid regulations associated with formal employment."[1] Workers' share of national income is in decline worldwide, in tandem with union density. Only 7 percent of the world's formal economy is organized into free and independent trade unions. With a sharp decline in union density and collective bargaining coverage, inequality has increased dramatically and threatens global growth and stability.

In the Global North, perhaps nowhere are these trends more clearly illustrated than in the expansion of low-wage workplaces, many of which employ a majority immigrant workforce. With globalization, many workers have seen their local economies devastated and been forced to seek employment in richer economies. International migration has become a large and growing phenomenon, with more than 200 million people now living outside of their home countries for extended periods.[2] Few poor migrants from rural areas can secure formal jobs or a path to citizenship. They rely instead on low wages from temporary, contingent, and informal employment to survive. Often this is in unseen and underappreciated jobs in agricultural, domestic work, the service sector, subcontracted maintenance services, or atomized supply chains.

The authors, however, also make clear that one of the front lines against the current crisis in capitalism has been the "countermovement" of union campaigns in immigrant workplaces. In order to build a more democratic and equitable society out of the crisis, workers and their organizations must lift up the bottom of the labor market and build new models of worker representation in those sectors. Unions, struggling to reverse declining membership and account for the growing contingent and informal workforces, have developed creative organizing strategies for protecting and representing workers in changing workplaces. This has often been done by embracing community-based organizations, building trust with immigrant workers, and taking on their unique challenges in societies where immigrants are too often excluded from basic rights.

In the United States, from the time of Samuel Gompers until 2000, official union policy too often reflected national immigration policies and was discriminatory and protectionist in nature. This closed perspective on collective bargaining extended to women and workers of color in many cases. Yet, historically, immigrant workers have also been a source of activism, creativity, and power in organized labor. In recent years, union practitioners in nearly every sector have had to face the obvious conclusion that in a globalized economy, the strength of the labor movement depends on organizing and fighting for all workers, regardless of national origin.

From my time with the United Food and Commercial Workers International Union to my current role at the AFL-CIO, I have seen a remarkable transition in the labor movement. After years of seeing employers use immigration law and "employer sanctions" to undermine organizing drives among undocumented immigrants, thus jeopardizing standards for all workers, I was involved in the hard internal politics behind the labor movement's historic call for legalization and immigration reform in 2000. I drew hope from the 2003 Immigrant Workers Freedom Ride. In 2006, with a small delegation of union officials, I witnessed a group of Latino immigrants in a chapter of the National Day Laborers Organizing Network (NDLON) employ the strategies and tactics of an earlier era of the labor movement and reach a consensus not to work for less than a $15 an hour. Subsequently, the national AFL-CIO passed a resolution that encouraged worker centers to affiliate with its national and local labor union bodies. This dramatic change in labor union politics has resulted in connecting AFL-CIO affiliates with worker centers and their networks like NDLON in dynamic partnerships to expand the labor movement and adopt new organizing strategies.

The resolution was both a recognition of the growing importance of worker centers in immigrant and other marginalized communities left behind by industrial unionism, and an admission that labor's institutions needed to embrace aspects of worker centers' movement-based approach to organizing workers. In the process of building partnerships, encouraging examples have emerged of workers rebuilding power through movement-based community unionism. The CLEAN Carwash Campaign,[3] for example, has evolved from a fight to enforce labor standards to a comprehensive initiative to address the structural exploitation of the industry and ingrained inequities in the *carwashero* community. By building trust with a network of community-based organizations, it has utilized the institutionalized power of a labor union to begin to reshape the carwash industry and has adopted movement-based aspects of worker center organizing to address broader issues in the immigrant community.

In other cases, too, the AFL-CIO has found that worker movements are often in need of institutional support. Established institutions can bring not only expertise and funding, but also can open political spaces not available to immigrant workers and local organizations. When movement and institution forces come together in this way workers can build power even in informal or contingent employment relationships.

For example, the National Domestic Workers Alliance built relationships with local unions to gain support for organizing and policy initiatives. These relationships eventually led the AFL-CIO to push for the International Labour Organization's (ILO) Domestic Workers Convention (Convention 189) and the inclusion of domestic workers in the ILO process, ceding a seat to a domestic worker and encouraging eleven other representative organizations to do so as well. In 2011, the National Taxi Workers Alliance was granted an Organizing Charter by the AFL-CIO, giving it affiliate status in the Federation, despite being an organization made up of independent contractors. The New York City Taxi Workers have used powerful movement building and their union affiliation to leverage demands for a fare increase and the establishment of a health fund with the NYC Taxi and Limousine Commission. The Alliance is now working with the AFL-CIO Organizing Department to build thirty locals of taxi drivers across the United States in the next seven years—all unified under the national charter.

To be sure, as *Mobilizing against Inequality* lays out, the challenges associated with organizing immigrant workers are many and it is often difficult to navigate competing institutional and movement priorities. When intentional collaborative work is done, true partnerships and affiliations will be meaningful. But, after affiliations began in 2006, some partnerships stagnated as they were formed prior to building a meaningful relationship. At the first Worker Center Advisory Council meeting on January 25, 2013, between the AFL-CIO and worker center leaders, one representative stressed that active worker centers do not want to be junior partners in a static state federation of central labor councils.

Unions must address this fundamental tension as we work to build an inclusive movement for a just economy. Unions will need to learn new ways of doing business, experiment with new forms of worker representation, share power with community partners, and build trust in historically underrepresented communities. This is a challenge that will need to be addressed across national boundaries, in globalized industries, and in the vast informal economy. It is in this regard that this volume brings considerable value, as it begins the serious global conversation on how organized labor must respond to the capitalist crisis and its ravaging of immigrant workers and their families.

For readers in the United States, this is also a timely reminder that unions must begin to prepare for an unprecedented organizing opportunity on the horizon. Despite the fall 2013 difficulties in gaining passage of the Senate immigration bill in the House of Representatives, we are still closer than ever to winning far-reaching, if imperfect, reform of our immigration system. This has been a top institutional priority for the labor movement and its allies. After decades of gridlock and human suffering, more than 11 million undocumented immigrants currently living in the United States may be able to win a roadmap to citizenship. Unscrupulous employers may no longer be so easily able to pursue a race to the bottom in wages and standards by exploiting vulnerable immigrant workers and dividing working people. Unions must prepare to work as equal partners with the immigrant community and its allies to aid in this transition period and ensure that their rights are protected in the legalization process.

With progressively less density in most industries, the labor movement is at a critical juncture in its history. Building a renewed movement with the ability to represent workers in today's economy will be a monumental challenge. Will labor respond to this crisis as it did in the 1930s with the growth of industrial unionism, or will workers increasingly toil in exploitative conditions in a corporate-driven society? With the rampant growth of low-wage work and lawmakers chipping away at already eroded social safety nets, the labor movement, now more than ever, needs to forge strategies that bring workers out of a state of precariousness and train them to become informed agents of change.

The bold workers and organizers in these campaigns and elsewhere remind us that the economy is not out of our control, shaped solely by the dictates of business interests, Wall Street bankers, and macro-level market forces. In California, New York, Paris, and London, the most vulnerable workers are building a new kind of power and are challenging us to rethink the way we evaluate the role of unions in representing workers. We must take this collection as both a nascent expression of hope for the future and a challenge for practitioners to take up in the coming years of struggle.

Acknowledgments

For a four-country research project that stretched across four years, there are many colleagues, practitioners, and institutions to thank. Footnotes in selected chapters offer specific acknowledgments. Because not everyone will read the full text, let alone the footnotes, we highlight our most significant acknowledgments here.

Funding for the research was more than generous: a large grant from the Hans Böckler Foundation for comparative work, following seed funding from the Carnegie Corporation and the Public Welfare Foundation that launched the project.

Institutional support—hosting, resources, contacts—was provided by the ILR School at Cornell University (our primary base of operations), the Worker Institute at Cornell, two CNRS research institutes in France—IDHE at the Ecole Normale Supérieure in Cachan/Paris and LEST at the University of Aix-Marseille, and the Fondation Maison des Sciences de l'Homme.

Insightful comments on the complete manuscript were provided by Ana Avendaño at the LERA conference in San Diego in January 2013, by Ruth Milkman at the March 2013 International Labour Process Conference at Rutgers University, by Melanie Simms at the June 2013 Council for European Studies international conference at the University of Amsterdam, and by Miguel Martinez Lucio, who commented in detail on all chapters and in so doing made significant contributions to our final revisions.

With research from the four countries virtually complete, we met at a workshop in Frankfurt in November 2011, hosted by the Hans Böckler Foundation and the German Metalworkers Union (IG Metall). We invited union commentators from each country, including Wilf Sullivan from the British TUC, Francine Blanche from the French CGT, Ana Avendaño from the AFL-CIO, along with German unionists Peter Bremme from ver.di, Wolf Jürgen Röder, Petra Wecklik and Bobby Winkler from the IG Metall. Academic commentators included Sébastien Chauvin, Steve French, and Otto Jacobi.

Along the way, research findings were presented at various university workshops and academic conferences, including meetings of the Transatlantic Social Dialogue (cosponsored by the European Trade Union Institute, Hans Böckler Foundation, and the ILR School/Worker Institute at Cornell) in 2010 at the ETUI in Brussels and 2011 at a training center of the IG Metall in Inzell, Germany.

Case study reports and country literature reviews by field researchers who are not contributors to this volume include Mirvat Abd el ghani, Chiara Benassi, Zyama Ciupijus, Laetitia Dechaufour, Ian Greer, Nathan Lillie, Emilija Mitrovic, Marion Quintin, and Oliver Trede. Their work, along with full case study reports and literature reviews by authors of this book, are posted in full at http://www.mobilizing-against-inequality.info.

In addition to the colleagues and practitioners named above, others who provided valuable information, insights, and contacts include Rosemary Batt, Omar Benfaid, Elodie Béthoud, Maud Billon, Liz Blackshaw, Matthew Bolton, Paul Bouffartigue, Hélène Bouneaud, Mary Catt, Sylvie Contrepois, Isabel da Costa, Pierre Coutaz, Claude Didry, Laurent Grognu, Lena Hipp, Neil Jameson, Maria Jepsen, Annette Jobert, Anousheh Karvar, Harry Katz, Annalisa Lendaro, Jean-Louis Malys, Geri Mannion, Paul Marginson, Sonja Marko, Ariel Mendez, Paul Nowak, Pat O'Neil, John Page, Philippe Pochet, Daniel Richter, Carl Roper, Catherine Sauviat, Penny Schantz, Agnes Schreieder, Kurt Vandaele, Yves Veyrier, and Jane Wills.

Noel Harvey, Roland Erne, and Bill Roche of the Irish Industrial Relations Association invited Lowell Turner to present an early draft of the introductory chapter as the Countess Markiewicz Memorial Lecture, in Dublin in November 2011, drawing an audience of about 100 academics and trade unionists who provided valuable questions and criticism in the early stage of writing and framing for the book.

At Cornell University, Vicki Errante and Anne Sieverding provided able administrative assistance throughout, and Anne pulled together our references into the book's bibliography. Bonnie Hockenberry and Ricci Curren guided us through the financial morass of sponsored projects with patience and good humor.

At Cornell University Press, Fran Benson provided strong editorial support and promoted this book with enthusiasm. Katherine Liu, Karen Laun, and Susan Barnett at Cornell University Press, plus Irina Burns, copyeditor, also provided important support during the production process. Do Mi Stauber did a splendid job putting together our index.

We especially want to emphasize the contributions of Otto Jacobi, Wolf Jürgen Röder, and Nikolaus Simon, who supported this project in various ways with great enthusiasm from start to finish.

Finally, we coeditors would like to thank our coauthors—Gabriella Alberti, Daniel Cornfield, Michael Fichter, Janice Fine, Jane Holgate, and Denisse Roca-Servat—for their fine work and collegiality. Over a four-year period, as collaboration and relationships deepened, deadlines were consistently met and hard feelings were virtually nonexistent even in our disagreements. It was a great pleasure for us to collaborate with a team of such outstanding and personable colleagues.

Lowell Turner, Maite Tapia, and Lee Adler

Acronyms and Abbreviations

ACORN	Association of Community Organizations for Reform Now
AFL-CIO	American Federation of Labor and Congress of Industrial Organizations
AFSCME	American Federation of State, County, and Municipal Employees
AMP	Asylum and Migration Policy
APEX	Association of Professional, Executive, Clerical and Computer Staff
BAVC	Bundesarbeitgeberverband Chemie e.V. (German employer association)
BIS	Department of Business, Innovation, and Skills
BME	black and minority ethnic
BNP	British National Party
C11	Collectif des Onze (coalition of five union confederations and six NGOs in France, 2009–2010)
CFDT	Confédération Française Démocratique du Travail (a French union confederation)
CGT	Confédération Générale du Travail (a French union confederation)
CLEAN	Community-Labor-Environmental Action Network
CLIWA	Coalition of Low Wage and Immigrant Workers Advocates

CNRS	Centre national de la recherche scientifique (national center for scientific research)
COMET	Construction Organizing Membership Education Training
CoVe	Commission on Vulnerable Employment
CSEA	Civil Service Employees Association
CTW	Change to Win
CWOC	Carwash Workers Organizing Committee
DGB	Deutscher Gewerkschaftsbund (German Labor Federation)
DWU	Domestic Workers United
EEC	European Economic Community
EMWU	European Migrant Workers Union
ESOL	English for Speakers of Other Languages
EU	European Union
FEETS	Fédération d'Equipement, Environment, Transports et Services (a branch of the French union confederation Force Ouvrière)
FN	Front National (National Front)
FO	Force Ouvrière (a French union confederation)
FSU	Fédération Syndicale Unitaire (a French union confederation)
GMB	Originally General Municipal Boilermakers; now known simply as GMB
HERE	Hotel Employees and Restaurant Employees Union
IBT	International Brotherhood of Teamsters
ICE	Immigration and Customs Enforcement
IDHE	Institutions et dynamiques historiques de l'économie, French research institute linked to CNRS
IG BAU	Industrie Gewerkschaft Bauen-Agrar-Umwelt (Industrial Union of Construction and Agriculture)
IG BCE	Industrie Gewerkschaft Bergbau, Chemie, Energie (Industrial Union of Mining, Chemicals and Energy)
IG Metall	Industrie Gewerkschaft Metall (Industrial Union of Metalworkers)
IOM	International Organization for Migration
IREM	Italian construction company
IWW	Industrial Workers of the World
JfC	Justice for Cleaners
KFC	Kentucky Fried Chicken (fast food restaurant)
LAWAC	Los Angeles Workers Advocates Coalition
LC	London Citizens
LEST	Laboratoire d'Economie et de Sociologie du Travail (French research institute linked to CNRS)

LGBT	lesbian, gay, bisexual, and transgender
LIUNA	Laborers International Union of North America
MigAr.ver.di	immigrant drop in center
MRNY	Make the Road New York
MWSU	Migrant Workers Support Unit
NAFTA	North American Free Trade Agreement
NAWJC	Northwest Arkansas Workers' Justice Center
NDLON	National Day Laborers Organizing Network
NGO	nongovernmental organization
NIP	National Integration Plan
NLRA	National Labor Relations Act
NMTDA	Nashville Metro Taxi Drivers Alliance
NOWCRJ	New Orleans Workers Center for Racial Justice
OECD	Organization for Economic Cooperation and Development
ONS	Office for National Statistics
PSI	Policy Studies Institute
PWD	Posted Workers Directive
RESF	Réseau d'Education Sans Frontières (French network of organizations fighting for the rights of immigrants and immigrants' children)
RESPEKT	"Respect" (anti-racist IG Metall campaign)
RMT	National Union of Rail, Maritime and Transport Workers
ROC-NY	Restaurant Opportunities Center New York
RWDSU	Retail, Wholesale, and Department Store Union
SEIU	Service Employees International Union
SMIC	Salaire minimum interprofessionnel de croissance (minimum wage in France)
SOAS	School of African and Oriental Studies
SSA	Social Security Administration
SUD	Solidaires Unitaires Démocratiques (a French union confederation)
T&G	shortened version of TGWU
TELCO	The East London Communities Organization
TGWU	Transport and General Workers Union, now known as UNITE
TLC	Transportation Licensing Commission
TUC	Trades Union Congress
UBC	United Brotherhood of Carpenters
UD	Union Départementale (regional union)
UFCW	United Food and Commercial Workers

UFT	United Federation of Teachers
UFW	United Farm Workers
ULR	Union learning representative
UMF	Union Modernisation Fund
UNISON	UK public service union
UNITE	New name for TGWU after merger with Amicus in 2007
UNSA	Union Syndicale (a French union confederation)
USW	United Steelworkers
ver.di	Vereinte Dienstleistungsgewerkschaft (United Services Union, Germany)
WASH	Workers Aligned for a Sustainable and Healthy New York
WSJ	*Wall Street Journal*

Part I

UNIONS AND THE MOBILIZATION OF IMMIGRANT WORKERS

ORGANIZING IMMIGRANT WORKERS

Lowell Turner

At this historical turning point, when global economic governance driven by market expansion and deregulation has failed, the ongoing battle for a sustainable economy hinges on two profound challenges: rising inequality and environmental destruction. In this book, we focus on the former, while acknowledging that solutions to the two central problems must be linked. Where economic growth is targeted and how the rewards are distributed will determine whether economic and social development is sustainable.

Rising inequality is well illustrated in a juxtaposition of contemporary concentrations of wealth, on the one hand, and workforces facing increasingly precarious circumstances, on the other. Labor markets in the Global North today have reached new levels of fragmentation, stagnant in the middle, with expanding low-wage workforces not benefiting from any kind of collective representation. The contributors to this volume share the belief that collective action is essential in battles to turn things around in the years ahead. Unions and other organizations of collective representation, however, will succeed only if they can overcome divisions and rally workers together in common purpose and organization. We also believe that a litmus test for success will be the ability to push up the low end, to give voice and bring unity to the millions of women, young workers, older workers, immigrants, and migrants who face the most vulnerable conditions of employment. This is no easy task, but as long as so many are lacking in representation, to be played off against each other and against more settled workforces, there can be little hope for an effective pushback against the economic injustice that characterizes our era.

To frame the chapters in this volume, this introductory chapter includes two separate but closely interrelated areas of emphasis: the context—the crisis of free-market capitalism—and an introduction to our research findings concerning union strategies toward immigrant workers. The two parts are separate but in today's global economy tightly linked.[1]

Unions and Immigrant Workers: A Four-Country Study

This book presents findings from a comparative study of union strategies toward immigrant workers in four countries: Germany, France, the United Kingdom, and the United States.[2] The work began in 2008 and has included researchers from across the four countries, producing four country literature reviews, about two hundred interviews with practitioners, twenty in-depth case studies, and four country summary papers.[3] In early November 2011, we met at a two-day workshop in Frankfurt, both researchers and invited commentators from trade unions in each of our countries, to discuss findings and work out comparative analysis and policy implications.[4] The book is a product of our research as well as workshop and email discussions that have helped develop the comparative analysis. We also decided at the workshop to link this book to a "living" website, so that we could post literature reviews and case studies in full, as well as updates and links to related publications by researchers working in the same area. Our hope is that this book will not "freeze" with publication but rather will stimulate ongoing dialogue based on research findings and policy implications.

The Context: Free-Market Capitalism in Crisis

Our research showed us very quickly that the challenges facing both unions and immigrant workers in today's fragmented labor markets are extremely difficult, and cannot be understood out of context: thirty years of global liberalization driven by unsustainable economic policies that brought us to a deep crisis of capitalism.[5] It is therefore important to step back for a moment and take a look at the crisis and its causes, the context in which the development of union strategy must take place.

Although the crisis spread quickly across the globe and took on many different forms, including a sustained crisis in the Eurozone, the financial collapse of

2008 that triggered escalating global crises was very much "made in America." And if we look beneath the many details, I believe that crisis can be explained by two interrelated factors: long-term average wage stagnation and financial deregulation, both integrally related to the collapse of the postwar social contract and a massive upward redistribution of wealth and power.

In its very essence, taking liberties with the complexity of modern economic development, the narrative of financial and economic collapse in the United States can be summarized as follows: "Had it not been for thirty years of average wage stagnation and an extraordinary upward redistribution of wealth in the United States, people would not have needed subprime loans. And if it had not been for thirty years of deregulation, culminating in financial free for all, people would not have been able to get subprime loans." As we now know, bad loans, with no effective regulators in sight, were packaged into toxic mortgage-backed securities, to spread the risk around. So effectively did the risk spread that financial collapse in the United States soon crashed the global economy.

The crisis is thus closely linked to the great concentrations of wealth and power that have come to dominate national and global economies alike.[6] Concentrations of wealth that have diminished sustainable buying power and demand-led economic growth even in the rich countries of the Global North; and related concentrations of political power promoting the market fundamentalist ideology that led us into reckless deregulation and the dead end politics of austerity.[7]

And here we tip our hat to the Occupy encampments of the fall of 2011. Many occupiers were young and untested, unclear on what they wanted, and could not camp out forever. Nonetheless, they succeeded in doing what many others had tried and failed to do: change the discourse, shine the light of crisis and causation on the extraordinary inequalities in contemporary society, on the concentrations of wealth and power that dominate policymaking and threaten our economic, democratic, social, and environmental futures. Whatever else follows in the years ahead, the Occupy movement provided a great service at a critical moment in the history of postwar capitalism.

How did things get to this point? It is a familiar story: the Reagan and Thatcher "revolutions," thirty years of global liberalization, a fertile context for employers to challenge unions. Widespread union decline in numbers and influence in much of the Global North left labor unable to prevent the spread of low-wage workforces. Low-wage work, much of it temporary and most of it lacking in any kind of collective representation, became the norm in expanding private sector services such as retail, hospitality, building services and domestic care, and spread also through outsourcing, privatization, and "union avoidance" into traditional union strongholds such as manufacturing, construction, transportation, and communication. What Guy Standing (2011) and others have called a vast new "precariat" expanded at the low end of a fragmented labor market. The politics of increasingly unequal societies have concentrated financial, economic, and political power in fewer and fewer hands.

The crisis reflects a fundamental tension between markets and democracy, between capitalism and social stability (Polanyi 1944). Temporary solutions to the inherent contradictions led to the serial crises of postwar capitalism in the Global North: inflation (1970s), public debt (1980s, 1990s), private debt (2000s), and finally financial collapse in 2008 (Streeck 2011a). In the United States, households dealt with stagnant average wages first by the entry of women into the workforce, then by working overtime and sometimes multiple jobs, and finally by running up unprecedented credit card and mortgage debt (Reich 2010). Weakly regulated financial institutions were all too willing to channel the gains of rising productivity—no longer claimed by the workforce—back into loans that fueled rising household debt. After the 2008 crash, with no ready new buffers in place, the crisis appeared to call the very sustainability of capitalism into question in the United States, Europe, and elsewhere.

What about varieties of capitalism? Comparative political economists and labor researchers have devoted much energy, especially since the early 1990s, to debating the continuing importance of contrasting national institutions, in liberal and coordinated market economies, against the forces of growing convergence in a global economy.[8] Clearly, differences in national political and economic institutions remain important. Yet on many dimensions, similarities have become more important than differences. Such dimensions include growing inequality, the growth of low-wage nonunion workforces, the expansion of precarious work often populated by immigrant workers, the inability of unions to speak with a coherent voice on behalf of all workers, a growing demonization of foreigners and especially Muslims in Europe and the United States. Germany is held up as a model, yet inequality has grown substantially there too since the mid-1990s, as low-wage, precarious work expanded across the economy.[9]

Wolfgang Streeck (2009), for one, has broken dramatically with the varieties of capitalism literature to remind us that capitalism's contours are constantly contested. Exceptional circumstances in the most economically developed countries produced apparent institutional equilibrium in the early decades of the postwar period, yet stability masked underlying dynamics and lulled social scientists into static crossnational analysis. Meanwhile, the very logic of capitalism drove actors to push against, and beyond, the constraints of regulation, even in the most coordinated of market economies. As political economists from Karl Marx to Karl Polanyi to Milton Friedman might have predicted, capitalism in the late twentieth century increasingly burst the bonds of social regulation, at both sector and national levels in a reinforcing context of global liberalization.

Thus runaway capitalism carried us all into economic crisis, including, for example, the supposedly well behaved Celtic Tigers of Ireland.[10] When the depth of the crisis became apparent in 2008, it was easy to believe that neoliberal ideology and policy would now be discredited, that we could introduce reforms and build toward a more sustainable society. In the United States in that year, people voted in large numbers for change. Many believed, and especially the millions of engaged young Americans who flocked to the Obama campaign, that with the dominant set of policies discredited and a new government in power, we could look forward to transformation toward a clean energy, inclusive, more socially balanced society.

In retrospect, Obama could have given us better leadership. It took him too long to figure out that bipartisanship was not an option. But it is not primarily Obama we should blame. Few of us anticipated the massive countermobilization—of interests, ideology, obstructionism, and right-wing populism—that would gather steam and choke off change in the United States so quickly.

But when we look back at similar crises and conflicts in the twentieth century, there is little reason to be surprised that transformation would be so difficult.[11] After the stock market crash of 1929 and the Great Depression that followed, it took until the mid-1930s for New Deal policy consolidation in the United States and until the late 1940s for managed capitalism to take hold throughout Western Europe. After the economic crises that began in 1973, it took until the 1980s for the Reagan/Thatcher governments to push things in a fundamentally new direction. And this is where we are now: in a sustained postcrash period of intense political conflict and experimentation that will determine the shape of a new order, if we are lucky enough to get there.

What we do know is that neoliberal capitalism as currently governed, with its extraordinary levels of inequality, is unsustainable even as it maintains policy dominance. It is *economically unsustainable* for the weak demand generated by the expansion of low-wage work. It is *politically unsustainable* for the concentrations of power that threaten the life of a vibrant democracy. It is *socially unsustainable* for the inevitable spread of protest, of social and labor unrest, whether from the left, right, or somewhere else. And most obviously: it is *environmentally unsustainable,* for there will be no stopping free-market capitalism from destroying the environment without a general shift toward greater social regulation.

We are looking then at perhaps a decade or more of political struggle between contending visions of the future. In the United States, for example, we might frame the conflict as tea party America, in Europe the politics of austerity, versus an alternative sustainable society. We know what neoliberal economic governance looks like but the alternative remains less clear. History does not move backward in time: it will not be the New Deal or the nation-based managed capitalism of the so-called Golden Years (which in any case were not so golden for everyone). If we are to find our way to an inclusive, well-regulated, sustainable global society it will be, like every other kind of social order, shaped in struggle.

The Challenge for Labor

If there is to be a successful mobilization against concentrated economic and political power, labor unions have an essential role to play. That role lies in helping to bring together the vast lower and middle segments of workforce and society—a good portion of what has come to be known as "the 99%." We believe that because immigrant workers occupy a central position in the low-wage workforces that reflect the growing inequalities of contemporary society, these workers and the organizations that promote their interests must surely have pride of place in the battles ahead.[12]

The particularities of immigration history vary from country to country. But processes of global liberalization since the 1970s have intensified the pressures in every context. We have witnessed a continuing push/pull of immigration from Latin America, Africa, the Middle East, and South Asia toward the richer countries of the Global North. Large flows of non-Caucasian—and thus more easily identified and stigmatized—workers and family members have entered Europe and North America, both with and without official documents. The open labor markets of the European Union have accelerated the movement of workers from poorer to richer regions within Europe. Immigrant workers, despite national policies that privilege skilled workers, typically enter at the labor market's low end, in the most precarious jobs whether or not they have officially sanctioned work documents.

The availability of low-wage immigrant labor has given employers a strengthened hand to push for freer labor markets and weaker unions, to play groups of workers off against each other, to fragment the collective cohesion and bargaining power of workers and their organizations of representation. Increasingly precarious workforces include large numbers of vulnerable immigrant workers everywhere in the Global North.

Thus the challenges facing unions to organize and advocate for immigrant and other low-wage workers are now in many ways similar across the Global North—despite significant national and local differences in union structures and the institutions in which collective representation takes shape. Unions have for the most part recognized the changing workforce realities and have changed their official policies, if not always their actual practice, accordingly. The change has come gradually, driven largely by the demands of immigrant workers themselves.

In the 1950s and 1960s, unions in Germany, France, the United Kingdom, and the United States tended toward restrictive orientations. This changed with the social movements of the 1960s and 1970s. Starting with the civil rights movement in the United States and sparked by 1968 strikes in France and across Europe, a contagion of protest was actively joined by immigrant workers fighting for their own interests, against discrimination in the workplace and society, for greater acceptance and incorporation.

The role played by immigrant workers in those earlier social movements launched internal union debate that to some extent changed the face of trade unionism across the Global North. The demands of immigrant workers, especially in the strike waves of the early 1970s, forced unions in many cases to move, if often haltingly, toward policies of inclusion. In parallel fashion, the social movements of that era included and contributed to a growing assertiveness of Hispanic workers in the United States, many of them immigrants, with long-term transformative effects for unions and politics in key parts of the country.

Progress was slow, but since the early 2000s major labor federations in much of the Global North have adopted policies that recognize immigrants above all as workers in need of organization and representation. In the United States in 2000, for example, the American Federation of Labor and Congress of Industrial Organizations (AFL-CIO), after a lengthy internal debate, threw off vestiges of protectionism to recognize workers as workers no matter the country of origin—and to emphasize the importance of organizing the millions of immigrants, with and without official documents, at work in the U.S. economy. The Trades Union Congress (TUC) in Britain and the German Labor Federation (DGB) in Germany have done the same.[13] Deeds do not always match words, still official policy statements are important, especially when they represent a break with the past and open the door for innovative strategy.

Mobilizing against Inequality

With such forces in play, we find great problems, limited progress, many defeats, but we also find some strikingly similar success stories for immigrant-based labor campaigns across our country cases. We began this stream of research in the United States, where some unions, beginning in the late 1980s and expanding in subsequent years, focused organizing efforts on low-wage, immigrant-based workforces in sectors such as building services and hospitality—driven by a recognition that in this arena lay significant prospects for labor movement revitalization.

Justice for Janitors, a comprehensive campaign that included strategic union leadership, grassroots mobilization, and coalition building, became a successful model for the Service Employees International Union (SEIU). First in Denver in 1986 and Los Angeles in 1990, then in numerous other U.S. cities, including in less union-friendly environments such as Houston and Miami, Justice for Janitors brought union representation and rising labor standards to tens of thousands of urban janitors, many of them immigrants. Hotel Workers Rising campaigns, led by the union Unite Here, have done the same for thousands of hotel housekeepers and other employees in cities across the country. In 2003, the AFL-CIO-sponsored Immigrant Workers Freedom Ride traveled 3,000 miles across the country to highlight the interests and the centrality of immigrant workers in the U.S. economy.

In the best cases, such campaigns transformed local politics. Thus by the early 2000s the Los Angeles County Federation of Labor had become an unrivaled political force in city politics. Ruth Milkman (2006, 2010) writes insightfully about the "LA model of organizing and advocacy" as a potential scenario for the future of the U.S. labor movement. One of our research case studies finds the United Steelworkers, in alliance with worker centers and other NGOs representing the interests of immigrant workers, pursuing a breakthrough campaign targeting thousands of L.A. carwash workers (Roca-Servat 2010).

We wondered to what extent similar processes, driven by similar problems and opportunities, might be taking place in other comparable countries of the Global North. The Hans Böckler Foundation shared our interest with a grant that enabled us to turn this study into a four-country comparison. We took our research on the road.

Everywhere we found similar problems, but in the United Kingdom, for example, we also found a successful Justice for Cleaners campaign, led by TGWU/Unite (the Transport and General Workers Union, now merged into Unite) and the vibrant community organization London Citizens (Holgate 2009a). In a sustained effort based in both workplace and community, the union brought in 2,000 new members from the immigrant-based ranks of cleaners at the Canary Wharf financial center and other locations.

We also found crossnational learning, as activists at TGWU and London Citizens brought over colleagues from the SEIU to offer lessons from campaigns in the United States. We were surprised to find unions in Europe learning from the U.S. labor movement, so heavily beaten down since the 1980s. One way to understand this phenomenon is that unions in the United States have what Alexander Gershenkron (1962) called the "advantages of backwardness": battered in the 1980s and 1990s, they were forced to innovate, and especially to return to the grassroots with strategic campaigning (Turner 2007a). As recent attacks on public sector collective representation show, the tide has not yet turned on the decline of labor movement in the United States, but if in the meantime others can learn from experiments in U.S. organizing, so much the better.

In France, we were deeply impressed by a union-led movement in support of undocumented workers that seemed to come out of nowhere in 2008. Chapter 2 of this book tells the story of a path-breaking effort on the part of a labor movement sometimes written off by labor scholars and even unionists in other parts of Europe. Research for this project has persuaded us that unions in France, weak in numbers but strong in mobilization capacity, organizationally fragmented yet increasingly collaborative in the wake of economic crisis, deserve to be taken more seriously. The *sans papiers* (without papers) movement of 2008–2010 brought together the demands of thousands of immigrant workers under a supportive umbrella led by the Confédération Générale du Travail (CGT) and subsequently joined by other union federations and NGOs in a Collectif des Onze. Workers came out of the shadows to occupy restaurants and building sites, to win surprisingly strong public support, and in many cases to secure work papers for legions of new union members (Barron et al. 2011; Quintin 2008, 2010).

In Germany, we were impressed by the effort made by unions and works councils to integrate immigrant workers into their ranks, especially through institutions of codetermination, vocational training, union membership, and leadership development. We found inspiring stories of immigrant worker integration by the IG Metall (Metalworkers Union) in Kiel, recent organizing efforts by ver.di (the united public and service sector union) in Hamburg, and the rise of immigrant workers to positions of leadership throughout the labor movement and the institutions of codetermination (Mitrovic 2011; Trede 2011). We did not find, however, cases of social movement mobilization on behalf of immigrant workers in Germany to parallel similar findings in France, the United Kingdom, and the United States. Understanding this difference is one of the puzzles we address in this book.

Successful Outcomes Are Possible: A Comparative Perspective

Divergent national union approaches are based on particular national histories and circumstances. Yet beyond the obvious differences, there are strong similarities in the fragmentation of today's labor markets, employer strategies, and the challenges facing unions. In the growing low-wage workforces where immigrant workers are so prominent, mobilization may not be easy but successful outcomes are possible. Key ingredients for Justice for Janitors and Hotel Workers

Rising in the United States, for Justice for Cleaners in the United Kingdom, and for the *sans papiers* movement in France include social justice framing and comprehensive campaign approaches. All of these campaigns were organized by innovative union strategists and at the same time grounded in both rank-and-file and broader social mobilization. In all of these cases, innovative union leaders viewed immigrant organizing as a vehicle for labor movement revitalization as well as a channel for efforts to bring representation to increasingly vulnerable workforces in fragmented labor markets. In each case, distinctive ethnic identities were accepted and even encouraged, ironically in pursuit of greater working class solidarity.

There is much work to be done. In the United States, we have witnessed successful union-led immigrant organizing campaigns, yet we have also experienced a nativist backlash fueled by anti-immigrant rhetoric that targets so-called illegal aliens. In the United Kingdom, Justice for Cleaners and other living wage campaigns have rallied immigrant workers, and the TUC has come out strongly in favor of more such efforts, yet most unions remain hesitant. In Germany, unions have done much to integrate immigrant workers in their strongholds but have yet to reverse inequality marked by the expansion of immigrant-rich, low-wage sectors not covered by codetermination or collective bargaining. In France, a breakthrough *sans papiers* movement has been powerful for its symbolism and lessons but remains small in relation to overall labor market segmentation and the limited influence of unions beyond their bases in the public sector and at large companies.

It is nonetheless possible to end this introductory chapter with a positive scenario based on credible causal implications. This may not be a likely scenario but there is no reason to think it is not a possible one. For social scientists whose interest extends beyond molecules, it is important to understand not only how we got into this mess but where we might go from here. Not only how market expansion has overwhelmed social regulation but where possibilities lie for pushback.

We see everywhere in the prosperous Global North an expansion of low-wage workforces, populated by immigrants, ethnic and racial minorities, women, and young workers, lacking in any meaningful collective representation (Jeffreys and Appay 2010). As unions wake up to this reality, decline breeds innovation in renewed efforts at organizing, advocacy, and coalition building. Successes foster internal union reform and strategic reorientation as well as the emergence of alternative forms of collective representation such as worker centers, alliances, and networks. Social justice framing highlights the politics of inequality and helps change a discourse so hopelessly misdirected at deficits, currencies, entitlements, and scapegoats such as civil servants and immigrants. Strategic mobilizations help overcome divisions across the middle and lower workforce segments. As neoliberal economic governance proves unsustainable, revitalized unions and their allies weigh in powerfully on the side of fundamental policy transformation in the drive for an inclusive, sustainable society (Reich 2010; Watt and Botsch 2010).

Not a bad scenario, although even in the best imaginable case we face rough waters ahead—years of campaigning and conflict. As global economic integration continues to drive immigration, immigrant workers who enter at the low end of the labor market can play a variety of different social roles. They can, for example, serve as a reserve army of labor to help employers keep costs down and workforces divided. They can serve as scapegoats for the political campaigns of flag-waving demagogues. In either of these or related situations, ongoing social conflict, economic instability, and deepening inequality are likely.

Alternatively, immigrants can be active agents and natural allies for other low-wage workers, and for unions and other organizations in campaigns to reduce economic and social polarization. Much recent research shows that a more equal society is a healthier, more stable society (Wilkinson and Pickett 2009). Union campaigns to join or lead the mobilization of immigrant workers carry the promise of a more integrated, sustainable society.

UNION CAMPAIGNS AS COUNTERMOVEMENTS

"Best Practice" Cases from the United Kingdom, France, and the United States

Maite Tapia, Lowell Turner, and Denisse Roca-Servat

Among the many challenges that global liberalization has posed for trade unions in the Global North, the growth of precarious immigrant workforces lacking any collective representation stands out as both a major threat to solidarity and an organizing opportunity (Munck 2010). Precarious immigrant workers, often termed "workers at the margins," make up a substantial and growing segment of the workforce in most developed countries (Thornley et al. 2010). Even though labor and immigration are inherently connected—people primarily migrate to find better employment opportunities—immigration as a topic has all too often been neglected by industrial relations scholars (McGovern 2007; for exceptions, see Fine 2006; Holgate 2005; Martinez Lucio and Perrett 2009a; Milkman 2006; Wills 2004).

In this chapter we compare recent innovative union campaigns in three countries: the CGT-led *sans papiers* campaign from 2008 to 2010 in France, the "Justice for Cleaners" campaign led by TGWU/Unite from 2005 to 2010 in the United Kingdom, and the CLEAN Carwash campaign led by the Community-Labor-Environmental Action Network and the United Steelworkers from 2008 to 2012 in the United States. It is surprising that despite deep differences in union traditions and structures as well as political-economic context, these campaign strategies are more substantially similar than different. From an analytical perspective, we consider the campaigns as examples of "countermovements" against the expansion of unregulated labor markets (Polanyi 1944).

All three cases took place in a context of economic instability following thirty years of global liberalization, and in the United States and France an emerging immigrant rights movement. In all three cases, unions broke with their past ambivalence and organizational inertia to craft comprehensive campaigns that moved beyond traditional channels to promote the interests of low-wage immigrant workers. In all three cases, unions deployed an arsenal of overlapping tactics: rank-and-file mobilization, coalition building, media attention, social justice framing that won public support, pressure on employers through strikes and demonstrations, and pressure on local and national governments. In addition, the unions also came up against limitations in internal resources as well as relationships with external allies. Specific goals varied from country to country—in France the focus was on the "regularization" of undocumented workers, in the United Kingdom the focus was on a living wage, in the United States on union recognition. However, in all cases unions stood beside immigrant workers fighting for dignity and respect in the workplace regardless of their place of origin, language, race, ethnicity, or citizenship status, enrolled new members, and raised the profile and promoted the interests of hard-working but vulnerable members of a growing service sector workforce. The result in each country was a broad comprehensive campaign of a kind that until recently has been far more common in the United States than in Europe.

We ask the following questions: How can we explain a simultaneous shift by three very different unions in distinct national contexts toward comprehensive strategies based on the grassroots mobilization of immigrant workers? And what common factors account for the considerable successes of these campaigns? More generally, how can and should unions relate to immigrant workers in an era where labor mobility is both intensified and contested (McGovern 2007)? To what extent might campaigns addressing the interests of growing immigrant workforces contribute to renewed union solidarity and vitality (Le Queux and Sainsaulieu 2010; Milkman 2006; Munck 2010; Turner and Cornfield 2007)?

More broadly, the following questions are addressed in this chapter and throughout the book: What can these cases tell us about contemporary debates in comparative political economy and industrial relations? What do similar mobilization-based responses tell us about the relative usefulness of a comparative institutional framework, compared to a theoretical perspective based on the dynamics of deregulation in a capitalist global economy (Hall and Soskice 2001; Streeck 2009, 2011b).

Unions as Countermovements

In his classic work, *The Great Transformation* (1944), Karl Polanyi argues that achieving a fully self-regulating market economy is a utopian goal. The economy is not autonomous; rather it is embedded in political, social, and cultural relations. Consequently, any attempt at disembedding the economy from society will encounter resistance and ultimately fail. Market societies thus necessarily include opposing movements: a laissez-faire movement to expand the scope of the market, and countermovements that emerge to protect society from the ravages of a free market. Countermovements do not necessarily lead to social democracy and protection, but can instigate fascism and authoritarianism (Polanyi 1944). Since the publication of *The Great Transformation,* however, discussion has centered primarily on the prospects of a counter hegemonic movement that could subordinate market economy to democratic politics (Evans 2000).

Recently, much academic debate has focused on the usefulness of the Polanyian theoretical framework to explain the emergence of an alternative to neoliberal capitalism (Burawoy 2010, 2011; Caspersz 2010; Clawson 2010; Lambert 2010; Waterman 2011; Webster 2010). More optimistic positions have identified characteristics of this emancipatory transformation within transnational labor networks, left-wing alliances, and new social movements (Evans 2010; Webster, Lambert, and Bezuidenhout 2010). More pessimistic accounts see "capitalism as a succession of small transformations and a complex intertwining of marketization and countermovements, but with no definite end in sight" (Burawoy 2010: 307).

This chapter contributes to this debate by moving away from the "pessimism" and "optimism" trap in which Polanyian renderings have stalled, instead relying on a comparative analysis that broadens the conversation to include other theories of labor and social movements (Waterman 2011). Recognizing the importance of Polanyi's critique of commodification and self-regulated market, we consider the following cases of organized labor revitalization through the struggle of immigrant workers as examples of innovative labor-related social countermovements. Union campaigns involving immigrant workers, like the ones analyzed here, portray social resistance, and human capacity to recreate cultural, social, and political alternatives (ideas and practices) to twenty-first-century capitalism's rapacious tendencies.

In their strongholds, with established channels of representation, unions play a key role in processes of social regulation that protect workers and society from the impacts of unrestrained markets. In the traditional industrial relations literature, collective bargaining is viewed as an orderly, constructive process aimed at promoting interests and resolving conflict in an otherwise disorderly or oppressive environment (Colling and Terry 2010; Katz et al. 2008). In different national contexts, unions have been oriented toward social partnership, "business unionism," or some other variant of an established order (Ebbinghaus 2002; Fantasia and Voss 2004).

Where no such channels exist, employers typically resist power sharing and workers may require a more active mobilization to promote their interests and win rights to collective representation. To mobilize power in the face of resistance, unions may behave more like social movements than established actors. In so doing, they become countermovements to the arbitrary power of employers in unrestrained markets. Collective representation can thus take on contrasting forms: as active social regulation through channels of collective bargaining and/or codetermination where it is well established; or as a contentious social movement where it is struggling for official recognition. In either case the goal can be seen in Polanyi's terms as social regulation (Figure 2.1).

In the cases considered here, unions have campaigned like social movements in contexts where basic worker rights and representation were missing. Facing market deregulation, the retrenchment of the welfare state, wage stagnation, and the expansion of precarious workforces, some key unions in the Global North chose to mobilize actively for social change (Turner and Cornfield 2007; Turner, Katz, and Hurd 2001; Waterman 1993), and reembed the economy in the social, cultural, and political fabrics of society (Polanyi 1957).

In the United Kingdom the trends are clear: a significant increase in the low-wage workforce from the late 1970s until the late 1990s. Low-wage work has been defined by the Organization for Economic Cooperation and Development (OECD) as earning less than two-thirds of the median earnings (usually hourly wage) of the employees of an economy. This definition has been adopted by many researchers, especially when conducting crossnational comparisons (e.g., Gautié and Schmitt 2010). In 2005, the incidence of low-wage workers was as high as 22.1 percent, which remained unaltered in subsequent years (Lloyd et al. 2008). Immigrant workers are more likely to end up in low-wage work than native-born

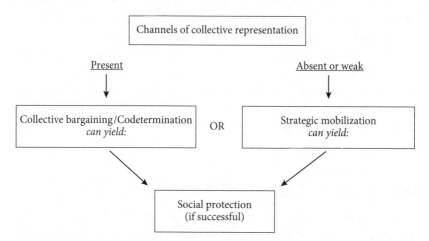

FIGURE 2.1 Contrasting channels of representation leading to potentially successful social regulation

workers, and the growth of foreign-born workers has been the fastest in relatively low-skilled sectors and occupations (Rienzo 2011). Similarly, there has been a considerable increase in precarious employment since the 1990s (International Labor Organization 2012) and immigrant workers are more likely to be exposed to precarious work than native-born citizens (O'Reilly et al. 2008).[1] Furthermore, since the 1970s, income inequality, measured by the Gini coefficient, has risen more rapidly in the United Kingdom than anywhere else in Europe (Wilkinson and Pickett 2009).

Very similar trends can be observed in the United States (Mishel et al. 2009; Wilkinson and Pickett 2009). But even in the prototypical coordinated market economy, Germany, the low-wage workforce increased from the mid-1990s up to 20.8 percent in 2004, one of the highest shares across continental European countries. So-called mini-jobs, a new form of precarious, atypical employment, are considered one of the main drivers for the expansion of low-wage work. France, by contrast, has a rather low incidence of low-wage workers (12.2%) and the share actually declined from the late 1990s to 2007 (Caroli and Gautié 2008). One of the main reasons for this is France's high minimum wage (known as SMIC). The minimum wage was introduced in France in 1950 and became indexed to inflation as well as to the growth of overall productivity in 1970. Between 1970 and 2005 the minimum wage real value doubled, whereas, for example, in the United States the federal minimum wage decreased in real value by 34 percent during that same time period (Caroli and Gautié 2008). Although income inequality in France declined over the 1990s (OECD 2008), this trend was reversed in the Sarkozy era, beginning with the 2008 economic crisis. In any case, in France there is a proliferation of precarious work, characterized by unstable and insecure employment. Consequently, France's labor market is deeply segmented, with foreign-born workers more likely to be part of the precarious workforce than native workers (Caroli and Gautié 2008).

Workforces at the low end—especially but not only in private sector services—are heavily populated by women, younger workers, ethnic and racial minorities, and to a significant extent these workers are foreign born. To gain representation for such workers, unions may have to move well beyond their comfort zones into sustained periods of conflict and mobilization.

Why Organize Immigrant Workers?

Despite national policies that favor the immigration of skilled workers, most immigrants, with or without work documents, skills or diplomas, enter the workforce at the low end—in retail, building services, hospitality, agriculture, construction, domestic care—often through employment that is temporary or subcontracted (e.g., Nicot 2007; Winchester 2007). Labor market segmentation has expanded as union membership and bargaining coverage have declined throughout much of the Global North.[2] In this context, unions have come up against two realities: that overall labor standards are threatened when some workers have rights but others do not; and that the expansion of precarious work has become deeply entrenched in today's fragmented labor markets.

The intensification of international competition has weakened unions in their manufacturing strongholds where jobs and production are mobile. Future organizing prospects for unions should in principle be better where jobs cannot be moved—in construction, transportation, and private and public sector services such as health care, retail, hospitality, and building services. Yet these sectors are also impacted by globalization in the growth of immigrant workforces. Thus the mirror image confronting unions in today's world markets: if good jobs in manufacturing can flee the Global North, many of the remaining jobs can be populated by immigrant workers in precarious circumstances that allow employers to keep labor standards down. French anthropologist Emmanuel Terray (1999) has called this *délocalisation sur place*, broadly translated as domestic outsourcing, or outsourcing on the spot. Such employer strategies encourage a deepening of already segmented labor markets.

Unless economic globalization is reversible, and we do not believe that it is, unions have to organize the new low-wage workforces as they exist. According to Penninx and Roosblad (2000), over time, unions have encountered three dilemmas when first dealing with immigration: resisting immigration versus cooperating; excluding immigrants from their membership or including them; and providing equal versus special treatment. Since the late 1990s, trade unions have more or less "solved" the first two dilemmas as many unions today favor policies that promote rather than restrict immigration (Avci and McDonald 2000; Watts 2002). The challenges facing unions to organize and advocate for immigrant and other low-wage workers are now in many ways similar across the Global North—despite significant national and local differences in union structures and the institutions in which collective representation takes shape. Inspired in some cases by immigrant worker activism some unions made the decision to support immigrant workers and include them in organizing efforts. In some places, this alliance proved powerful, giving new life to labor movements in need of revitalization. In the United States in 2006, for example, "labor (both in the form of established unions and worker centers) and immigrant rights groups joined together with immigrant communities throughout the country to launch a series of mobilizations culminating in the largest demonstrations in U.S. history" (Narro, Wong, and Shadduck-Hernandez 2007: 49). Similarly, in 2008 the *sans papiers* movement in France brought together undocumented immigrants and organized labor, generating a dynamic and emancipatory social movement (Barnier and Perrin 2009). Rallies and demonstrations in places like France and the United States showed that immigrants were not only workers, but also children in public schools, stay-at-home mothers, and neighbors who contributed to society (Barnier and Perrin 2009; Narro et al. 2007). This social image helped persuade civil society, and more particularly unions, to see immigrants as low-wage workers with the same rights as other low-wage workforces.

Organizing immigrant workers is by far not the only thing unions have to do. But for overcoming workforce divisions, for bringing together the vast middle and lower segments of a fragmented labor market in the push toward a more socially balanced and sustainable society, helping immigrant and other precarious workers achieve basic rights and representation is an unavoidable challenge.

In the three cases discussed in this chapter, unions have made major efforts to bring representation to immigrant workforces at the low end.[3] The case studies are based on original field research conducted from 2008 to 2012. We draw on news stories and documentation, interviews we conducted, as well as published sources (e.g., Barron et al. 2011; Holgate 2009, 2011; Roca-Servat 2011). These are exceptional cases for the intensity of mobilization, strategic leadership, active rank-and-file engagement, coalition building, and a measure of success. They demonstrate possibilities and limitations for contemporary unions to serve as deliberate countermovements against the expansion of markets beyond society's capacity for regulation.

Justice for Cleaners in London, 2005–2010

By the mid-2000s, about 58 percent of the London cleaners were immigrant workers, a proportion that has since increased steadily (Asset Skills 2007). They are among the lowest paid and most vulnerable employees, qualities that make them attractive to many employers (Connolly 2010; Wills 2008).[4]

In 2001, the East London Communities Organization (TELCO)—a broad-based community organization—kicked off an innovative London living wage campaign to secure better living and working conditions for low-paid, mostly immigrant cleaning workers.[5] Inspired by two major urban-based movements from across the pond—Justice for Janitors campaigns led by the Service Employees International Union (SEIU) in selected cities since 1986, and the living wage campaigns led by coalitions of community and labor groups in over 100 U.S. cities since 1994—TELCO targeted public hospitals in East London as well as high-profile private banks located in the wealthy financial district Canary Wharf. By staging public protests (marches, demonstrations, public assemblies) and lobbying politicians and employers, TELCO achieved significant gains for the workers, such as the living wage and holiday and sick pay. The campaign gained enormous publicity, receiving the support of the mayor of London and attracting the attention of trade unions.[6]

In 2004, the Transport and General Workers Union (TGWU, now Unite), following the election of a new general secretary, decided on a "strategy for growth." The union allocated substantial resources to an organizing department and brought in experienced organizers from SEIU for advice. Whereas immigrant cleaning workers were once perceived as "unorganizable" due to high turnover, language barrier, or immigration status, the experiences of SEIU in the United States and TELCO in London revealed, on the contrary, the potential for organizing this growing low-wage sector.

The union decided on a "zonal approach": rather than organizing workplace by workplace or employer by employer, TGWU targeted the largest cleaning contractors to sign zonal agreements. Because intense processes of competition have led to massive consolidation in the cleaning industry, a handful of large national and transnational firms have acquired responsibility for at least 75 percent of the office space in financial centers at Canary Wharf and the City of London (Wills 2008). Rather than pressuring the contractors directly, the union put pressure on key clients by orchestrating daily "public shaming" demonstrations. As a result, to avoid damage to their reputations, the clients would push the contractors to sign the zonal agreements, locking them into one bargaining unit (Graham 2007).

Within each workplace, the union identified and developed workplace leaders, set up workplace committees, and eventually, in 2009, created a formal cleaners' branch consisting of about 3,000 members. The union recruited staff organizers, health and safety representatives, and union learning representatives from among the cleaners themselves, which resulted in an important change of demographics within the union structure. Meanwhile, the living wage campaign spread to other unions as well as other sectors. The National Union of Rail, Maritime and Transport Workers (RMT) and the public sector union Unison also focused on organizing cleaners. The campaign then further diffused from hospitals and banks to major universities such as Queen Mary, the London School of Economics, the School of African and Oriental Studies (SOAS), and Birkbeck College.

Even though TGWU/Unite was successful in gaining union recognition and ensuring better working conditions for thousands of cleaners, the majority of them immigrant workers, some challenges have arisen. First, different styles of organizing between unions, as well as between unions and community organizations, are sometimes hard to reconcile. Inter-union rivalry between the RMT, a union with a heavy industrial focus, and the TGWU has led to turf-based tensions.

The RMT wanted railway cleaners to join the railway union, even though they were subcontracted to large multinational cleaning companies. Tensions between TGWU and TELCO are ascribed to the union suspicion of faith-based groups within TELCO, different democratic structures, and contrasting organizing approaches (Holgate 2009b).

Second, the union has experienced heavy backlash as workplaces such as SOAS have been raided and undocumented cleaning workers deported. Even though TELCO initiated a conditional or "earned" regularization campaign, to create a path to citizenship for migrants who have been in the United Kingdom for at least five years without a criminal record and have references from employers, the TGWU has not fought publicly for the regularization of undocumented migrant workers.

Finally, although the initiative to organize cleaners began with the community organization TELCO, trade unions have picked it up, keeping the focus on the London living wage as the centerpiece of their campaigns. The extent to which the union strategies improved the immigrant workers' position in society is debatable. However, the formation of a cleaners branch and the recruitment of immigrant workers as staff organizers, health and safety and union learning representatives have been steps important to integrating immigrant workers into the union structure.

The *Sans Papiers* Movement, 2008–2010

Emboldened by public support in a 2006 campaign in France in support of immigrant schoolchildren and their parents, and in a context of intensified workplace pressure and fears of deportation, undocumented workers, the *sans papiers* ("without papers"), increasingly reached out to French unions for support. A few small battles at workplaces convinced activist-minded leaders at the CGT, the largest French union federation, that a broader campaign was possible. Careful plans were made in under-the-radar meetings between CGT leaders and growing numbers of *sans papiers* workers in the Paris region.[7]

With great fanfare and media attention, the campaign was launched on April 15, 2008, with strikes at seventeen work sites, many of them restaurants. About 200 workers occupied their own workplaces, while union supporters massed in front of the buildings. The key demand was for employer support for worker applications to local government offices for legal work permits, known in France as *régularisation*. Social justice framing was brilliantly successful: these were workers with jobs but without papers no workplace rights to contest conditions of exploitation. Union strategists, for example, "helped" the media to focus on restaurants on the Champs-Élysées, to highlight the contrast between wealthy patrons and the immigrants working at low wages and with no rights who served them.

In the face of much public support for the strikers, employers reclaimed their workplaces by writing letters confirming employment status and their own demonstrated need for these workers. A second wave of strikes broke out in May, followed by many more in the months to come. From posh establishments such as La Grande Armée and La Tour d'Argent to fast food KFC, *sans papiers* workers learned that with public and union support they could occupy their workplaces with less danger than they had previously imagined, and employers learned that the workers and their union supporters would not back down until demands were met.

From April 2008 to October 2009, the union claimed about 2,000 regularizations and about 2,000 new members. Still, other undocumented workers and advocacy groups protested the CGT focus on specific workplaces rather than general solutions, and the exclusion from the movement of unemployed and isolated workers not employed at target firms. The CGT faced an occupation of its own by dissatisfied workers not included in the demands.

It was necessary to broaden the campaign. Other unions and nongovernmental organizations (NGOs) that had been wary at first saw the successes and the potential for more. The CGT saw the need for a broader coalition of support. Together they announced formation of the Collectif des Onze (Collective of the Eleven, or C11), including five union confederations—CGT, CFDT, SUD, UNSA, FSU, and six NGOs—Cimode, RESF, Femmes Egalité, Autre Monde, Droits Devants! and Ligue des Droits de l'Homme. On October 12, 2009, about 2,300 workers went out on strike, in building services, construction, and catering, at small and medium enterprises as well temporary agencies that in many cases supplied the workers. Backed by the C11, the focus now shifted to the state, with demands for the negotiation of clear, expanded regularization criteria that would be binding on often arbitrary local government offices.

The strike grew to include over 6,000 by the end of the year, with demonstrations through the winter and spring of 2010, high profile political and celebrity support, and finally an occupation at the Place de la Bastille beginning on May 27. On June 18, 2010, representatives from the C11 reached an agreement with the national government that ended the strike and the encampment at the Bastille. This was not a full victory but it was a breakthrough: the government agreed to specified work permit criteria, to protect workers with applications in process, to accept the validity of the strike as a labor conflict (allowing strikers to return to their respective workplaces), and expand possibilities for regularization for temporary and informal workers.

We do not want to romanticize this movement. About 5,000 workers have received work permits—these are workers who would probably not otherwise have received them and would have continued to toil with no workplace rights. Employers and the state have been put on notice that undocumented workers are capable of successfully demanding rights. Unions have discovered new potential constituencies and strategic possibilities. But this is still small progress in an overall picture of labor market segmentation and exploitation.

The *sans papiers* campaigns of 2008–2010 are important as breakthroughs, as symbols, and as opportunities for organizational learning and strategic development on the part of French trade unions. In research of this kind, it is difficult to get union officials to talk about the internal debates that lead to acceptance of high-risk innovative campaigns. One point we repeatedly heard emphasized was the threat to the labor standards of all workers if some workers have no rights. In today's global labor markets, unions may be learning that it is no longer possible to exclude immigrants without papers, any more than it is possible to exclude temporary workers. The symbolic importance of the *sans papiers* victories lies in demonstrating that it is possible, through strategic mobilization, to bring rights to the most precarious workers. A focus on inclusion, argue campaign activists, offers the best route to overcoming workforce divisions and weakened bargaining power.

Campaign success was based on a combination of ingredients similar to what we found in organizing successes in the United States and the United Kingdom: carefully planned strategic union leadership in sync with active rank-and-file engagement, gaining strength in the Collectif des Onze period through a new focus on coalition building.

French unions are promising future campaigns based on lessons learned. And they claim that immigrant worker organizing has opened new doors for them. Like most unions, organized labor in France has its strongest base in large companies and in the public sector. Organizing the *sans papiers* has taken French unions into small- and medium-size enterprises, into the informal sector, and into the agencies that supply growing shares of today's temporary workforces. A new focus on immigrant workers has brought unions lessons for expanding their presence in parts of the labor market from which they have previously been excluded.

To summarize, the recent participation of French unions in mobilizing and empowering immigrant workers can be viewed as a breakthrough in efforts for broader social cohesion. At the same time, progress is halting, regularizations are still often subject to the whims of local government offices and in any case only a first step toward greater social acceptance, government and employers continue to throw up obstacles, and the nationalistic political party Front National has gained renewed traction playing the antiforeigner card. Union campaigns in support of the demands of immigrant workers, especially the undocumented, are innovative and significant but still only a small step toward the greater equality of a more sustainable society.

The CLEAN Carwash Campaign in Los Angeles, 2008–2012

Washing cars is big business in Los Angeles. This city has the highest car density in the United States, with ninety-two cars per square mile and one car for every 1.8 persons. With 330 clear days per year, the city enjoys the ideal car-washing weather. More than 400 carwash establishments in L.A. have reported combined revenue of over $250 million per year in 2002 (CWOC 2008). Yet carwash workers have a far from glamorous existence, facing systematic wage and hour violations, health and safety violations, and even sexual harassment. This very fragmented industry (the majority of firms consist of single establishments) employs between 7,000 and 10,000 workers in L.A. County, the majority of whom are first generation immigrants from Latin America, and at least one-fourth of them are undocumented (CWOC 2008; Narro 2008).[8]

At the end of the 1990s, the poor working conditions of the carwash workers were first exposed by public interest lawyers, working for community organizations and worker centers (Garea and Stern 2010). A first attempt to regulate the carwash industry was drafted in California Senate Bill 1097 (SB 1097) by Senator Tom Hayden. Fierce opposition by the Western Carwash Association and a lack of data concerning the abuses, however, led Governor Gray Davis to veto the bill (Narro 2008). In 2002, the Los Angeles Workers Advocates Coalition (LAWAC)—a group of legal aid services and community organizations dealing with low-wage workers, labor violations and labor enforcement—decided to target the carwash industry. This second attempt led to the Carwash Worker Law, or AB 1688, and in October 2009, Governor Arnold Schwarzenegger signed the bill into law, establishing minimum labor standards for carwash workers through 2014.

Passing this law was critical, but it was not enough. The coalition sought the support of the labor movement to address chronic noncompliance with wage, hours, and health and safety regulations. After much discussion, the American Federation of Labor and Congress of Industrial Organizations (AFL-CIO) and the United Steelworkers (USW) committed to organize the carwash workers. In March 2008, the CLEAN Carwash campaign officially took off as a joint effort between the Community-Labor-Environmental Action Network (CLEAN), and the Carwash Workers Organizing Committee (CWOC) of the USW and the AFL-CIO.

On October 25, 2011, a breakthrough campaign victory gave CLEAN and CWOC its first union contract at a carwash in Santa Monica.[9] This pioneering collective bargaining agreement included wage increases, health and safety protections, grievance and arbitration procedures, and protections for the workers in case of ownership change. In February 2012, two more union contracts were negotiated with L.A. carwashes (Semuels 2012). Following these critical union gains, community advocacy groups and unions in other cities, such as New York, have launched similar campaigns. An investigative report showed that New York City carwash workers, the majority of whom are Latino immigrants, face similar abusive practices, including wage and hour violations and unprotected exposure to hazardous chemicals (WASH 2012).

While union recognition and the spread of this campaign to other cities are significant outcomes, equally important is the way the CLEAN Carwash campaign operates as an innovative blend of community and labor organizing. Besides pushing for economic gains and improved labor conditions, CLEAN has incorporated a strong emphasis on immigrant workers' social and political rights. The adoption of social justice discursive framing emphasizing worker and immigrant rights rather than just economic justice; the campaign's involvement in discussions about immigration reform and immigrant legalization; the use of popular education techniques or critical pedagogy to empower the workers; and, finally, the workers' own participation in city hall meetings and lobbying of state officials and legislative representatives are important elements that have pushed the campaign beyond traditional union organizing (Roca-Servat 2011). As a result, CLEAN—an amalgamation of over 100 faith-based, neighborhood, legal advocacy, immigrant rights, environmental and labor organizations—has gained widespread support and solidarity, ranging from religious leaders and high school and college students to an array of other unions based in the Los Angeles County Federation of Labor.

Furthermore, the campaign consisted of important labor-related strategies, such as the formation of health and safety committees among the workers, the creation of a Carwash Worker Leadership Brigade to develop union organizers and leaders, the hiring of organizers with previous experience from the day labor movement, and workers on the ground boycotting and picketing carwash violators. The CLEAN Carwash campaign, based on integrating immigrant workers' economic, social, and political rights and building a successful alliance between immigrant and community organizations and trade unions, thus offers a promising "best practice" case: a community-labor alliance that has managed to improve the labor conditions of carwash workers as well as to ignite civic participation and discourse on social inclusion among the (mostly immigrant) workers.

A German Exception?

In contrast to the British, French, and U.S. stories told in this chapter, we have found less emphasis on the mobilization of immigrant workers in Germany. Yet we know there has been substantial growth for a large nonunion low-wage sector in Germany—in retail, hospitality, building services, construction, domestic care, manufacturing suppliers, and elsewhere—also populated by significant numbers of immigrant workers. This finding limits a convergence argument as it applies to union strategies. Yet convergence is also clear in growing inequality and the expansion of low-wage work, and there are clearly similar problems and future challenges—as well as inspiring stories from places like Hamburg, Kiel, and the rise of immigrant workers to positions of union leadership throughout the German labor movement.[10]

Are strongly embedded institutions of social partnership preventing German unions from moving outside their comfort zones, in the areas of the economy where they are entrenched, to organize the growing immigrant-rich precarious workforce lacking in representation? For now, we simply note the difference and raise the question for consideration: To what extent is the German case fundamentally different? We do know that German institutions have also benefited immigrant workers in important ways: in the integration of immigrants into unions and work councils in union strongholds, and in Germany's unparalleled vocational training system that has offered opportunities, especially to second generation immigrants, that do not exist in other countries. Yet we also know that, just as in France, the United Kingdom, and the United States, inequality is growing, precarious work is expanding and includes many first and second generation immigrants, and that anti-immigrant, especially anti-Muslim, attitudes are widespread. Yet in Germany we do not find breakthrough cases of mobilization parallel to what we have found in the other countries.

Comparative Analysis

How can we compare these three campaigns? Despite obvious differences in union structures and traditions, as well as the distinct institutional settings in the United Kingdom, France, and the United States, we find important commonalities in the contexts, characteristics, and significance of these campaigns. We suggest that for starters, Polanyi's framework of the "double movement" provides a useful approach for understanding these union campaigns. And a social movement framework also helps make sense of strategies, tactics, resources, framing processes, cultural consequences, and extra-movement dynamics employed and present in the campaigns.

First, immigrant worker struggles appear to be similar in certain ways and to occur against a comparable background of heightened levels of global liberalization. Immigrant workers, especially at the low end, have been described as "invisible workers": they literally remain unseen, cleaning banks, hospitals, or universities while the city sleeps (Hearn and Bergos 2011; Pai 2004). Their invisibility often goes hand-in-hand with precarious, exploitative working conditions or, in the worst cases, forms of modern quasi-slavery. Although cleaning buildings and washing dishes and cars are nonmobile jobs that cannot be shipped abroad, immigrant workers all too often become the object of "social dumping" practices. Employers who choose low-road labor strategies may hire immigrants, with or without work documents, to take advantage of exploitative labor practices and gain competitive advantage.

Immigrant workers are typically more vulnerable than native-born workers because they rarely have the same access to information regarding employment laws; they migrated mostly for employment reasons and are eager to accept any job offer; and especially if they are undocumented, they are less likely to complain in case of abuse. These layers of vulnerability make them an attractive workforce for employers seeking to bring down costs with low wages and minimal benefits. Such practices have proven commonplace for immigrant cleaners in the United Kingdom, for restaurant and construction workers in France, for carwash workers in the United States, and indeed for immigrant workers around the world.

The political-economic context shows similar trends as well. Since the 1980s, policymakers in all countries have operated within frameworks of neoliberal national and global governance. While in France processes of economic liberalization occurred at a slower pace than in the Anglo-Saxon countries, a "pragmatic neoliberalism" characterized by high levels of privatization has taken root (Prasad 2005). In addition, changes in global production and employment systems in both countries have led to processes of "precarization," in which flexible, part-time, fixed-term, temporary, or agency work, rather than full-time permanent work, all too often becomes the norm, and much of this precarious work is carried out by growing immigrant workforce (Thornley et al. 2010).

Thus neoliberal economic governance, combined with low-road employer strategies that take advantage of the invisibility of migrant workers, has been important factors in pushing trade unions to act. In Polanyi's terms, the expansion of the self-regulated free market is confronted with countermovements, such as the ones described in this chapter, demanding social protection.

These countermovements, which intertwined immigrant and labor rights struggles, stand as important social movements in opposition to market fundamentalism. More specifically, these countermovements also contained political, cultural, and social claims, rooted primarily in recognizing immigrants as bearers of rights and political subjects. Social movement theory, therefore, provides insightful elements for comparing the emergence and success of these campaigns.

Unions used similar strategies and tactics in each case. TGWU/Unite in London, the CGT and later the Collectif des Onze, in Paris, and the USW and NGO activists in Los Angeles adopted comprehensive campaigning approaches based on sustained grassroots mobilization of immigrants, a rights-based framing that challenged low-road employer strategies. The assumed powerlessness of immigrant workers was transformed into concrete sources of leverage. Indeed, the assumption that immigrant workers are "unorganizable," and afraid to step forward because of fears of deportation, has proven false in a variety of contexts (Chun 2009; Milkman 2006). Justice for Cleaners, *sans papiers*, and CLEAN Carwash campaigns provided the economic resources, legal expertise, and institutional experience that supported immigrant workers' voice, actions, and struggle, to demand the recognition of their rights in workplace and society even in the most dangerous of circumstances. The campaigns received intense media coverage and gained broad public support. The unions did not simply fight for union recognition, but framed their issues in terms of social justice and fairness.

Through sustained campaigns including demonstrations, strikes and civil disobedience, vulnerable workers and their union supporters were able to pressure employers and policymakers to win significant concessions. In all cases it was important to get some employers on board, who then set an example of good behavior to push others in the same direction. These campaigns were a victory not only for the workers themselves—gaining a living wage, regularization, and union recognition—but also for the trade unions, who achieved breakthroughs in working with immigrants.

Furthermore, the campaigns took place in global cities, accentuating the heightened levels of wealth and capital, on the one hand, and the miserable working conditions of much of the immigrant workforces that keep the cities running, on the other (Sassen 2001). This blatant contrast shaped the consciousness of workers as they came out of the shadows demanding the right to a decent living. All three campaigns have since diffused to other cities, involving new actors, new sectors, and generating a potential shift in scale from a local to a regional or national level.

In addition, extra-movement dynamics and coalition building played an important role on all three campaigns. While in the United States trade unions have for two decades engaged in comprehensive campaigns involving immigrant workers (including Justice for Janitors and Hotel Workers Rising; see, e.g., Milkman 2006; Turner and Cornfield 2007), in France and the United Kingdom this is a rather new phenomenon. Outside influences were important in opening the doors for these campaigns. In the United Kingdom, the unions learned a great deal from the U.S. union SEIU and from the community organization TELCO. In France, key "bridge-building" CGT activists refocused the organization on the demands of immigrant workers in the wake of a nationwide NGO-led immigrant schoolchildren support campaign. And, in the United States an umbrella of public interest law organizations, community associations and worker centers were at the basis of the Carwash campaign creating the CLEAN alliance.

These innovative cases also brought with them significant cultural consequences. On the one hand, working with immigrant workers gave the labor movement an opportunity to transform itself into a more inclusive force. Especially in the United Kingdom, the campaign opened the door for immigrant workers to take up new positions within union structures, thereby significantly changing the union from within. In the United States, the CLEAN Carwash campaign implemented a popular education program that trained immigrant workers as union organizers, and safety and health representatives in their workplace. Moreover, even though these campaigns had only a minor impact on overall union membership (in each case the unions gained at most a few thousand members), they carry potential for a "qualitative revival" of unionism, with increased levels of union involvement based on bottom-up initiatives by local activists across different groups (e.g., Le Queux and Sainsaulieu 2010). On the other hand, these campaigns served to transform the social imagery about immigrants. In this regard, all three campaigns allowed immigrants to break through invisibility and silence, and posit themselves as fellow workers, family members, and next door neighbors, bearers of rights.

The unions engaged in these campaigns also faced similar challenges. Relationships with external allies were at times ambivalent. Tensions between different unions revolving around control, territory, or distinct democratic structures, or between trade unions and community or immigrant associations, resulted in episodes of backlash, especially in the United Kingdom and France. In addition, unions in all three cases were restricted in terms of internal resources.

Aside from the general goal of bringing rights and representation to precarious workers, specific goals varied based on national circumstances and opportunity structures. In the United Kingdom, TGWU focused not on regularization but on a living wage. Although TELCO initiated a "path to citizenship" campaign, neither U.K. nor U.S. unions made the public defense of undocumented workers a central campaign issue. In France, by contrast, the CGT took a bold stand publicly defending the *sans papiers* and promoting their struggle as a union issue. For immediate outcomes, the British union provided a structural solution for migrant workers by setting up a separate cleaners' branch. In France, the outcome consisted mainly of regularization of undocumented workers and their inclusion as individual members in local union branches. In the United States, the most visible success came in union recognition and collective bargaining contracts, but the carwash campaign evolved beyond fighting poor labor conditions. Immigrant, community, and labor organizations were also pushing for immigration reform and legalization, emphasizing immigrants' social and political rights.

Although differences in demands and outcomes are important, we want to stress the greater significance of similar, broad goals and strategies that go beyond these immediate differences. These campaigns emerged as social movements in the absence of established channels of representation. Unions fought not only for increased union membership but for labor market reform, demanding better social protection for immigrant workers and by extension for all workers.

Conclusion

Our findings reveal blind spots in a crossnational comparative perspective based on institutional equilibrium (Hall and Soskice 2001). The cases point rather toward common dynamics in the development of global capitalism as well as the independent role of actor choice. We suggest that our case studies can be viewed as examples of countermovements against a neoliberal global order and the commodification of social life (Polanyi 1944; Stiglitz 2006; Turner 2011). Our crossnational comparison reveals fundamental similarities underlying the campaigns and their socioeconomic contexts, even given very different national institutions (Bertossi 2010; Gumbrell-McCormick 2011). The cases presented in this chapter highlight union decisions about whether and how to mobilize in the face of employer opposition in increasingly deregulated labor markets (Baccaro et al. 2010). Moving beyond the stale debate on unrealistic optimism or unqualified pessimism (Waterman 2011) with regard to the possibility of a new world order, we offer these fine-grained case studies of union strategies toward immigrant workers to enhance understandings of the challenges and limitations for traditional and non-traditional actors in an era of heightened global liberalization.

If market expansion has driven labor market fragmentation and the growth of immigrant-rich precarious workforces, unions have choices about how to respond. In today's world markets, it may no longer be possible to pursue policies of restriction, whether of immigrant labor or temporary work. Watching it all happen, letting the ground slip away while clinging to strongholds is one choice. Strategic mobilization is an alternative, as union and rank-and-file activists in the Justice for Cleaners, *sans papiers,* and Clean Carwash campaigns have shown.

Part II

CASES AND NATIONAL CONTEXTS

THE UNITED STATES

Tackling Inequality in Precarious Times

Lee H. Adler and Daniel B. Cornfield

U.S. immigration policy has been race or nation-based for almost its entire history. Exclusion of immigrant workers from China and India, severe restrictions on Eastern and Southern Europeans, and a variety of containment policies directed at south of the U.S. border populations have characterized the 200-plus-year set of ad hoc policies.

There was a thawing of these restrictions for nearly two decades beginning in the mid-1960s, but tougher laws and enforcement arrived in the late 1980s and only intensified with the passage of NAFTA in the early 1990s. The past twenty years have seen a rise of the Right in U.S. politics, which in turn has spawned a variety of local and state anti-immigrant measures in all regions of the country. Legislative and other attacks have been directed at work solicitation by day laborers, rent and housing concerns, health care and education for immigrants without papers, and arrests for status alone.

Political and legislative impasse in Washington has precluded any national approach to the issues surrounding immigration. In the early 2000s, the U.S. labor movement and worker centers, led by unions involved in organizing low-wage and service sector workers, pushed a resolution through the national American Federation of Labor and Congress of Industrial Organizations (AFL-CIO) endorsing immigrant workers' rights as U.S. workers' rights.[1] That coalition has persisted in national reform efforts as well as state and local initiatives, some of which are mentioned in our findings.

Change has come slow to the AFL-CIO and Change to Win (CTW) affiliates, whose structures in the United States must be the real change agents. Still, we have identified a number of instances where different unions have undertaken workplace struggles that have advanced internal union integration of immigrant workers. Summaries of those efforts follow the observations made in this chapter (see also Fine and Tichenor's [2009, 2012a] overviews of the U.S. labor movement's dynamic approach to immigration over the past 150 years).

Postwar Historical Context

Immigration

Contemporary immigrant labor organizing in the United States occurred against the backdrop of a liberalized, post-1965 national immigration policy that increased immigration from Mexico, Central America, the Caribbean, Africa, and Asia. The 1965 national immigration law reforms replaced the forty-year-old system of national-origin quotas with the present entry criteria based on family reunification. Immigration to the United States had virtually ground to a halt during the four decades before 1965.

Organized labor supported both the restrictive national origins system during its nativist phase of the 1920s to curb the immigration of nonskilled workers from Eastern, Central, and Southern Europe, and the family-unification system during its pro-civil rights and human rights phase of the 1960s. Similarly, organized labor supported the 1980 liberalization of national refugee policy, which expanded the eligibility criteria beyond refugees of communist nations, but then supported the strong border controls and sanctions against employers who hired undocumented workers in the 1986 national immigration reforms (Briggs 2001: ch. 6; Watts 2002: ch. 7).[2]

The number of legal and undocumented immigrants to the United States continued to increase through the mid-2000s due to strong labor demand in the growing U.S. service economy until the onset of the Great Recession. Continuing refugee resettlement efforts, the persistence of cohesive immigrant social networks, and the contraction and deindustrialization of the Mexican economy (Cornfield 2006, 2009a; Portes 2009; Portes and Rumbaut 2006: chs. 2 and 10; Waldinger and Lichter 2003) contributed to this trend. Indeed, Portes and Rumbaut (2006: 367) conclude that "Mexico has become the de facto low-skilled labor reservoir for the American economy." Between 1970 and 2010, the percentage of the foreign-born U.S. population increased from 4.7 percent to 13.0 percent, with 53 percent from Latin America, and 55 percent, or 11.7 million, from Mexico.[3]

Supplementing this remarkable increase in Latin American immigrants has been a smaller but surprisingly large number of Muslim immigrants. The growing numbers of Muslim immigrants to the United States from Africa, Asia, and the Middle East have prompted the U.S. labor movement to give some attention to organizing these as well as Hispanic immigrant workers. Friedrich Ebert Stiftung (2009) estimated that 3,000,000 Muslim immigrants arrived in the United States mainly from Arab nations during the 1990s. According to the U.S. Bureau of the Census (2010, table 75), the number of adults who self-identified as Muslims more than doubled to 1.3 million between 1990 and 2008.

Somali political refugees from the ongoing civil war that began in 1991 are among the fastest growing Muslim immigrant groups in the United States. Between 1991 and 2008, some 60,000 Somali refugees and asylum seekers obtained legal permanent resident status in the United States (Dagne 2010; U.S. Bureau of African Affairs 2010; U.S. Bureau of the Census 2010, table 51). By 2008, the number of U.S. residents claiming Somali ancestry had grown to 80,774 (U.S. Bureau of the Census 2008).

Muslim immigrant workers are disproportionately employed in personal transportation (e.g., taxi cab drivers) and the food-processing industry, which have been the sites of cultural conflicts and religious accommodations in the workplace (Appelbaum 2008; Eyck 2009; Greenhouse 2008d, 2010; Mathew, 2008; Ness 2005: 34; Semple 2008). Success in organizing these Muslim workers has been quite limited throughout the country. In October 2011, the AFL-CIO issued a charter to the National Taxi Workers Alliance, a union whose multiethnic and multireligion, immigrant urban membership and jurisdiction of independent contractors effectively include Muslim workers among its ranks (Mathew 2008; Ness 2005; Stan 2011).

The U.S. Situation

Meanwhile, more than three decades of wage stagnation, income disparity, and decline in the U.S. labor movement's density, especially in the private sector, characterized nearly all parts of the labor market for middle and lower middle class U.S. workers.[4] Coupled with the steady increase in immigration in its many forms, public resentment of immigrant workers reappeared, accelerated by the fears following the 9/11 World Trade center attacks.

As mentioned earlier, the AFL-CIO shifted its stance on immigration policy from perceiving immigrants as threats to U.S. workers toward treating immigrants as integral members of the labor force and nation. This policy shift evidenced, in part, a labor union revitalization initiative. U.S. trade unions sought to recoup union membership losses from the globalizing and shrinking manufacturing sector by organizing workers in the growing service sector.[5] Low-wage service workers were disproportionately foreign born and Hispanic, lacked union protection, and their jobs were physically anchored and less vulnerable than factory jobs to being exported abroad.

The national AFL-CIO's progressive turn in 2000[6] reflected pressure throughout the 1990s applied by service and hospital workers (SEIU), hotel workers (HERE), and home health-care workers (SEIU and AFSCME [American Federation of State, County, and Municipal Employees]) who pushed considerable organizing efforts in these workplaces. This progressive "turn" of the national AFL-CIO, however, was often limited to speeches, legislative lobbying efforts, legal interventions, and studies and expressions of concern, as its national federation structure required and requires leaving the actual incorporation of immigrant workers to its activist affiliates.[7]

Separate from these structurally imposed limitations on the national AFL-CIO's ability to be the agent for migrant worker incorporation was its outstanding work on the 2003 Immigrant Workers Freedom Ride. This remarkable event, initiated[8] by and a part of HERE's campaign to both organize and protect the mostly immigrant worker populations at nearly every major U.S. hotel chain, caught fire, as busloads of activists traveled along several intercoastal, West-to-East itineraries of immigrant labor organizing rallies that converged in Washington, D.C. Although certainly subject to debate, the AFL-CIO's massive, nationwide mobilization for the Freedom Ride represents its most outstanding progressive work. Nearly every staffer, wherever located, joined the effort and worked with the federation's affiliates, throughout the country, resulting in massive outpourings in many locations. It was mobilization with a focus, that is, to achieve passage of immigration reform that would include a predictable path to some type of citizenship rights. It was the labor movement as a whole at its best. Ultimate rejection of that legislation was disappointing, and although national trade unions again in 2006 mobilized tens of thousands of its members in coalition with the immigrant worker community seeking legislative reform, it, too, was not successful.

The effects of the Immigrant Workers Freedom Ride organizing effort were still felt in 2006. Then, a nationwide May Day immigrant worker protest led to the defeat of the anti-immigrant Border Protection, Antiterrorism and Illegal Immigration Control Act pending in the U.S. Senate. The May Day protest of some 4,000,000 protesters, thought to be the largest protest in U.S. history, emanated from Los Angeles and coursed eastward across the nation along roughly the same itinerary of over 160 cities as that of the Immigrant Workers Freedom Ride. Protest mobilization was facilitated by labor unions, but also included the active support of immigrant groups, worker centers, the Catholic Church, and Spanish-language radio (Voss and Bloemraad 2011).

The described proimmigrant stance within the AFL-CIO is especially strong among unions representing janitors, garment workers, and hotel and restaurant workers. These unions, along with unions representing immigrant workers in other physically anchored sectors, including farm workers, grocery stores, food processing, and construction laborers, broke from the AFL-CIO in 2005 to form the rival labor federation CTW, which promised increased labor organizing in these sectors.[9] Following the split, there were few AFL-CIO affiliates whose organizing agendas explicitly focused on organizing or incorporating migrant workers.[10] Although this chapter does include reference to two AFL affiliates' successful efforts with immigrant workers (Roofers in Arizona and United Steelworkers [USW] car wash workers in Los Angeles), in neither case does it represent a significant shift[11] in the resource allocation of those unions.

Union structural experimentation also occurred as U.S. trade unions focused more intently on immigrant workers. Laborers International Union of North America (LIUNA) developed and pursued a multifaceted approach to immigrant labor organizing. Beginning in the mid-1990s, LIUNA conducted Spanish-language organizing campaigns in coalition with the National Day Laborers Organizing Network (NDLON) and worker centers among day laborers in residential construction in the U.S. regions of greatest immigrant concentration, namely, the southwest and the northeast.

In certain of its regional efforts, LIUNA undertook significant internal change, even chartering a couple of local unions that allowed for a membership of day laborer workers, and seriously considered a major residential housing campaign in the Southwest. These activities occurred over several years midway through the 2000s, but they were not sustainable due to organizational and economic constraints.[12]

Other Developments, 1990–2012

The Justice for Janitors stunning SEIU organizing success in the early 1990s "highlighted the potential for a broader nationwide labor resurgence" (Milkman 2006: 2). And, for a while, it appeared that this might be the case. Considerable immigrant worker organizing took off in a variety of workplaces in Los Angeles, and there were also significant drives in the Southern states of Texas (janitors) and Florida (health care and janitors). SEIU's success in these campaigns played a key role in helping John Sweeney, then union's president, get elected president of the AFL-CIO in 1995.

Post-1990 immigrant labor organizing strategies varied by geographical context, and by scale, issue breadth, coalition complexity, and degree of local initiation

(Cornfield 2009a; Reynolds 2007). Three generic types of immigrant labor organizing strategies predominate:

1. *Urban labor-community coalitions.* These large-scale, multiunion, top-down and bottom-up social coalitions with multiple community groups address communitywide issues such as living wage campaigns, and occupation and sectorwide issues, including working conditions for janitors, home health care and construction workers. Examples of urban labor-community coalitions are the multiple campaigns conducted by both the SEIU and the Houston-based Harris County AFL-CIO beginning in the mid-1990s on immigrant rights, worker development, and minimum wage (Reynolds 2007: 77, 80);[13] multiple communitywide and sectorwide campaigns in Los Angeles, beginning in the early 1990s, such as the Los Angeles Manufacturing Action Project, the organizing campaigns for home health-care workers,[14] drywallers, and janitors; the Los Angeles Alliance for a New Economy (Milkman 2000, 2006; Reynolds 2007); and the initiation in 1999 of the South Florida Jobs with Justice movement (Nissen and Russo 2007).

2. *New organizing in rural manufacturing.* This single-plant organizing campaign is implemented in a large, rural, nonunion branch factory of a unionized (multi)national corporation. This strategy has been deployed as a corporate campaign with a national consumer mobilization at a food-processing factory in a new destination (for immigrant workers) place by a national union that already has union contracts at other factories of the same corporation. For example, the United Food and Commercial Workers (UFCW) succeeded in organizing the 5,000-worker, multiethnic workforce in its fifteen-year campaign at the Smithfield (world's largest) hog slaughtering factory in Tar Heel, North Carolina in 2008. The UFCW, which already represented some 10,000 Smithfield workers at twenty-six other Smithfield-owned facilities, conducted a national Justice for Smithfield consumer campaign to mobilize public support for the North Carolina workers (Greenhouse 2008a, 2008b; Kromm 2008; UFCW 2008, 2009).

3. *Worker centers.* These are "community-based mediating institutions that provide support to low-wage workers" through service delivery, advocacy, and organizing, especially among newly arriving immigrants (Fine 2006: 2, 11). Unlike labor unions, they do not engage in collective bargaining. Reminiscent of the Jane Addams-era settlement houses, worker centers are place-based organizations that are mainly established by communities, ethnic NGOs, faith-based groups, and social and legal service

agencies. Many have collaborated with unions and participated in the 2003 Immigrant Workers Freedom Ride (Fine 2006). In her exhaustive study of U.S. worker centers, Fine (2006: 11) shows that a "third wave" of worker centers have emerged since 2000 "in suburban and rural areas and in southern states in response to the large concentration of Mexican and Central American immigrants working in the service, poultry, meat-packing, and agricultural sectors." Worker centers have been established, for example, in Southern gateway cities, such as the New Orleans Workers Center for Racial Justice (NOWCRJ 2011), established around 2007 and organizes day laborers and guest workers, and the Miami Workers Center (2011), established in 1999 in the African American community and has since expanded its outreach "to build the collective power of low-income African American and Latino communities" (see also Nissen and Russo 2007: 154).

A further example of third-wave worker centers is the Northwest Arkansas Workers' Justice Center (NAWJC) established in a new-destination community of Latino immigrants and other low-wage workers employed in manufacturing, services, and construction. Established in 2002, NAWJC (2011) works "to improve conditions of employment for low-wage workers in northwest Arkansas by educating, organizing, and mobilizing them, and calling on people of faith and the wider region to publicly support the workers' efforts."

Before turning to the detailed section of union-immigrant worker campaigns, we note that incorporation efforts since 2009 must take into account a national political and economic context, which continues to push the country rightward. In the U.S. workplace "galloping" to the Right might be more accurate. The attacks on both sectors of U.S. workers are vicious, sustained, and manifold across nearly every work location.

The wage stagnation, the accelerated austerity measures, and the continuing, profound economic inequality characterizing the U.S. social and workplace reality have constricted the development of a progressive movement. Shrinkage of union density and even its vaunted electoral power have made it more difficult to fund the AFL-CIO's—and its affiliates—progressive immigrant worker policies and legislative initiatives. Although the UFCW and the SEIU (CTW affiliates) have found a greater degree of organizational comfort in organizing low-wage workers, only AFSCME,[15] LIUNA (which now holds joint membership with CTW and the AFL-CIO), and the USW have struggled with the needs of low-wage, immigrant workers in the much larger federation.[16]

Even so, since 2005 considerable resources have been allocated by the national AFL-CIO which, in conjunction with worker centers, has fought for immigration reform, and in the innovative campaigns with the USW to organize car wash workers on both coasts. Change to Win and its affiliates have acted similarly, as the UFCW (poultry workers), SEIU (building service, hotels,[17] and health care), and LIUNA (day laborers, weatherization, residential housing) have each undertaken serious campaigns to organize immigrant workers previously overlooked by U.S. trade unions.

Perhaps the most interesting development is the political space created by the national federations' willingness to partner with immigrant worker advocacy groups. On the U.S. East Coast, these include a reliable segment of New York City unions' financial and other support for the Domestic Workers United (DWU)[18] political and organizing campaigns, the immigrant worker organizing accomplished by Brandworkers of New York City retail stores, Make the Road New York in the City's car washes,[19] ROC-NY's restaurant organizing,[20] and LIUNA's uncertain but important relationship with NDLON.

Key Campaigns

Our research includes five case studies of immigrant labor organizing. Immigrant labor organizing in right-to-work and new-destination states empowers and serves the immigrant workers with the deepest deficits in social, economic, and political resources and, consequently, are most vulnerable to the greatest nativist abuse by employers, the state, and local communities. Two of our cases, written by Denisse Roca-Servat, are Latino worker campaigns in Arizona (Justice for Roofers, 1996–2006) and in Los Angeles (CLEAN Carwash Campaign). Two other cases—written by Dan Cornfield—take place in new-destination places, among Muslim Somali workers, first at a UFCW plant in the Middle Tennessee region, and the other in Nashville, by taxi cab drivers.[21] Janice Fine wrote the fifth case, which tracks both the significant innovative efforts by LIUNA to link up and organize immigrant workers, as well as the internal and external difficulties that made success difficult.

Los Angeles CLEAN Carwash Campaign, 2008–2012

The CLEAN Carwash Campaign[22] is a joint effort between the Community-Labor-Environmental Action Network (CLEAN), the Carwash Workers Organizing Committee (CWOC) of the USW, and the AFL-CIO. One of the campaign visionaries, Victor Narro refers to it as a "cooperative, industry-wide strategy" that grew out of years of advocacy on behalf of L.A.'s carwash workers by progressive lawyers working through community organizations and worker centers. The CLEAN Carwash Campaign embodies the effort of carwash workers to assert their right to organize in order to improve labor conditions in the industry.

There are many reasons why this campaign has received national attention from immigrant communities, social justice activists, and labor unions. In large part, it is because these groups were each needed in order to attain success. Especially noteworthy was the positive way that worker center messaging, emphasizing immigrant worker social and political needs, was honored by the USW and the AFL-CIO. Trust was thus built early and often. As a coalition, these key groups complemented the efforts of progressive lawyers who have fought for many years on behalf of this mostly undocumented workforce, attacking wage and hour violations, wage theft claims, and multiple health and safety concerns.

The campaign has carefully focused on building civic participation and social integration. Coalition partners have helped immigrant workers navigate the world of work and the larger U.S. society. They have succeeded by "broadening out" the campaign to include collaborations between labor and community alliances, political integration, and sociocultural integration, while stressing workers' rights and their health and safety on the job. Essentially, the campaign was able to explain to members of the immigrant communities involved that what happened to carwash workers really mattered to all.

At the same time, within the union's internal structure, the campaign required the USW to include Latino immigrant workers as organizers and union representatives to incorporate culturally appropriate union organizing strategies. It also served as a key building block between the USW and Los Angeles' progressive labor movement.

The campaign surely has had its difficulties, ranging from a stubborn and highly diffuse set of employers, to an impoverished workforce that must be careful due to its overwhelmingly undocumented status. This is not a workforce in which U.S. trade unions have been historically interested, but in this coalition unions played an exemplary role as "listening" outsiders who had a lot of strategic skill and political power to bring to the struggle. That, coupled with a serious commitment, resulted in a historic first union contract in the carwash industry late in 2011, with two others signed in 2012.

The modest success, covering fewer than 100 workers, is significant for other reasons. Unlike the Justice for Roofers campaign described below, or either of the Muslim campaigns, we see a stronger and more lasting connection to the community in the Los Angeles campaign. Part of that is because of the incredible work done since at least 1995 by progressives in the community's labor movement and the immigrant rights movement. The other part is attributable to the resolve of the USW/AFL-CIO organizations, as they realize that success of incorporating migrants into U.S. trade unions requires a certain degree of elbow grease, and they are prepared to use it.

The unions truly learned from this experience that they bring value even when they are not "in charge" of the community coalition, and the victory for the workers, the community, and the USW/AFL-CIO has been quite inspirational.

Arizona Justice for Roofers, 1999–2006

The lengthy Justice for Roofers campaign[23] also involved Latino workers—many of whom were undocumented—in the anti-immigrant state of Arizona. It deployed a comprehensive union-organizing model tailored to the industry, characterized by unusually collaborative efforts of several construction unions undertaking immigrant organizing in a manner respectful toward the culture of the workers involved. Examining the different actors, strategies, and actions used helps us understand the possibility of immigrant worker union organizing in the construction industry in the United States.

As slow as other U.S. trade unions have been to realize the importance of organizing immigrant workers, the construction unions have been even slower. Even in large cities in union-friendly political environments, the building trades have been reluctant to undertake inclusion of migrant workers into their affiliates (Gordon 2005). Arizona seemed an odd place where the traditions of the building trade unions might be set aside.

The roofers union in Arizona faced a highly transient work force where low wages, unsafe conditions, overwhelming numbers of undocumented workers, and extreme weather resulted in a yearly turnover rate of 90 percent (Roca-Servat 2010). The lead organizers, schooled in construction campaigns in Las Vegas and with the Farm Workers years earlier, saw hope in this rough terrain, and the Roofers International president, together with the newly anointed AFL-CIO Organizing Institute graduates, forged an alliance not unlike the USW/AFL-CIO, with each organization offering considerable resources to advance the campaign. The organizing model pursued was bottom up, also referred to as community organizing, as the lead organizers rejected the construction industry "old reliable," the so-called COMET program.[24]

There is special value in studying this case and allowing it to inform those interested in unions and immigrant worker organizing. The author of the case was an organizer in the campaign, and she was able to observe and listen to the organizers, the workers, and the worker-leaders. Being on the "ground level" permitted Roca-Servat to write about and understand at a very deep level the importance of the union's bicultural approach and its cross-cultural sensitivity. Workers who sensed that the union organizers were not very different from them stepped forward and undertook more risk, which lead to a higher chance of organizing success.

The roofers' organizers also pursued, like the L.A. carwash campaigners, a legal strategy around minimum wages, failure to pay overtime, and wage theft. This kept the pressure on at another front, and proved to be helpful in bringing an important contractor to the bargaining table. As the campaign strengthened, it spread into other, non-Latino segments of the community, and even traveled across state lines where other leverage possibilities existed. Some of the campaign's early successes seem to influence other trade unions, as sheet metal workers, painters, and iron workers also succeeded in organizing alongside the roofers in the home and commercial construction industry.

During the organizing drive, this roofing contractor grew from 350 workers to more than 700. This growth of significant numbers of residential roofers as union members, the majority of them first generation Latino immigrants, posed a tremendous test for proper union representation and communication.[25] With the support of the International and the Local Roofers' Union, not only were Spanish-speaking representatives and an office assistant hired, but some English-only speaking union officials such as the Local's treasurer made an effort to learn Spanish in order to communicate better with new union members.[26] Union member meetings were initially conducted in both English and Spanish and eventually in Spanish only. All these changes signified important restructuring within the union.

This case is one that could serve as a model for how U.S. trade unions might proceed with their immigrant worker organizing. With the correct research, culturally astute union leadership, proper logistical support, a strategic legal component, and substantial horizontal engagement with the work force, undocumented workers "become" workers and are amenable to being organized. The value of all elements of a grassroots campaign, immersion in the community with the workers, their neighbors, their community associations, coupled with recognition of their culture and heritage, all create trust, a condition precedent to organizing success.

The roofers' struggle in Arizona was "the first attempt to build a participatory[27] union movement not only in the midst of a very anti-immigrant and antiunion setting but also in the face of some internal union opposition" (Roca-Servat 2010: 361). In this regard, it represents a story "of guts and willingness to experiment in the face of tremendous odds" (Gordon 2005: 4). Although its sustainability will not be easy, its methodology offers considerable hope for future efforts that evidence the preparation, care, and thoughtful selection of staff.

LIUNA, 1996–2012

LIUNA's efforts to redesign its relationship with immigrant workers have taken many complex and at times confusing turns. The union was an early supporter of the push inside the AFL-CIO to change the federation's policy on immigrant workers. It was among the first, if not the first, of the building trade unions to recognize that altering the sharp decline in union density in this sector required pursuit of both a legislative (immigration reform) and organizing (immigrant workers, including the undocumented) strategy. It was also perhaps the most forward U.S. trade union in reaching out to nonstandard, undocumented workers as it forged alliances in parts of the country with NDLON.[28]

Research of these activities by the author of this case and one of our editors revealed LIUNA organizers melting into immigrant worker communities in the Southwest and in New Jersey, respecting the biculturalism discussed in the roofers case, and assisting workers with police, housing, and wage theft problems. A sophisticated organizing structure was set up in Arizona, which evidenced the national officers' serious commitment to organize immigrant workers who were building homes before the 2007 economic crash. However, by overlooking LIUNA regional officials in launching the campaign, which caused considerable internal bickering, coupled with the huge layoffs reflective of the housing crisis, the drive ground to a halt.

During this same time, in New Jersey LIUNA began to experiment with the establishment of new locals that for the most part consisted of day laborers recruited to the union. One local was set up in New Jersey and another in New York City. By setting these up as separate locals, with a focus at least in New Jersey of anticipated work in weatherization, the organization sought to both acknowledge the importance of day laborers and bypass stubborn regional parts of LIUNA that did not think organizing immigrant workers, especially undocumented ones, was a high priority. This effort, too, sputtered, despite remarkable and courageous behavior by a number of Spanish-speaking organizers who used the LIUNA "brand" in community, police, and union meetings to tamp down hatred directed at the migrants and tried mightily to incorporate them into civil society.

Despite LIUNA's earlier immigrant worker organizing successes in the North Carolina poultry and New York City asbestos industries in the late 1990s, economic, legal, and structural problems prevented actualizing the hoped for relationship between the union and NDLON. The economic crisis has all but eliminated any funding for further house building or weatherization and forced day laborers into small renovation jobs that preclude a union presence. The same was and is true of residential construction that has slowed so considerably that the dreams of LIUNA organizers had to be shelved.

The somewhat unexpected heavier reliance during the Obama years of both E-verify[29] and ICE raids[30] has also made it more difficult to strengthen and make operational the NDLON partnership. Greater risk has now become a part of the discussion, and reluctance to deepen the NDLON-LIUNA relationship has replaced the hope that characterized their 2008 joinder. The fact that immigration reform has not occurred, nor is it likely, strengthens the position of those in LIUNA who believe, especially in a time of economic crisis, that pursuit of immigrant workers is not a successful strategy to pursue.[31]

The Case of Somali Workers in Middle Tennessee

During the mid- and late 2000s in Middle Tennessee, first generation Somali immigrant workers participated in labor campaigns among Nashville taxi drivers and Tyson poultry-processing factory workers in rural Shelbyville. In both places Somalis faced intense nativism and employer resistance (Cornfield 2008; Greenhouse 2008c; Jordan 2009; Tobia 2006). In each setting they experienced adverse relations with native local authorities, such as police and landlords, and reside in highly segregated neighborhoods (Cornfield 2009a; Cornfield and Arzubiaga 2004; Cornfield et al. 2003; Hinton 2005; Lena and Cornfield 2008; Marx 2005; *Next Door Neighbors, Somali-Soomaali* 2009). The taxi drivers are independent contractors who continue to shape their model of "nontraditional" self-organization, whether it is trade unionism, entrepreneurialism, or a blend of these models. The case of poultry workers is a case of already unionized factory workers who developed what is thought to be the first contractual recognition of Muslim holiday observance in a U.S. labor agreement. The Tyson poultry-processing plant workers are represented by the Retail, Wholesale, Department Store Union (RWDSU), an affiliate since 1993 of the United Food and Commercial Workers.

Nashville Taxi Cab Drivers

The case of Nashville taxi cab drivers is a case of self-organization of an occupational association among the predominantly Somali and Ethiopian immigrant owner-operators.[32] As owner-operators and independent contractors, the drivers have been stymied in their efforts to unionize and bargain with the union-resistant, oligopolistic taxi cab industry that is regulated by the municipal government in a city that is polarized in its acceptance of immigrants.

In the Nashville taxi industry there are seven taxi companies, a Transportation Licensing Commission (TLC) that regulates transportation safety and taxi rates, and the Nashville Metro Taxi Drivers Alliance (NMTDA), a nonprofit organization, 40 percent of whose members are Somalis and Ethiopians. They earn on average under $12,000, which is twice below the federal five-person family poverty guideline (Franklin n.d.). Efforts to unionize on a craft or occupational basis and to realize collective bargaining were unsuccessful due to an unresolved determination of the drivers' independent contractor status, cab company resistance, and TLC nonresponsiveness (*Nashville City Paper* 2008; Tennessee Immigrant and Refugee Rights Coalition 2008).

The establishment of the independent NMTDA occurred at a meeting of taxi drivers, labor officials, and immigrant rights advocates on August 5, 2007 in Nashville. In attendance at the meeting were four taxi drivers; Lewis Beck, president of the Middle Tennessee Central Labor Council that was collaborating with the United Automobile Workers in a taxi cab drivers campaign; Steelworkers legal counsel Lynn Agee; and Ahmed Dahir of the Tennessee Immigrant and Refugee Rights Coalition. The NMTDA was established as an independent nonprofit organization with a temporary board and has remained unaffiliated with the labor movement. The drivers' chief concerns were and have been police racial profiling of drivers, difficulties with their insurance, support for a living wage, better opportunities at the airport, and the prevention of unauthorized cabs and drivers.

The NMDTA have joined with unions, civil rights groups, and trade unions to fight for a living wage, neighborhood safety, and the right to unionize. The drivers have called at least one strike in support of their various demands, but as of 2013 they had not succeeded in organizing into a union. Still, their efforts to organize, and the support they received from the Nashville area trade unions, signified a big change in the local labor movement's efforts to incorporate the aspirations of these African immigrant workers.

Poultry Workers in Shelbyville, Tennessee

The case of Islamic holiday collective bargaining in Republican rural Middle Tennessee is a case of the industrial-union role in promoting local labor solidarity among its multiethnic and religiously diverse factory workforce. The union pursued labor solidarity with the immigrant Muslim workers' religious practices by designating Eid al-Fitr as one of eight paid holidays in the contract. This was subsequently dismantled in response to the vehement, local and national, nativist rejection of immigrant cultural practices by the community, compelling the company and the union to renegotiate and restore the previous, conventional schedule of paid holidays. Nonetheless, the bargaining parties agreed to inscribe Eid al-Fitr in the contract as an optional paid personal holiday, making this the first contractual recognition of a Muslim holiday in a U.S. labor agreement.

A growing number of Muslim Somali refugees in the United States have sought employment in the U.S. food-processing industry. They joined Latino workers in increasing the percentage of foreign born people in this county from 1.1 percent in 1990 to 9.0 percent between 2005 and 2007. The Somalis were mainly recruited to Bedford County with the assistance of Nashville refugee resettlement agencies by Tyson Foods as workers in the Tyson poultry-processing factory (Mosley 2007a, 2007b, 2008a). Prior to the arrival of Somalis, and after 1972 when Tyson acquired the plant, Tyson hired in succession white, African American, and Hispanic workers (Ross 2008). Immigrant-native tensions in Bedford County have arisen with increasing immigration and the deterioration of local macroeconomic conditions. Portions of the local civil society have emerged to promote positive group relations and offset the growing tensions. No labor-community coalition was a part of this effort.

It is within this context that in October 2007, the union and management at the Tyson poultry-processing plant negotiated a new contract provision that substituted the Muslim holiday of Eid al-Fitr for Labor Day as one of the eight paid holidays. This historic agreement, according to the RWDSU, "was the first union contract in the U.S. to recognize the holiday" (RWDSU 2008).[33] The union-initiated holiday provision was an accommodation for the Somali workers. As fifty-four-year-old Abdillahi Jama, a Somalian refugee employed at the plant, put it, referring to the prayer rooms and the holiday provision, "This new contract is good because it allows me to work on the second shift and still pray when I need to . . . It's very important to us, and the Eid is one of our most sacred holidays. It shows how the union helps us" (Mosley 2008b; Tyson Foods 2008b).[34] The twelve-person union negotiating committee, which included three Somali members, unanimously proposed the new holiday provision and 80–90 percent of the union members supported the new contract provision.

As Labor Day approached in August 2008, local newspaper coverage of the new Shelbyville Tyson holiday provision touched off a local and national nativist outcry against the union and the company. The local community reaction received national media attention that would compel union and company to renegotiate the historic holiday provision. Labor Day was restored as a guaranteed paid holiday for all workers, and Eid al-Fitr was made an optional paid personal holiday (Mosley 2008c; Tyson Foods 2008a).

Concluding Observations

Whether Briggs's "restrictionist" or Fine's more nuanced view of the labor movement "wrestling" over the past 150 years with itself about the incorporation and support of immigrant workers is correct, both would likely agree that something quite significant has changed. The AFL-CIO's public and emphatic pronouncement in 2000 supportive of a broad range of rights for immigrant workers at work and in civil society continues today.[35]

The politics, demographics, organizational successes, and the moral imperative of the immigrant worker movement for equality and justice in the United States are not likely to be overlooked by the U.S. labor movement for a long time. A number of U.S. labor organizations, led by SEIU, have all but made organizing heavily weighted immigrant workplaces a priority. Other unions' efforts described in this chapter reveal a broad range of involvement and experimentation in support of immigrant workers. How surprising it is that a building trade organization like the roofers applied such an innovative set of strategies and succeeded in the reactionary labor climate of Arizona! Or that LIUNA created alternate forms of membership, not too successfully, for day laborers and other immigrant workers. And that both the AFL-CIO and the USW undertook a long term and continuing struggle, coalescing with community organizations, to organize the nonstandard immigrant workers who comprise the carwash industry in Los Angeles.

These developments, along with the legislative efforts and civic organizing and demonstrations in support of immigrant workers tell us that U.S. trade unions' incorporation efforts are quite determined, when undertaken. Surely key questions and concerns remain. We doubt that these positive developments have significantly impacted many U.S. workplaces. And we wonder to what extent the immigrant worker organizing, struggles to accomplish legislative reform, political demonstrations, and structural innovation since 2000 by U.S. trade unions has resulted in an increase in workplace or political and civic space for immigrant workers and their families.

We cannot reply with "yes" to these questions. Certainly, there have been real gains in the SEIU organizing successes in Los Angeles, Miami, Houston, and elsewhere with regard to building and health-care workers. Likewise, the hotel workers union—although much more modestly—where successful, have truly changed the working and economic conditions of the immigrant workers assisted by their organizing gains. And, yes, there is civic meaning to the Arizona roofers' campaign, and to the LIUNA's effort to create alternative structures to incorporate immigrant workers into their union, even if not sustainable.

But it is also hard to not remember that most AFL-CIO and CTW organizations are not engaged in organizing or incorporation efforts on behalf of immigrant workers. These unions are in daily fights for their survival, as the protracted economic downturn and harsh political reactions pummel their institutions and their members' well-being. All of the USW resources directed toward the L.A.

car wash fight, including its expansion to New York City,[36] as well as the LIUNA, roofers, and UFCW undertakings, have resulted in the organization of very few workers.

Meanwhile, 390,000 immigrants were deported in 2011 by the federal government headed by a Democratic president, suggesting that United States' progressive forces, including the country's trade unions, have not been able to alter the governmental attacks on these workers and their families. Somewhere, in the calculus of civic incorporation, this development means something.

Our study neither underestimates the remarkable organizing successes and efforts at structural innovation, nor overestimates what they really mean to immigrant workers and their families. Organizing any workers in the United States is extremely difficult, and many believe that only labor law reform legislation will change this. Likewise, many immigrant worker advocates believe that only by immigration reform will organizing these workers be possible. Both of these hoped for changes have remained elusive, in good and bad times, and one wonders whether trade unions and their immigrant worker colleagues need to consider different approaches or strategies in order to succeed.

THE UNITED KINGDOM

Dialectic Approaches to Organizing Immigrant
Workers, Postwar to 2012

Maite Tapia

> I do not think we need in this country a "melting pot," which will
> turn everybody out in a common mould, as one of a series of carbon
> copies of someone's misplaced vision of the stereotyped English-
> man. . . . I define integration, therefore, not as a flattening process
> of assimilation but as equal opportunity, coupled with cultural diver-
> sity, in an atmosphere of mutual tolerance.

—Speech by Roy Jenkins, UK Home Secretary, 1966

Since the 1970s, Roy Jenkins's vision, known as the "Jenkins formula," has signified a shift for British policymakers, establishing laws and guidelines within
a model of multiculturalism rather than assimilation. Multiculturalism, that is,
recognizing distinctive cultural and ethnic traditions (Taylor 1994), has been
contrasted with assimilation, often described as "absorbing" minority groups
into the larger established community. Even though there is variation within each
country, it is widely claimed that policy in France is based largely on a Republican
model of assimilation, whereas in the United Kingdom it is based on a model of
multiculturalism.[1]

The United Kingdom, unlike France or the United States, has not been a traditional country of immigration. Up until the 1980s, it was a country of net
emigration (Schain 2008; Winder 2004). The Trades Union Congress (TUC),
representing the majority of the UK's trade unions, did not even discuss issues
surrounding immigration or racial discrimination until 1955 (i.e., the postwar
Caribbean immigration). From then until the 1970s, however, the labor movement favored selective, exclusionary, and restrictive policies (Wrench 2000). Mir-
roring official UK policy, only since the early 1970s have the trade unions shifted
their debates from assimilation to a more multicultural vision of society.

The trade unions' conventional strategy toward minorities was one of "pas-
sive assimilation and race blindness: the collective problems of workers transcend

whatever differentiates them along race, gender, or cultural lines" (Virdee and Grint 1994: 208), to counter that tendency some unions developed special structures to deal with race or issues affecting black members. This dialectic still persists today: on the one hand, British trade unions set up self-organizing structures, guaranteeing the autonomy of ethnic minority groups; on the other, they stress a more integrative approach, considering workers as workers, regardless of their background.

Postwar Historical Context

As in other European countries the United Kingdom actively recruited migrant workers to rebuild the economy after 1945. Initially, Britain recruited Polish ex-servicemen and European Voluntary Workers from refugee camps, and from Southern and Eastern Europe. The TUC, and especially the miners' union, however, insisted on strict conditions, arguing that these immigrants could be employed only if there was no British labor available (Wrench 2000). Facing discrimination particularly in industries where unions were strong, immigrants often held low-skilled, manual jobs. Migrant workers were seen as a threat to jobs and working conditions, undermining the high wages and benefits won by the trade unions (Freeman 1997; Kalecki 1943).

Labor migration came from ex-colonies as well: West Indies, India, and Pakistan—the Commonwealth. According to the 1948 British Nationality Act all subjects of the crown had the right to enter Britain. These workers, through their commonwealth citizenship, had the right to live and work in Britain without restrictions. Indeed, they had the same political and legal rights as the British citizens (e.g., voting rights in local and national elections). This colonial status was thus very different from the guest workers in other European countries. Although they had the same rights in theory, the Commonwealth workers took subordinate positions in employment compared to white British workers and were over-represented in low-paid, insecure jobs (Wrench 2000).

During the 1950s and 1960s, the UK trade unions' position can be categorized as "racist exclusive": some trade unions' preference was, first, to keep migrant workers out of the labor market, since that was not possible; second, to keep them out of the union; third, since many became union members, to exclude them from the entitled union benefits (Wrench 2000).[2] The hostility of the TUC was based on social rather than economic grounds. Although the immigrant workers did not constitute a threat to the jobs of British workers, the TUC argued that black workers did not integrate with white workers, which helped to stereotype black migrant workers as "problem" and "other" (Holgate 2009b; Wrench 2000).[3]

Furthermore, during the 1950s there were numerous race riots and attacks on immigrants by white youths and neofascist organizations and a populist wing of the Conservative Party was on the rise (Geddes 2003).

Since 1962 there has been a shift toward immigration restriction through legislation (this took place before the economic downturn of 1973). Control legislation was introduced by the Conservative government and rested on the assumption that all those who could potentially move to Britain would actually do so (approximately 800 million people). The TUC failed to oppose the legislation until the early 1970s, when industrial disputes, pressure from within the labor movement, and the growth of the National Front pushed the TUC toward policies against racism and discrimination, to reconsider their color blind approach, and to produce educational material on the subject of migration.

Key conflicts occurred in 1972, 1974, and 1976 with a discourse around "race," rather than immigration. In October 1972, 500 South Asian workers went on strike at the Mansfield Hosiery Mills. Even though the workers received eventual support from their union, the importance was the support from the community and other Asian workers rather than from their fellow white workers. In a similar vein, in 1974 Asian women at Imperial Typewriter went on strike without support from their union. This conflict illustrates again the racist attitudes from union reps, on the one hand, and the necessary support from the community for the Asian workers, on the other. Finally, in 1976, the APEX (Association of Professional, Executive, Clerical and Computer Staff) strike at Grunwick, a photo processing plant, has been historically very significant. Asian women demanded union recognition through a strike that lasted over a year. This time, however, they received full support of the labor movement. The APEX strike can be considered a watershed moment for both black and white workers—for whites to see "blacks" (as they were called then) striking for union recognition, and for "blacks" to see unions as allies. Some scholars argue that the support from the union movement came to stop an attack against the labor movement as a whole, rather than out of antiracist sentiments. However, it is important to recognize that while the union was fighting for basic union rights, it had to confront its own past failures concerning migrant workers—an important step forward in the development of their antiracist strategy (Holgate 2009b).

In the 1980s, the low participation of black workers in the unions led to debates concerning separate structures or self-organization within unions to ensure that black issues and the rights of other marginalized groups are being addressed by the trade union (Wrench 2004). According to a 1984 Policy Studies Institute study (and more recent data from the UK government), the density of union membership is higher among black workers than white workers, but black members are much less likely to hold an elected position within the union, particularly at senior level. These self-organizing structures are considered a strategy to increase participation and facilitate the participation of black members (and other marginalized groups) into the mainstream union structures more easily (Virdee and Grint 1994). Furthermore, since 1993, the TUC also has an annual black workers conference (referring to all nonwhite people).

Finally, since the 1990s, there has been more immigration from Europe, especially from the east after the European enlargement in 2004. One-third of the migrant workers are from Poland. A majority, however, end up in low-paid service sector and construction jobs and many are being hired through agencies as temporary workers (Anderson et al. 2006; Fitzgerald and Hardy 2010). It has been a tough organizing environment for unions: Thatcher antiunion laws are in place, union density has declined, and economic restructuring, such as geographical fragmentation, makes it hard to organize workers. Furthermore, the public sector is undergoing waves of privatization. Many civil service jobs, such as nursing or street cleaning, are now contracted out to private companies, making it harder to organize these workers.

Current Context

In the United Kingdom, trade union density fell precipitously through the 1980s and early 1990s and is currently about 26 percent. The difference between the sectors is striking with 14.2 percent union density in the private sector and 56.5 percent in the public sector. Furthermore, collective agreements covered 16.8 percent of private sector employees in 2010, a fall of 5.7 percentage points compared with 2000, and 64.5 percent of public employees, a fall by 3.6 percentage points from 2009, and by 9.7 percentage points compared with 2000 (BIS 2011; ONS 2010).

In 2010, an estimated 7,000,000 people in the United Kingdom were foreign born, or about 11 percent of the total population. The biggest group comes from India, followed by Poland (ONS 2010). Although numbers of Eastern Europeans have grown in the United Kingdom, they still form a comparatively small part of the workforce or 472,000 workers (1.63% of the workforce) by the end of 2009, compared to 13,000 (0.05% of workforce) at the end of 1997 (ONS 2010).

Between 2008 and 2012, the United Kingdom slipped into a "double-dip" recession. Consecutive quarters of negative economic growth in 2008–2009 and then again in 2011–2012 pushed the United Kingdom into a long and deep recession. Unemployment rose significantly from just over 5 percent in 2007 up to over 8 percent in 2012. This high unemployment rate has dire consequences for the labor movement as well, costing it at least hundred thousand members (interview with a TUC national organizer, June 17, 2009). The harsh economic situation, the austerity-related job cuts, and job insecurity have significantly affected the health and well-being of workers (TUC 2012). Meanwhile, the narrative of the UK government has been focused on austerity measures, spending cuts and increasing taxes. Conversely, trade unions have challenged this narrative, emphasizing how the austerity cuts represent a political choice rather than an economic necessity. Marches and demonstrations have erupted against these harsh economic and political measures taken by the government. Although migrant workers have not always been on the forefront, they are often in the weakest position, suffering the most from these austerity cuts.

In 2009, a new labor dispute concerning migrant workers swept across the British isles. On January 28, 2009, hundreds of (nonmigrant) protesters demonstrated outside the Total Lindsey oil refinery in Lincolnshire, in the east of England. These wildcat strikers held up placards echoing Gordon Brown's 2007 "British jobs for British workers" Labor Party conference promise. The refinery, owned by the oil company Total, subcontracted a £200 million construction project to an Italian firm, IREM. This firm brought in its own Italian and Portuguese workforce and was perceived as "stealing" local jobs, cutting labor costs, thereby undermining British jobs. The inflow of migrant workers at a time of high unemployment angered local communities. Within days, a strike wave spread quickly across the United Kingdom. Thousands of British, Scottish, and Welsh workers at over a dozen energy sites walked out in solidarity with their fellow employees. These series of protests attracted heightened media attention and were portrayed in a particularly xenophobic fashion. During the Lincolnshire dispute, the two main unions involved—Unite and GMB—purposefully shunned any debates on migrant workers, but rather emphasized the detrimental character of the European Directive on "posted" workers. They tried to accentuate the role of the employer who was taking advantage of migrant workers by paying them less than British workers.

Following the Total experience, the 2009 TUC Black Workers Conference issued a report stating that the slogan "British jobs for British workers" has no place in the labor movement. In addition, the report warned that the recession could have a "disproportionately adverse impact" on black workers and the rise in racism might lead to black workers being scapegoated. Furthermore, they are at risk on the labor market and are more likely to become unemployed than white workers due to their position in low-paid insecure jobs (TUC report 2009).

In 2010, after thirteen years of Labour Party rule, a Conservative/Liberal Democrat coalition came into power. The government's response to the economic crisis has been mainly to cut public spending. These austerity measures have led to several big demonstrations and protests across the United Kingdom.

Between November 2010 and February 2011, students protested against the increase in college tuition fees. The unions supported these demonstrations, though they were slow to react. Eventually, the TUC called for a big demonstration on March 26, 2011. This "March for the Alternative" came in response to the governments' public spending cuts and was attended by an estimated 500,000 people, making it the biggest demonstration in London since the 2003 anti-Iraq war protest.

Furthermore, the dire socioeconomic conditions have led to social unrest. In August 2011, riots broke out in England, starting in Tottenham, North London, and spreading across London and other areas of the country. Prime Minister David Cameron declared these riots as "criminality, pure and simple," many blame the harsh austerity measures imposed by the government and the increasing inequality in the United Kingdom (Alternet 2011). The riots were triggered by police killing of a young black man in a country where black people are twenty-six times more likely to be stopped and searched by police than white people (Townsend 2010). In addition, Tottenham is an area with the highest unemployment in London, where youth clubs have been closed due to 75 percent cut in youth services. As current research has shown, highly unequal societies are far less stable than more equal societies (Wilkinson and Pickett 2009). In the United Kingdom, the richest 10 percent are now 100 times better off than the poorest (Gentleman and Mulholland 2010) and according to the OECD (2010), social mobility is worse than in any other developed country.

Union Strategies since the 1990s

Diverse approaches to the organization and inclusion of immigrant workers between and within UK unions are clearly noticeable from the research. Even though there have been some successes, a comprehensive trade union strategy concerning migrant workers has yet to be developed. First, debate in this area is often lacking; it is framed in such terms that migrant workers are workers, regardless of their nationality, which leads to relatively few specific organizing approaches among migrant workers. Second, trade unions are often dependent on government funding for their migrant workers' projects, which often limits what the union can do in this regard. Third, historically, the UK unions have focused on lobbying government rather than mobilizing workers. The Labour Party was considered the political expression of the labor movement. Even though some decades ago, the natural political arena for union activists was to automatically join the Labour Party, now this no longer holds, creating challenges for the trade unions (interview with a TUC national organizer, June 24, 2009).

Overall, UK unions have been most successful in organizing migrant workers through educational channels, for example by offering English for Speakers of Other Languages (ESOL) classes. A large majority of trade unions have used ESOL classes to enhance the employability of migrant workers as well as to foster social cohesion among the workforce (Report UnionLearn 2007). As some scholars have shown, these union learning initiatives can be a means to stimulate membership as well as organize migrant workers (e.g., Heyes 2009; Mustchin 2012). Furthermore, many scholars have shown a positive correlation between union education and labor revitalization (e.g., Findlay and Warhurst 2001; Moore 2009b; Rainbird and Stuart 2011; Stuart et al. 2010; for exceptions, see McIlroy 2008). Even though these learning initiatives have value, they remain small scale and highly volatile as they are often dependent on government funding (Perrett and Martínez Lucio 2008). The Labour government established the Union Learning Fund in 1998, developing a new type of union activist (union learning reps or ULRs) similar to that of the general union representative or shop steward. These ULRs are more likely to be women, blacks, young, or recent hires. Currently in the United Kingdom there are about 24,000 ULRs and they are paid by the employer (TUC 2012). The Union Learning Fund, through the Department of Business, Innovation, and Skills, is still in existence at the time of writing. Finally, the Union Modernisation Fund offered support for projects involving "vulnerable workers." The funds were allocated by the government between 2005 and 2009 and have been used by TGWU/Unite for their Justice for Cleaners campaign, by UNISON to set up a Migrant Workers Participation Unit, and by the GMB for their migrant worker project. In 2010, however, the new Conservative-led coalition government abolished the union modernization funds.

Finally, scholars have called on trade unions to engage with civil society, working outside their traditional structures (e.g., Tapia 2012; Wills 2001, 2004). Fitzgerald (2009), for example, emphasized the innovative trade union strategies for organizing the new Polish migrant workers in the north of England, showing how the unions approached the Polish church and used the Polish UK media to organize the migrant workers. Unions remain wary, however, of working outside their existing structures. Although some trade unions have begun to build alliances with community organizations, for the most part these have been short term and on a small scale. Most efforts of community-labor alliances are still in early stages.

One important example of a community organization is London Citizens (LC). This organization will "organize people where they are already organized"— churches, community centers, schools, unions. LC has worked together with trade unions on campaigns, such as the Justice for Cleaners campaign (Holgate and Wills 2007). Tensions, however, come to the forefront. Union representatives remain often suspicious of working with faith communities. In addition, there is a different form of decision making between the two organizations. Trade unions are based on a representative model, whereas London Citizens tries to enforce a broader participatory model (Holgate 2009c).

The Transport and General Workers Union (TGWU/Unite)[4] has been one of the most active unions in bottom-up organizing and in mobilizing workers. Since 2003, with the election of the then general secretary Tony Woodley, the union has taken on a "strategy for growth" approach, emphasizing committed leadership, allocation of financial resources toward organizing, and the establishment of an organizing department. The emphasis is on "organizing the unorganized" in different sectors—food industry (red and white meat), building services (cleaners), or aviation (low cost airlines)—focusing on membership and numbers to assess its growth. This greenfield organizing is supplemented by "brownfield organizing," or expanding the membership where there is already a union in place. Migrant workers become part of the union through these organizing drives inspired by both the U.S. "organizing model," based on collaborations with the U.S. trade union SEIU, as well as by the efforts of LC. Although efforts are not specifically directed at organizing migrants, the latter in fact make up the majority of the workforce in those sectors. The strategy of the union is to focus on migrant workers as workers, trying to identify "deeply felt, widely felt, and winnable issues."

In addition, the union has benefited from government funding to provide training and education for its members. For example, during the Justice for Cleaners campaign, the union received financial support through the Union Modernization Fund and UnionLearn, which has been used to provide services to migrants such as, advice on rights, social services and language training as well as putting in place new union learning reps. Furthermore, between 2007 and 2009, the union set up a Migrant Workers Support Unit (MWSU). Finally, Unite wants to be known as the migrant workers' union, envisioning an international transferable union membership card (interview with a TGWU/Unite's international programs coordinator, March 17, 2009). It has also introduced limited membership for the unemployed and young people in an attempt to reach out further into the wider community (Unite 2011).

In sum, the focus of TGWU/Unite is on organizing and grassroots mobilization; although mainly workplace-based, the union has forged temporary alliances with civil society actors such as London Citizens. The union set up a MWSU, which mainly focuses on servicing migrant members, whereas the union branches focus on organizing all workers, regardless of their identity. Consequently, a discrepancy is noticeable between the MWSU (mainly service oriented) and the organizing work that is done by the branches.

Unison, the biggest public sector union with over 1.3 million members, has more of a project-based approach to migrant workers. The focus of this union is on offering services to migrant workers, rather than conducting big organizing drives, as a way to involve them within the union structures. Again, with funding from the Union Modernization Fund, it carried out both national and regional projects and set up the Migrant Workers Participation Project, a three-person unit within its national office. The projects consisted mainly of providing services to migrant workers such as ESOL classes, skills development, and training. In addition, Unison has set up separate, self-organizing structures for women, black, disabled, and LGBT (lesbian, gay, bisexual, and transgender) members as a way to deal with minority issues.

There has been a collaboration between the Migrant Workers Participation unit and academics from the Working Lives Research Institute at London Metropolitan University to look at the relationship of newly recruited migrant workers to their union branches (Moore 2009a). Unison is having some success in recruiting members into the union, but branches are less successful at integrating migrant workers into branches or union activity. Despite some pockets of success (e.g., Filipino migrant nurses network in Scotland), a systematic, comprehensive approach to the integration of migrant workers is still missing.

In sum, Unison is more oriented toward servicing members and lobbying government rather than mobilizing workers. Most of the work is workplace-based, although Unison had some success in building alliances with community groups such as the Filipino community. Often, however, this is the result of single bridge builders within the union rather than a developed strategy at the national, regional, or branch level.

The general trade union GMB caused some controversy by establishing the first migrant workers' trade union branch. It was set up in 2006 through the collaboration of the Southern Region Education Department of the GMB and the Polish community in Southampton. The project workers were financed by the Union Learning Fund and the main channel through which the GMB has been able to organize these workers was training and education. More than 500 of the 600–700 migrant workers who have taken ESOL classes have joined the union. Furthermore, the GMB sub-branch appeared to have led to a much higher attendance than is usual in union meetings and a greater number of activists. The creation of this sub-branch for Polish workers should be considered as a transitional process that would eventually lead to these workers becoming fully integrated into the union. However, the main activity of the branch was to deliver services to the mostly Polish members (e.g., helping with work documents, language). Consequently, once the services were delivered, a transfer to other union branches did not occur and the migrant branch remained unsustainable and eventually dissolved in 2012.

In sum, the GMB uses educational channels to organize migrant workers. They tried to go beyond servicing their members by setting up a special migrant workers' branch and forging alliances with the migrant workers' community. However, unable to reconcile organizing and servicing members, after about five years the migrant workers branch dissolved.

Finally, the Trades Union Congress (TUC) is the umbrella organization representing the majority of the UK's trade unions, or over 6,000,000 workers. The TUC has been important in opening the dialogue concerning migrant workers and providing some of the necessary funding. In 2007, the TUC established a Commission on Vulnerable Employment comprising members from business, academia, trade unions, and civic organizations, and produced a report on the precarious work situation of about 2,000,000 people, many of them migrant workers. This report opened space for trade union debate and action concerning the integration of migrant workers. In addition, unions received funding from the TUC to work on projects affecting vulnerable workers. The TUC frames the debate in terms of "exploitation," shifting the focus toward the exploitative employer instead of the migrant worker: workers are workers, regardless of their nationality.

Key Campaigns

This chapter discusses five case studies: The Justice for Cleaners campaign led by TELCO (part of London Citizens) and the TGWU/Unite, two campaigns led by Unison, one failed campaign led by the hotel workers branch of TGWU/Unite and London Citizens, and a case study of the migrant workers' branch set up by the general union GMB.[5]

The Justice for Cleaners Campaign, 2001–2010

In 2001, the community-based organization The East London Citizens Organization (TELCO)[6] kicked off a living wage campaign, revolving around the poor pay and working conditions of cleaners at big banks at Canary Wharf.[7] The broad public support and small victories attracted the attention of the unions. In 2004, the TGWU/Unite started the Justice for Cleaners campaign to unionize the cleaners—the majority from minority ethnic groups—at the financial center Canary Wharf. The union received the support of the U.S. trade union SEIU and poured many resources into organizing migrant workers. As a result of the campaign, the union set up a specific cleaners branch with about 2,000 cleaning members. Furthermore, the campaign spread beyond Canary Wharf to other sectors and was picked up by other unions such as the Rail, Maritime, and Transport union (RMT) who also began to organize cleaners, many of whom where migrant workers.

Unison and the Anti-BNP Campaign, 2009

This campaign revolved around the 2009 European election when Unison worked to prevent the election of members of the right-wing British National Party (BNP). In its efforts to raise the awareness of the elections and the threat of the BNP, Unison decided to target the largest European migrant voter group in the United Kingdom—Polish workers. The union made use of the new Polish media; began to build strong ties with Polish associations, and sponsored and organized social and educational events to increase the visibility of their campaign. This campaign was a first attempt to encourage political integration into UK society. Unison's main aim of the anti-BNP campaign was to enhance activism and participation of Polish workers in general and, more specifically, within the trade union. Although the results in terms of Polish voter turnout or new Polish membership were rather minimal, the anti-BNP campaign definitely raised the union's profile within the Polish associations. This campaign can be considered a first attempt of Unison to reach out to the Polish community in the United Kingdom, going beyond the workplace and moving toward a more community-inclusive model.

Unison and the Filipino Care Workers Campaign, 2007

In 2000, massive skill shortages in the United Kingdom induced the government to open up its borders and recruit about 20,000 overseas care workers, primarily senior-care workers from the Philippines. In 2007, the immigration policy changed, and the UK government suddenly asked these workers to show a level three vocational training certification. Although some of the care workers had a diploma in the Philippines, they could not provide this certificate and, consequently could not renew their work permits. Some care workers got deported, while others managed to stay but became undocumented or irregular workers.

As a response, the Filipino community—which is very well organized— decided to take action. Under the leadership of Kanlungan, the Alliance of Filipino Organizations, they pioneered in opposing such legislation, primarily through lobbying Parliament. Eventually, Unison was very supportive and worked alongside Kanlungan, doing background research, case work, and lobbying.

As one of the union officers explained, "It was hard to get Unison on board. Most trade unionists have no experience with working with the community. They don't know how to do it because it is so different from routine work. . . . Their routine is about representing members in the workplace and negotiating collective bargaining agreements. . . . Unions are not used to work with migrant workers or refugees. These workers are regarded as peripheral."

Unison's key tactic in this campaign was lobbying Members of Parliament to achieve substantial change in the immigration policy. Unison's involvement with the Filipino care workers can be considered a push for economic integration of those migrant workers into the UK labor market. Because of intense lobbying in 2007, the government changed its policy, and the Filipino care workers were able to stay in the United Kingdom to work. Many of the Filipino migrant workers became members of the union.

Hotel Workers Campaign, 2007–2009

TGWU/Unite and London Citizens attempted to unionize low-paid, precarious migrant workers in large hotels belonging to the Hilton and the Hyatt international chains. The campaign ended in a failure, however, as it was mainly led by officers and civil society actors and there was inadequate involvement of the migrant workers themselves. During the campaign there was exaggerated pressure on workers to join the union, management heavily retaliated, and the union treated migrant workers as workers, without acknowledging their specific situation. The existing internal divisions between the long-term settled migrant workers and the newly arrived more mobile Eastern European migrant workers were reinforced by the union and community organization, considering these new temporary migrant workers too weak to be successfully organized. Furthermore, the emphasis was put on certifying and awarding living wage employers, taking the focus away from the workers themselves. Finally, the union's Migrant Workers Support Unit had only weak ties with the hospitality branch of union. The unit focused mainly on servicing migrant workers and did not have any influence regarding the organizing strategy. Even though the unit was based in the organizing department, there was no proper relationship between these two structures.

The GMB and the Migrant Workers' Branch, 2006

The GMB has been the first union to set up a migrant workers' trade union branch in the United Kingdom. In 2006, the branch was set up in Southampton, the south coast of England, where about 30,000 Polish workers reside, representing about 10 percent of the local population. The migrant workers' branch was not limited to Polish workers, but comprised members from Pakistan, Lithuania, the Czech Republic, Slovakia, and several other countries, making up about 500 migrant workers. The main channel through which the GMB has been able to organize these workers was through training and education, offering free skills and ESOL classes. Setting up a separate migrant workers' branch has aroused some controversy within the unions, blaming the GMB Southern Region for having separatist, instead of integrative, approaches to migrant workers. According to the regional secretary of the GMB, the branch should be considered a holding branch: once the confidence of the workers is raised, they should transfer to local branches. However, the Southampton model has not been able to sustain itself. Once the services were delivered, a transfer to other union branches did not occur and the migrant branch remained unsustainable and eventually dissolved (Karmowska and James 2012).

Barriers to Integrating Migrant Workers

What are some of the difficulties to integrating migrant workers within the union and the broader society? Characteristics regarding the migrant workers themselves, as well as retaliating actions of employers, interunion rivalries, lack of funding, and structural barriers come to the forefront.

There is a continuous back and forth movement of migrant workers between the country of origin and the receiving country. This so-called challenge of "circular migration" (Holgate 2011) makes it difficult to organize these workers. Due to high turnover in certain sectors such as the cleaning industry, there is constant organizing needed. Furthermore, many Eastern European migrant workers are temporary workers hired through agencies, making it again difficult for unions to organize them.

More troublesome, employers have tried to intimidate migrant workers and blocked union organizing efforts by calling the immigration police. Consequently, workplaces have been subjected to raids by the immigration police leading, in some cases, to the deportation of migrant workers. In June 2009, for example, in the realm of the living wage campaign at London universities, nine cleaners at the School for Oriental and African Studies were taken by immigration officials and eight of them were deported within days.

In addition, rivalries between unions (e.g., TGWU/Unite and RMT) as well as between unions and community-based organizations (e.g., TGWU/Unite and TELCO) challenge the organizing process. The rivalries between unions stem from different organizing cultures as well as different structures (e.g., TGWU/Unite focuses on zonal-based agreements whereas the RMT functions as an industrial union and wants the cleaners of the railway within the RMT). Between unions and community-based organizations conflicts concerning territory, ideology, and structure come to the forefront (Holgate 2009c).

One of the persistent challenges is the lack of funding. Many migrant workers' projects depend on external, short-term government funding (Perrett et al. 2012). In addition, UK unions often have difficulty in providing the necessary resources for a longer period of time that is needed to organize migrant workers (Eldring, Fitzgerald, and Arnholtz 2012). As a result, migrant projects are allocated to a small number of union officers and the initiatives are not embedded within the larger union renewal strategies (James and Karmowska 2012). Furthermore, with the Conservative-led coalition government some of the funding channels such as the Union Modernization Fund have been aborted.

Finally, structural barriers are noticeable as well. First, large parts of the public sector have been privatized. Thus, many public service jobs lie outside the "traditional" public sector structure, representing great challenges for unions such as Unison to organize these workers in the periphery. Second, within Unison there are four self-organizing groups (women members, black members, disabled members, and LGBT members). There is, however, no special structure for the recent migrant workers or nonblack workers from Eastern Europe. The lack of a self-organized group of migrant members within the unions creates problems in dealing with migration issues or racial discrimination. Third, trade unions often lack community-based union structures to engage with migrant or BME (black and minority ethnic) workers inside or outside the workplace (Martínez Lucio and Perrett 2009).

Labor Movement Revitalization

Between 1979 and 1997, the British trade unions were faced with an antiunion and neoliberal agenda of the Conservative prime minister Margaret Thatcher, and to a lesser extent of her Conservative successor, John Major. Legal restrictions were placed on trade unions' ability to engage in industrial action; most sectoral collective agreements were dismantled; and many areas of the public sector were privatized. This ideological and political attack contributed to a catastrophic decline in trade union membership, undermining the unions' legitimacy as the representatives of the working people (Laybourn 2009). Since the end of the 1990s, to counter this decline, the U.S. model of organizing has been adopted by some unions in the United Kingdom emphasizing the importance of organizing workers and empowering them through campaigns and mobilization (e.g., Fiorito 2004; Heery et al. 2003; Simms, Holgate, and Heery 2012).

Following Turner's concept of union revitalization or "mobilization-based initiatives aimed at renewing union influence" (2005), these are important indicators and limitations of revitalization:

Indicators of revitalization include:

Renewed focus on organizing, especially in TGWU/Unite; recruiting and training new organizers from among the workforce;

Setting up workplace committees, specific branches (e.g., cleaners' branch);

Emphasis on education and training of members (e.g., ESOL classes);

Creating new roles for new activists such as union learning reps;

Seminal efforts of union to engage with community actors (e.g., Polish community, London Citizens).

Limitations of revitalization:

Internal divisions within the workforce, for example between the long-term settled migrant workers and the new Eastern European migrant workers;

Unions sometimes focus on employers (e.g., Living Wage Hotel Employer) rather than mobilizing the workers themselves;

Whereas some campaigns resulted in significant membership gains (e.g., Filipino care workers campaign, Justice for Cleaners campaign), others have not significantly increased union membership (e.g., anti-BNP campaign targeting Polish workers);

Unions have not yet developed a comprehensive strategy to integrate migrant workers in society;

Migrant projects are allocated to a small number of union officers, separating migrant workers issues from the broader union strategy;

Often a thorny relationship between the unions and community actors exists; issues of territory, different structure, and culture prevent long-term collaborations.

Unions, Immigrants, and a Sustainable Society

At the beginning of the twentieth century, the British trade unions created the Labour Party and not the other way around as in France or Spain. The Labour Party is therefore considered the political expression of the labor movement. Lobbying, more than street mobilization, has always been the way to get things done in the United Kingdom (interview with a TUC national organizer, June 17, 2009). Changing the spin of this traditional political wheel, for example, by greater collaboration with civic associations or self-organized migrant groups on political issues, will naturally encounter resistance. Consequently, the British unions are taking small but important steps toward breaking out of their corroded structure and starting to build alliances with other movements.

Three critical tensions face UK unions in their efforts to organize immigrant workers. First is the tension between opting for a *separatist versus an integrative approach*. Although these two approaches are not mutually exclusive, a union is likely to have one dominant strategy. TGWU/Unite for example, will mostly favor the integrative approach, claiming that workers are workers regardless of their identity, while other unions, such as Unison, have put in place self-organizing structures for minority groups; going a step further, the GMB has set up a separate migrant workers' branch. As Fonow (2003) argued with regard to the women within the U.S. Steelworkers Union, it is important to find a balance between integration and autonomy or, in practice, building solidarity and alliances across worker groups (integration) without, however, suppressing the significance of these differences among the workers (autonomy).

The second tension concerns the unions' strategies toward *servicing versus organizing* their members. Again, while this has been considered a false dichotomy (Fletcher and Hurd 1998), some UK unions such as TGWU/Unite have clearly shifted from a servicing to an organizing model. As the case study on the hotel workers campaign shows, a gap was created between the union's Migrant Workers Support Unit, focusing mainly on servicing the migrant workers, and the hospitality branch of the union, trying to actively organize the workers. Conversely, Unison is a service-oriented union that will lobby Parliament rather than engage in street mobilizations to achieve their gains. In the United Kingdom, the main avenue for bringing migrant workers into the union structure has been through learning initiatives such as ESOL classes. Taking advantage of these services might be an opportunity to go beyond the servicing/organizing dichotomy. However, as the GMB example shows, migrant workers were drawn to the union because of the free English classes, but once these services were offered, workers lost interest in the union and the branch dissolved.

This brings me to the third challenge, or the extent to which UK trade unions focus on the *workplace or the society*. Even though the British trade unions have their roots within the community, many focus strictly on workplace issues without involving the larger community. In the late nineteenth and early twentieth century, the British trade unions were based in the communities, playing critical roles in shaping those communities (Hobsbawm 1987). This period of "community-based trade unionism" evolved into a "representational community unionism" during the twentieth century, when the Labour Party was formed (Wills and Simms 2004). The trade unions, through the Labour Party, were represented in local and national government, working on issues of public policy and the redistribution of wealth. The trade unions were able to shape community life directly through worker representation or indirectly through the political power of the Labour Party. The erosion of occupational communities, the decline of union membership in strongholds such as manufacturing, and the challenge of organizing workers in nonunionized sectors such as retail and health care have pushed the labor movement away from this representational form of community unionism toward a stricter form of workplace-based unionism. Organizing migrant workers offers an opportunity for the trade unions to go beyond the workplace and engage civil society actors. Building alliances with community actors is not part of a comprehensive labor movement strategy, but in some cases efforts have been undertaken to build stronger ties with migrant communities, applying thereby a more integrative model of "community unionism."

FRANCE

Battles for Inclusion, 1968–2010

Lowell Turner

The dominant French views toward immigrant workers, of both unions and government in the postwar period, are rooted in a republican tradition dating from 1789. The Revolution produced legislation banning "intermediate associations" that might interfere with the "liberté, egalité, and fraternité" of the French citizen. Although legislation passed in 1901 encourages and regulates the activity of thousands of contemporary associations, French unions have remained hesitant about working with community organizations including immigrant advocacy groups. An often exclusive focus on the workplace has in the minds of some critics hindered the broad social solidarity necessary to sustain mobilization efforts in fragmented labor markets where precarious workforces include large numbers of immigrants. More than two centuries after the French Revolution, the two primary contending views toward immigrants, in both workplace and society, remain assimilation and exclusion.[1]

In the postwar period, unions have favored assimilation, with some concessions toward recognition of different immigrant identities and cultures. Changes in union strategies that have encouraged acceptance and integration—in whatever context or form—have occurred in part because of the mobilization of immigrant workers themselves. Two watershed moments provide bookends for the postwar struggles of immigrant workers in France, and corresponding changes in union attitudes and strategy: May 1968 and subsequent strike waves, and the campaign for the "regularization" of undocumented workers that began in 2008.

Despite republican traditions of equality and solidarity, immigrant workers—especially but not only from outside the European Union—remain all-too-often second-class citizens, in both workplace and society. Unions have joined anti-racist campaigns against the far right *Front National* and have gradually integrated immigrants into union membership, participation, and leadership roles. The fragmentation of organized labor into contending federations has at times played to the interests of immigrant workers, as unions compete for membership and influence. At the same time, organizational rivalries have often stood in the way of cohesive strategies and comprehensive campaigns to organize and integrate immigrants.

Given the active role of the state in the French economy, the demands of immigrant workers and supportive unions have almost always targeted the state as well as employers.

The research focus in this book is on first generation immigrant workers, with and without legal work permits. As of 2006, of a total French population of 61.5 million, 11.6 million—which is about 18.8 percent—were foreign born (Bouchareb and Contrepois 2009; Meurs, Pailhé, and Simon 2005). Working conditions are often harsh for such workers because of many factors, especially legal status and country of origin. Undocumented workers (*sans papiers*) from outside the European Union face the biggest obstacles to workplace and social integration; dramatic campaigns for "regularization" led by French unions from 2008 to 2010 have taken primary place in our case studies. Agency-based temporary workers have become more typical than "atypical" in the French workforce, as in the United States, Germany, and the United Kingdom, and large numbers of these are immigrants—with and without papers, from inside and outside the European Union (Gumbrell-McCormick 2011; Holgate 2011). Problems faced by first generation immigrants overlap with continuing workplace and social discrimination against second and third generation immigrant workers, especially from outside the EU.

As in other countries of the Global North, the expansion of a low-wage immigrant workforce is a defining characteristic of economic globalization in the current era, as well as a central component of inequality within French society. Large numbers of foreign-born workers toil in low-wage jobs in construction and private sector services such as hospitality, building services, and domestic care.[2]

Postwar Historical Context

Looking back at postwar history, we see a familiar western European story. As in West Germany and the United Kingdom, postwar reconstruction and rapid economic growth in the 1950s and 1960s produced labor shortages that led French governments to encourage the immigration of foreign workers, from poorer European countries as well as from the former colonies of North and West Africa (Noiriel 1988). For most of this period, union policy was largely protectionist, including an arms-length approach toward the new waves of immigrant workers.[3]

The active participation of immigrant workers, typically positioned in the least desirable jobs in manufacturing, in the strike waves that began in May 1968 forced unions to pay attention and move haltingly toward greater acceptance, including within their own organizations. In a context of economic crisis in the 1970s, labor shortages disappeared and the state moved toward more restrictive policies on immigration. At the same time, in response to immigrant worker activism, the two largest labor confederations, CGT (Confédération Générale du Travail) and CFDT (Confédération Française Démocratique du Travail), issued a joint declaration of solidarity with immigrant workers in 1974.[4] The focus now was to combat discrimination in the workplace, based largely on a republican ideal of assimilation: workers as workers, equal in principle, without reference to differences of ethnicity, race, national origin, or gender.

Immigrant workers themselves, in the wake of 1968, continued to fight for their own interests at the grassroots, in both workplace and society. Ongoing efforts included sustained social movements such as rent strikes by immigrant workers living in state housing (1973–1980) and major strikes initiated by immigrant workers, especially in the auto industry, between 1975 and 1983 (Schain 1994).[5] In the first case, the CGT played a major role, but in a workplace-based committee that contended for influence with a broader immigrant-led committee that put forward social as well as workplace demands. In the second case, both the CGT and CFDT, together and in conflict, played active roles in supporting and leading the campaigns. These and similar movements pushed forward the interests and participation of immigrant workers in French unions.

Although immigrant workers continued to push for rights and interests in the workplace, often with union support, the primary focus of immigrant rights movements in the 1980s shifted to society. The organization SOS Racisme, founded in 1984 in the wake of youth anti-racist marches and in opposition to the rise of anti-immigrant demagoguery led by Jean-Marie Le Pen and the National Front, worked with the Socialist government to influence policy on immigration and discrimination. In the 1990s and 2000s, immigrant rights movements focused on schools, churches and communities, and included high-profile demonstrations and occupations. While individual trade unionists were active in these campaigns, unions as organizations supported but did not play a leading role in what they perceived as civil rights movements not based in the workplace (Iskander 2007).

A turning point for these movements came in a campaign that gained public traction in 2005 for the settlement rights of the immigrant parents of students attending school in France. Led by the Reseau d'Education Sans Frontières (RESF), a coalition called Reseau Associative organized demonstrations that won broad public and political support—for the demand that children educated in France should not have to worry about one or both of their parents being deported (Benoit et al. 2011). The campaign raised awareness of the presence of undocumented workers at the heart of the French economy and society—and provided the context in which public support for the subsequent undocumented workers' movement would develop.[6]

A sustained movement for the rights of *sans papiers* workers, starting from the grassroots and given coherence and momentum by the CGT—joined later by other unions and social groups—provided a dramatic breakthrough for union participation in battles for the rights of immigrant workers. Our case studies concentrate on this most recent period in which immigrant workers provided a new focus for union strategy (see also Barron et al. 2011; Le Queux and Sainsaulieu 2010; and Nizzoli 2009).

Current National Context

The economic crisis that began in 2008, following many years of European integration and intensified economic competition, provided increasing opportunities—and incentives—for employers to hire, and in many cases exploit, immigrant workers. This is especially true for undocumented workers in low-wage sectors such as building services, cleaning, restaurants, domestic care, and construction. These sectors provide the arena in which *sans papiers* workers began to push French unions for support in the years after 2006.

Although foreign-born immigrants and citizens accounted for 18.8% of the French population in 2006 (Bouchareb and Contrepois 2009), by definition it is impossible know how many workers are undocumented. Estimates vary widely: in the spring of 2011, our union sources estimated from 200,000 to up to a million undocumented workers in France. While workers from other countries in the European Union (EU) circulate more freely than in the past, undocumented workers come from North (Mahgreb) Africa and West (sub-Sahara) Africa, Latin America, the Middle East, and Asia.

The political context has long weighed heavily against the interests of immigrant workers. Nicolas Sarkozy was elected president in 2007 in part by drawing voters from the far right, based on promises such as deportations of 25,000 per year. During its five-year term, his government kept this promise, with annual deportations ranging from 25,000 to 30,000—devastating for the deportees but still small in relation to overall numbers in France, including steady streams of new entrants. In local elections in 2011, the National Front, under the new leadership of Marine Le Pen, showed growing strength, and in the first round of presidential elections in 2012 Le Pen finished third, with 17.9 percent of the total vote. In the final round, in a runoff with the Socialist Party candidate Francois Hollande, Sarkozy again moved to the right to cater to anti-immigrant sentiment. This time he lost to the more immigrant-friendly Hollande in a close election (51.6% to 48.4%). It is not yet clear what difference the Hollande presidency is making for the rights and interests of immigrant workers, both documented and undocumented. One positive sign was that Hollande was elected despite right-wing attacks during local elections on his support for voting rights for immigrants.

One way the Sarkozy government played to anti-immigrant sentiment was in a loud but largely symbolic debate on *laicité*—secularism as a core principle of French society. Both the left and right in French politics support this concept, but the rhetoric of the Sarkozy government covered a thinly veiled attack on the role of Muslims in France. The ban on burkas, for example, that went into effect on April 11, 2011 was largely symbolic for a population of about 5,000,000 Muslims in France, of which about 2,000 wore burkas (and many still do).

Public opinion is fluid. On the one hand, voting for the National Front in both 2011 local elections and in the 2012 presidential election approached 20 percent nationwide. On the other hand, the big winner was the left, especially the Socialist Party that dominated local elections in 2011 and took national power in 2012. To the left of the Socialists, a new Front de Gauche surged to 11 percent in the first presidential round in 2012, led by Jean Luc Mélenchon who praised France for its history of *métissage* (cultural, ethnic, racial mixing) and attacked the anti-immigrant politics of Le Pen and her allies. In the waves of strikes by *sans papiers* workers that began in 2008, polls showed substantial public support (typically 50–60%) for the regularization demands of striking workers.

With the exception of high-profile expulsions of small numbers of Roma, the integration of workers from other parts of the European Union no longer appeared to be such a hot-button issue, for either political parties or unions. This could change as Marine Le Pen and the "new" National Front nurture a growing pro-France, anti-Europe sentiment. Increased labor mobility within the European Union, however, does enhance the ability of employers to play national and ethnic groups off against each other—with undocumented workers from outside the EU at the bottom of the pecking order.

Under pressure from unions, employers, and especially from the *sans papiers* movement, the Sarkozy government engaged in periodic negotiations and reformulations of criteria for legal immigration and regularization. By late 2009, the

Collectif des Onze (C11)—a coalition of five labor federations and six nongovernmental organizations (NGOs)—emerged as a primary bargaining partner for the French government (Barron et al. 2011). The main demand, subject to shifting government responses, including differing positions of ministries of immigration and labor, was for clear criteria for the regularization of workers without papers. Although some progress was made at the national level, local governments (prefectures) continued to impose contrasting interpretations of agreed criteria and other rules in issuing work permits.[7]

Union Strategies in Recent Years

Critics of a "national models" analysis of immigrant integration—contrasting, for example, French republicanism with Dutch multiculturalism—have emphasized variation within countries (Bertossi 2010; Deeg 2010).[8] Postwar strategies of French governments, employers, unions, and other organizations have clearly shown variation as well as changes over time. Nonetheless, our research does point toward a fairly consistent orientation toward a distinctly French tradition of republican assimilation: citizens as citizens, workers as workers, regardless of other identity characteristics. The breakthrough represented by the CGT-led *sans papiers* movement modifies but does not appear to change fundamentally a deeply entrenched orientation on the part of unions. And to a significant extent, the demands of activist immigrant workers themselves seem consistent with a drive toward inclusion in the dominant national framework of citizenship. At least three distinct contemporary approaches, lodged in three of the main French union confederations, can be identified.

The most significant change in recent years was the emergence of an active, public movement led by CGT on behalf of undocumented workers in low-wage sectors (Barron et al. 2011). Although the CGT was active in immigrant worker campaigns in the 1970s and early 1980s, workplace efforts lost momentum as immigrant rights movements shifted toward a broader social focus in the late 1980s and 1990s. Not until the mid-2000s did key "bridge-building" CGT activists begin to refocus the organization based on the demands of immigrant workers. The effort to address low wages and poor working conditions crystallized in demands for "regularization": legal status to afford protection for the promotion of workplace interests. The *sans papiers* movement included public strikes and occupations; demands that not only addressed wages and working conditions but also insisted that employers support the work permit applications of individual workers; open declarations by undocumented workers, going public with union support; a close collaboration between worker activists and union, including union membership for many current and former undocumented workers; union demands on local governments for work permit approvals; and ongoing negotiations with national government ministries over criteria for regularization. CGT activists insist that strikes and occupations are initiated only when workers ask the union for support. After early skepticism, other union confederations signed on to the campaigns in 2009, joining the C11 in national bargaining. The primary locus of action was in Paris and surrounding areas, although CGT pushed similar efforts in other urban regions such as Marseille and Lyons.

The CFDT has taken a more modest approach.[9] Wary at first, CFDT signed on in 2009 in support of the CGT-led *sans papiers* movement, and participated in strike support and in national and local bargaining. Local activists in certain areas have a history of support for the demands of undocumented workers, but have also been critical of the more aggressive, public role of the CGT—which they claim has put workers at risk and in some cases hardened the positions of local governments. The issue of immigrant worker support and organizing did not appear on the agenda of the national confederation's annual conference in 2010. CFDT claims a primary interest in results rather than mobilization, and points to internal policies to promote women as well as young and ethnically diverse workers within the organization.

Force Ouvrière (FO) stands out as the most visible French union confederation not to participate in the public campaigns that started in 2008, and it did not join the Collectif des Onze. The FO is critical of the CGT-led campaign for putting undocumented workers at risk in the interest of politics, publicity, and building up its own membership. The FO case study conducted for this research found that active local engagement with immigrant workers, both with and without papers, focused on individual empowerment. This has included educating workers about their rights, supporting individual campaigns for worker delegate positions (in the various representative bodies that characterize the French workplace), bringing immigrants into the union, teaching them the French language so they can put forward their own demands. FO has in a sense kept these efforts "under the radar" to protect precarious workers, and claims that this is the best way to advance worker interests and organizational presence.

Although our research does not include case studies of the involvement of SUD (Solidaires Unitaires Démocratiques), this combative confederation was the first to join in support of the CGT-led *sans papiers* movement. Originally formed by a left-wing breakaway from CFDT in the 1980s, SUD is a lively, activist confederation with anarcho-syndicalist roots, and has been active in the support of immigrant worker rights (Connolly 2010, 2012).

Key Campaigns

This chapter focuses on five in-depth case studies: Acts I and II of the *sans papiers* movement, as well as three separate cases led respectively by the CGT, CFDT, and FO. The cases focus mainly but not only on the rights, standards, and demands for work papers of undocumented workers in France. In every case, immigrant workers with papers also play an important role, both in demands for better working conditions and in solidarity with their undocumented coworkers. Indeed, building that mutual support, overcoming the divisions, was essential to progress made. This is not always an easy task for trade unions especially when employers play one group off against another. Key to persuading documented workers to support their *sans papiers* colleagues is the argument, advanced by activists both within the unions and at the workplace, that the rights of all are threatened when some workers have no rights.

Sans Papiers Act I, 2008–2009

Launched with great fanfare on April 15, 2008, this breakthrough movement began with orchestrated strikes and occupations by undocumented workers mostly in Paris, especially in restaurants but also in other low-wage occupations.[10] The CGT provided active union support for demands of "emerging" undocumented workers, mainly from North and West Africa but from other regions as well. In an innovative strategic campaign led by Raymond Chauveau and Francine Blanche of the CGT, the union worked closely with the demands and participation of activists from among the ranks of the *sans papiers*. Campaigns focused on wages and working conditions but most important on the demand for legal work documents, with pressure on employers to support worker applications to local prefectures. Clear social justice framing produced strong public support for the demands of striking workers. Accomplishments included successful pressure on employers and government, improved working conditions and pay levels, about 2,000 regularizations for workers previously without papers and a roughly equal number of new union members, as well as expanded public awareness of the plight of exploited immigrant workers, a significant component of the growing precarious workforce that in the U.S. narrative is often referred to as the "working poor." The events of 2008–2009 also laid the groundwork for an extension of the movement into Act II.

Sans Papiers Act II, 2009–2010

Act II included the expansion of the *sans papiers* movement into a broader strike by over 6,000 undocumented workers, including many in isolated workplaces (such as domestic workers). In support of the campaign, CGT was joined in the summer and fall of 2009 by four additional union confederations (CFDT, SUD, UNSA, FSU) and six NGOs (Cimade, RESF, Ligue des droits de l'Homme, Femmes Egalité, Autre Monde, Droits Devants!), to form the C11. Still focused on the workplace—now in many locations and industries—but with demands that targeted the national government, the mobilization expanded into a broader social movement, with strikes and occupations that culminated in a high-profile encampment at the Bastille from May 27 to June 18, 2010. In negotiations with government ministries, backed by the demands of over 6,000 striking workers, the C11 gained concessions including modest improvements in clarity for regularization criteria and an extension of criteria scope to include, for the first time, temporary and domestic workers. Striking workers returned to work with protections in ongoing legal support from the CGT and other groups.[11] In a hardening political context, however, as the Sarkozy government approached the 2012 presidential election, local prefects in many cases continued to interpret rules in contrasting ways in different areas.

Strike and Occupation at Griallet, 2008

In May 2008, in a campaign not directly related to the simultaneous Act I *sans papiers* movement, twenty-one workers went on strike at the fiercely antiunion construction company Griallet, on the outskirts of Paris.[12] The striking workforce, made-up of nineteen undocumented workers and two workers with papers, occupied company premises and later built an encampment just outside the door, while engaging in union-supported legal proceedings against the company. The seven-month-long campaign was led by a key "bridge-building" CGT activist, Josselyn Loubli (a black worker who was a French citizen and thus protected from deportation threats) and won strong support and solidarity from a workforce engaged in high-risk action. In the end, this "gangster" company (as it came to be known at CGT headquarters) was put out of business and all jobs lost, but the workers gained key demands for back wages, certification of exposure to asbestos, and residence permits for previously undocumented workers to allow them to stay in the country and search safely for legal employment elsewhere.

Sustained Support Efforts at Yvelines, 2008–2011

Under the leadership of Maud Billon, the CFDT regional/local (union départementale or UD) in Yvelines, west of Paris, engaged quietly for many years in support of undocumented and other immigrant workers.[13] In particular, Daniel Richter, a retired Renault engineer, worked tirelessly on a volunteer basis to prepare and submit dossiers in support of work permit applications for undocumented workers. The union engaged in careful campaigns to avoid putting workers at risk and remained critical of more aggressive CGT approaches. In some cases CFDT-Yvelines worked in collaboration with NGOs and other unions to pressure employers and local government. This is an unusually engaged case for CFDT, which has not given this issue the same kind of organizational priority as CGT. Although the confederation at national and other levels has moved deliberately to integrate foreign-born workers into union leadership positions, there appeared to be little communication among branches in this area, and the colleagues at Yvelines were disappointed to find no consideration of the specific problems of immigrant workers at the 2010 CFDT national congress.

Organizing Cleaners at FO-FEETS, 2006–2010

At the FO sector local FEETS (Fédération d'Equipement, Environment, Transports et Services) in Paris, Laurent Grognu and colleagues worked actively for several years to organize workers and sign up members in the cleaning industry (and were still doing so as our field research ended).[14] In an under-the-radar campaign, these activists have focused on empowerment, teaching workers about their rights, bargaining skills, the French language. The emphasis on rank-and-file education is reminiscent of parallel efforts in the United Kingdom. From 2003 to 2009, FO membership in the cleaning industry in the Paris region grew from 80 to 1,400, in grassroots recruiting efforts aimed at a multinational workforce that included workers both with and without papers, mainly from Africa and Latin America. Membership included workers in hospitals, hotels, roads, transport, and other private enterprises. The local union supported the FO decision not to join the Collective des Onze, arguing against a CGT approach that puts workers at risk by bringing them out into the open. The core idea advanced in this case is about avoiding unnecessary risk while empowering workers with the tools necessary to stand up for themselves.

Integration Profile

Since 1968 and especially after 2005, French unions have made important positive contributions to breaking down barriers and opening up society to immigrant workers. They have done this at the workplace by defending the interests of immigrant workers, individually and in ongoing campaigns, large and small, visible and under the radar. They have signed up foreign-born members and encouraged empowerment and activism. In some cases, immigrant workers have risen to positions of union leadership. Beyond the workplace, union activists—and sometimes unions as organizations—have supported antiracism movements and immigrant rights campaigns targeted at schools and government agencies. Most dramatically, unions led high-profile campaigns from 2008 to 2010 for the regularization of undocumented workers.

Unresolved is the tension between integration as assimilation and the acceptance of "non-French" cultural identities, or a more group-based incorporation. This tension underlies much of the debate—within and across unions and in coalition efforts with immigrant advocacy organizations—that accompanies campaigns that bring together unions and immigrant workers.

Separate union structures such as those encountered in some British, Dutch, and Italian campaigns are virtually unknown in France.[15] Our own case studies as well as an examination of other cases available from secondary sources persuade us that, although attitudes are changing slowly, by and large French unions remain reluctant to acknowledge and incorporate distinct ethnic identities. This is true despite the fact that successful strikes and the promotion of the interests of immigrant workers by other means are typically rooted in ethnic social networks that bring workers together. Notable victories in the *sans papiers* movement of 2008–2010 and at Griallet, along with support provided and the empowerment of immigrant workers we have seen at Yvelines and among Paris cleaners, include both strategic leadership on the part of key union activists and an openness to mobilizing social networks and ethnic identities. Such efforts have produced breakthrough models of innovation for a labor movement still wary of recognizing distinct ethnic identities.

Republican traditions remain dominant, even as recent campaigns appear more accepting of cultural differences and identities. For the most part, the orientation of French unions pits itself against the exclusionist ideology of the far right by insisting on the inclusive integration of immigrant workers as French workers and citizens (or future citizens), quite apart from distinctive ethnic, racial or cultural identities.

Services versus Mobilization

Throughout the case studies conducted in this and other countries in the course of this research, as unions respond to the demands of immigrant workers in precarious workforces, we find a recurrent tension between the need to provide services to individuals and efforts to mobilize workers in collective action. Wage recovery, referrals for language training, and support for work permit applications are important services unions can provide to immigrant workers. Such services can help build trust and lay the groundwork for collective action.

Conversely, like immigrant advocacy NGOs, unions can also get bogged down in service provision, in lieu of mobilization aimed at changing working conditions and power relations more broadly.

For the CGT, the *sans papiers* movement of 2008–2010 brought a new focus on grassroots mobilization, to support the collective efforts of undocumented workers in their demands for work documents and better working conditions. The innovation inherent in this movement-building effort is perhaps unprecedented in the postwar history of the French labor movement. The CGT worked closely with activist workers to support and lead this social movement, resulting both in new membership and in substantial gains for many immigrant workers. Although the emphasis was on groups of workers stepping forward together with union support, the CGT soon found itself, especially after the broader strike ended in 2010, immersed in protracted "servicing" of individual applications for work papers.

Although CFDT joined with CGT in the Collectif des Onze in 2009, confederation leadership claims a distinct interest, different from the CGT, in advancing the interests of workers by achieving concrete results rather than high-profile public action. This is a union confederation more oriented toward negotiation than mobilization. The Yvelines branch has demonstrated a rather exceptional commitment to promoting individual applications for work papers on behalf of undocumented workers.

In addressing the interests of immigrant workers, the FO is noteworthy for an explicit opposition to open mobilization. Where activists have supported the interests of immigrants, among cleaners in Paris for example, the union offers extensive services aimed at training workers for individual and collective empowerment. The emphasis has been on grassroots efforts to offer skills, including language training and rights awareness, to low-wage immigrant workers.

All three confederations, in the course of their work, have assisted immigrant workers in gaining unpaid wages and better working conditions—and claim this as an important service they can help provide. Even for the CGT, there was a noticeable drift from mobilization to service provision after the dramatic movement of 2008–2010. The loss of movement momentum is a danger inherent in processes of service provision. On the other hand, the CGT and other unions have been careful not to abandon the workers who put themselves at risk, a necessary condition for credibility in calls for future mobilization.

Workplace and Society

French unions have been unanimous and are distinct in our four-country cases for insisting on a workplace focus. Nonetheless, efforts to promote the interests of employees at work inevitably bring unions into "social partner" and other negotiations with the state, at all levels, as well as with employers. The *sans papiers* movement, for example, included active pressure on local governments to issue work papers and on the national government for clear criteria for regularization. French unions, however, including the CGT, did not play leading roles as organizations in the immigrant social movements of the 1990s and 2000s that focused more on social than workplace demands, on social targets rather than employers.

The CGT-led *sans papiers* campaign beginning in 2008 brought immigrant workers into the center of organizing efforts, still firmly rooted at the workplace. By contrast, the 2009–2010, in which unions and NGOs joined to negotiate with government, was a breakthrough for integration efforts that garnered broad labor and social support, including both workplace-based and civil society organizations.

What remains to be seen is the extent to which such coalitions between unions and associations of civil society will develop in future efforts to reform a fragmented labor market, one in which the workplace and social problems of precarious workers are closely linked (Béroud and Bouffartigue 2009a, 2009b). The *sans papiers* movement has brought French unions into new arenas of a precarious workforce based to a significant extent in small- and medium-size enterprises, including intermediaries such as agencies that provide temporary workers, as well as isolated domestic workplaces and the "informal" labor market (Noiseux 2012).

A new literature in the French sociology of work examines the need, and the potential, for the emergence of "civil dialogue" to complement the existing collective bargaining and "social dialogue" of employment relations (Didry and Jobert 2008; DeMunck et al. 2012). The innovative experience of the C11 is an example of collaboration between actors based in workplace and society. Efforts that combined a workplace-based strike with national negotiations addressing both workplace and social criteria may point toward a future integration of workplace and social demands.

Barriers to Union Engagement or Success in Integrating Immigrant Workers

Republican ideology has in the past sometimes blinded French unions to the particular needs and demands of immigrant workers. Unions have at times been accused by immigrant advocacy groups of racism, of a failure to focus on workplace and social discrimination, including within the union. CGT, for example, faced a substantial protest movement in 2009 by *sans papiers* workers not included in the strikes and demands aimed at employers and government. The protest included an occupation at the CGT itself and pushed the union toward a broader coalition-led strike in the fall of 2009 (Barron et al. 2011).

An exclusive focus on the workplace has sometimes isolated unions from broader support in civil society, and from the credibility and legitimacy with immigrant workers that such engagement could produce. At the same time, negotiations with state ministries (labor, immigration) take place far from the grassroots movements of immigrant workers, sometimes creating mistrust and charges of exclusion.

All French unions depend to a significant extent on state and employer funding—to free up time for union representation work as well as broader projects of "social partnership"—and thus they suffer from limited resources for discretionary use in the kinds of innovative efforts described in our case studies. Low membership levels mean that French unions, dependent as they are on various forms of state funding, have a limited capacity for activities that extend beyond the workplace. This includes a broader engagement in civil society and the expansion of social dialogue into the civil dialogue that some activists and labor scholars have advocated (DeMunck et al. 2012). Support for the demands of immigrant workers are sometimes seen as lip service, in the context of other organizational, political, and economic priorities.

Union fragmentation continues to plague the French labor movement. Contending confederations pursue different strategies, sometimes reinforcing, sometimes undermining each other's efforts. There is also great variation within each confederation regarding the commitment of local branches, both sectoral and regional. Unions typically have an active national office and presence—advocating policy, negotiating with state and employers, organizing demonstrations small and sometimes very large—yet confederations and member unions tend to be internally decentralized (e.g., Piotet 2009). Local, regional, and sector-level branches often go their own way, with little regard for reforms—such as a commitment to organizing immigrant workers—that may be advocated at the level of the national confederation.

Labor Movement Revitalization

Despite external pressures, internal conflict, organizational weakness, and the never-ending critiques of academic and other observers, the French labor movement refuses to die.[16] In campaigns to defend public services and pensions that followed the financial collapse of 2008, French unions demonstrated a capacity for mass mobilization that belied predictions of terminal decline. Campaigns to address the demands of immigrant workers have shown a surprising capacity for strategic innovation.

If union revitalization refers to "mobilization-based initiatives aimed at renewing union influence" (Turner 2005), French labor's engagement with campaigns in support of immigrant workers since 2008 can be seen as a promising development.

Indicators of revitalization include:

High-profile, successful strikes and occupations of restaurants, building sites and other places of work where immigrant workers predominate;

The emergence of thousands of undocumented workers from the shadows into the public arena, to promote their demands in union-supported campaigns;

Widespread support for demands for work permits, unpaid wages, and better working conditions—from the public and from other "legal" workers at worksites where immigrant worker strikes took place;

A new strategic formula that includes strikes, occupations, rallies, union backing, media attention, social justice framing, and public support, to pressure employers and government;

Organizational learning and the capacity for sustained mobilization (as opposed to "all out" one-day demonstrations of thousands or even millions);

Coalition success as other unions joined the CGT-led *sans papiers* movement, working together in a broad social effort to support immigrant worker demands;

The widespread development of "intersyndicale" efforts (campaigns and negotiations including two or more unions) at national, local, sector and firm levels—from increasingly unified calls for demonstrations and strikes to the dramatic breakthrough represented by the Collectif des Onze;

Active employer support in many cases (typically after strikes and occupations) for union-supported work permit demands;

Engagement of national government in peak-level negotiations for regularization criteria, resulting in concessions to accommodate the demands of striking immigrant workers.

Limitations on revitalization include:

Despite the two-year mobilization of the *sans papiers* movement and concessions gained in national negotiations, outcomes of individual work permit applications still often appear arbitrary, depending on the preferences or interpretations of local governments. This continuing pattern calls

into question the sustained influence and follow-up capacity of unions in
relationships with immigrant workers, especially those without papers;

The vibrant center for both the *sans papiers* movement and our other case
studies was the Ile de France, the area around Paris where national union
confederations are based. Secondary literature indicates that the decentralization of the French labor movement results in a slow diffusion of
innovative approaches toward immigrant workers and new organizing
efforts aimed at a growing precarious workforce;

The fragmented labor market itself, including large numbers of precarious
workers across a range of industries, strengthens the hand of employers
to play groups of workers off against other groups. Unions are only beginning to learn how to engage and represent cleaners, domestic workers,
restaurant employees, construction workers at "union-free" worksites,
agency, temporary and informal sector workers, and others in sectors
where unions have historically been weak or altogether absent. This is
especially true for the large numbers of immigrant workers, with and
without work permits, who populate these sectors;

Continuing divisions in strategic orientation among unions, within unions,
among the workers themselves, and their advocacy organizations make
innovative campaigns contentious (e.g., Béthoud 2009);

Peak negotiations at national, employer, and sector levels often engage
unions as institutions but at some distance from the base. A lack of trans-
parency sometimes undermines trust for unions at the grassroots, among
members and nonmembers alike.

Case studies presented in this chapter include breakthroughs for both unions
and immigrant workers, especially the undocumented, but have not added up to
any large increases in union membership or in fundamental changes in unions
as organizations (Le Queux and Sainsaulieu 2010). It remains to be seen how
transferable the new strategic capacity for mobilization is beyond these specific
campaigns.

Unions, Immigrants, and Sustainable Society

In the broader political, economic, and social context, union efforts that focus
on immigrant workers can be seen as one piece in a larger battle for sustainable
society—at local, national, and international levels. Thirty years of global liberalization have left France a more economically unstable society with an increasingly fragmented labor market. Current economic and political battles in France,

as elsewhere, form part of a mosaic of ongoing conflict over the terms of future economic growth.

As global economic integration drives growing immigration, both legal and illegal, immigrant workers who enter at the low end of the labor market in France, as elsewhere, can play a variety of different social roles. Through no choice of their own, they often work in jobs at well below their skill levels, without basic protections or enforceable rights, and in so doing help employers keep costs down and undermine union efforts at representation and growth. All too often, they are targeted as scapegoats by extremist groups such Marine Le Pen's National Front and candidates and office-holders of the center-right such as former president Sarkozy. When such rhetoric predominates and finds resonance in large numbers of an insecure workforce and society, social conflict and economic instability are likely results.

In the case studies presented here, immigrant workers have nonetheless been viewed as natural allies for other low-wage workers, and for unions and other organizations in campaigns to reduce economic and social inequalities. The recent efforts of French unions to join or lead the mobilization of immigrant workers carry promise for a more integrated, sustainable society.

The participation of French unions in empowering and mobilizing immigrant workers is a breakthrough in efforts for broader social cohesion. At the same time, progress is halting, regularizations are often arbitrary and in any case only a first step toward greater social acceptance, government and employers continue to throw up obstacles, and the far right has gained renewed traction playing the antiforeigner card.

Union campaigns in support of the demands of immigrant workers, especially the undocumented, are innovative and significant but still only a small step toward the better integration and greater equality of a more sustainable society.

GERMANY

Success at the Core, Unresolved Challenges at the Periphery

Lee H. Adler and Michael Fichter

Chapter 2 described union efforts to incorporate migrant workers by undertaking innovative organizing drives in building services, hospitality, restaurants, and carwashes in the United States, the United Kingdom, and France. An emphasis on social justice, coalition building with civil society organizations, strategic campaigning, and strong leadership in efforts to mobilize rank-and-file workers were all characteristics of union activities in these three countries. In each example there was a departure from traditional union organizing approaches, suggesting that unions operated as a countermovement to the arbitrary, unbridled employer prerogatives in these fragmented segments of the labor market.

The German case is in many ways different, largely due to the power, influence, and organizational status unions achieved in rebuilding and democratizing the country (West Germany) after 1945. In the expanding postwar economy, unions achieved and maintained a position of strength, bolstering their ability and willingness to foster the integration of the growing numbers of immigrants at the workplace. Migrant workers, largely unskilled, were recruited to do the backbreaking and worst paid jobs, but these were in the industrial heartland (Pries 2003), where unions were organizationally and institutionally anchored. There was no need for Service Employees International Union–style leadership or public campaigns in their efforts to ensure workplace integration for migrant workers.

At the same time, during the 1960s and even more so in the subsequent years, the issue of integrating foreign workers into West German society proved to be considerably more challenging for the unions. Indeed, as intolerance and xenophobia in the general population increased and political leadership faltered with regard to integration, union efforts on behalf of migrant and foreign workers were often stymied, even among their own members.

The repertoire of union activities was nevertheless wide-ranging, including billboard campaigns, training seminars, workplace programs, and demonstrations against antiforeigner and xenophobic manifestations. Indeed, the continuing need to combat right extremism represents the broader context of union activities in support of migrant workers. There is evidence of local initiatives such as our case study of the service union ver.di in Hamburg to fight for the economic rights of an undocumented (*sans papier*) au pair. However, a concerted nationwide campaign such as the one mounted by the French CGT in coalition with other social forces is just not on the union agenda in Germany today. Nor does it appear likely that unions would expend significant social or political influence or invest valuable resources on a broad campaign specifically aimed at rectifying injustices that immigrants suffer in the labor market and in society in general. As can be seen in the union campaigns since the early 2000's on behalf of national minimum wage legislation, the thrust was on eliminating the low wage sector as it affects *all* workers, regardless of their citizenship status.

Clearly, there are differences between union approaches in the other three countries and those we have found in Germany. But whether this makes the German case an "outlier" requires us to carefully examine what German trade unions have done to incorporate migrant workers at work and in civil society in the postwar era.

We have learned that from the earliest days of migrant workers coming to West Germany, the unions have been an effective countermovement in their efforts to integrate migrant workers at the workplace and in the unions. Unions have achieved equal legal status and contract coverage at the workplace, protected migrant workers from the arbitrary power of employers, and worked to open training, career, and integration perspectives. Throughout the affiliates of the German Trade Union Federation (DGB),[1] persons with migrant family backgrounds represent the membership as elected and appointed officials.

This chapter traces the history of German trade union efforts to incorporate migrant workers, arriving first from Italy, and then from Spain, Greece, Turkey, Portugal, the former Yugoslavia, and from the African countries of Morocco and Tunisia. Officially, the early migrants were expected, and many had as their goal, to return to their home countries with their accumulated savings. Most migrants, independent of their skill level, were contracted to do the low-paying, hardest, and dirtiest jobs; however, German unions ensured that these workers were covered by their collective agreements and were paid according to the same contractual standards as German workers.

Union incorporation efforts at the workplace have gone far beyond matters of wages and working conditions. Union powerhouses such as the metalworkers' union IG Metall, the service employees' union ver.di (including its five predecessors), and the IG BCE, which represents employees in mining, chemicals, and energy sectors, have consistently spoken out publicly and campaigned and run workers' education programs against racial discrimination and the ugly manifestations of right extremists, who regularly blame migrant workers for Germany's social woes. We learned of plantwide activities in every decade since the 1970s, with works council and trade unionists leading anti-racist campaigns. We were reminded of this long-standing and consistent effort of the IG Metall's antiracist Respekt! campaign, which requires employers to post on their bulletin boards that "racism is not allowed here." The fact that this campaign coincides with the ongoing engagement of the German Soccer League against racism is evidence of its broadly recognized basis.

As we broaden the context of the comparison of the four countries studied, and consider more fully not only the workplace but also the societal outcomes to date, the limits of union activity and influence in support of migrant workers in Germany are evident. At the same time, we argue that the positive developments reported from the other countries inspire but have not demonstrably changed migrant workers' overall economic or social reality. It is in this concrete sense that Germany is not truly an outlier and its trade unions' incorporation efforts constitute a counter-movement resulting from their associational and institutional strength as well.

The Historical Context of Worker Migration in Germany

Germany has gone through several phases of worker migration since 1945. Divided in the aftermath of World War II and Allied occupation, East and West Germany embarked on diametrically opposite paths, including union development. Prior to the (re)unification of Germany in 1990, we focus exclusively on union policies and migration in West Germany as the historically dominant and decisive arena. The first phase beginning in the mid-1950s and lasting until 1973 was marked by the active recruitment of migrant workers in the midst of a booming industrial economy. The second phase extended until the end of the Cold War, symbolized by the fall of the Berlin Wall in 1989. In this period, West Germany grappled with the presence of a growing migrant population in a no longer booming economy. The post–Cold War period was especially marred by violence against foreigners, political indecisiveness, and a more heated debate over a far more heterogeneous migrant population in terms of origin, settled-ness, skills, goals, and so on.

Migration to united Germany in the post-1989 or third phase occurred under less favorable economic and social conditions. As a country in reunification, Germany was politically unprepared, and many native Germans, especially from eastern Germany, were perhaps even unwilling to receive migrant newcomers. As part of the evolving relationship between the European Union (EU) and the transformation countries of Eastern Europe, many workers from those countries began to look for employment opportunities in the EU. At the same time, the number of persons claiming German ancestry, many of whom came from countries of the former Soviet Union, increased dramatically. In addition, asylum seekers from war-torn and dictatorial regimes around the world sought to enter the European Union, many coming to Germany until 2004 when the Eastern European countries became members of the EU. Legal restraints on migrating to Germany for employment—even for persons from the new member states of the EU—had been erected already during the latter years of the third phase, and those workers who were able to take up residence in Germany found a highly segmented labor market offering relatively few well-paying jobs for them in union-contract facilities. The jobs they were offered, often through subcontractors and agencies, were in construction and services, and in the growing segment of low wage, nonpermanent work.

Phase One: The Postwar Context

As the major showcase for rebuilding capitalist economies in Europe, West Germany was at the forefront of Marshall Plan aid from the United States. As it gained its economic footing following the war's devastation and embarked on a remarkable growth trajectory, West Germany's reindustrialization quickly experienced deep labor shortages. This occurred despite the increasing numbers of East Germans who fled to the West during the years before the Wall was erected in 1961. But the booming economy was not the only cause of labor shortages. The male population had already been decimated by World War II, and in 1955 the West German federal government signed a treaty allowing the country to join NATO. Thus, the induction of thousands of young men into the new army coincided with the beginning of the Government program to recruit foreign *Gastarbeiter* (guest workers) to work in industry.

That year, the West German government actively promoted the recruitment of workers to fill mostly low-skilled jobs in industry. The first agreement was signed with Italy (1955), followed by agreements with Spain and Greece (1960), Turkey (1961), Morocco (1963), Portugal (1964), Tunisia (1965), and with Yugoslavia in

1968. In each of these countries, the federal labor agency set up recruiting offices to offer able-bodied (male) workers two-to-three-year contracts in factories and services throughout the country.

The active recruitment program of foreign workers changed the ethnic composition of the workforce permanently. This became especially pronounced after the erection of the Berlin Wall in 1961. The number of foreigners increased from only 1.2 percent of the population to nearly 5 percent in the decade from 1960 until 1970.[2] When the West German government ended the recruitment program in 1973 there were 2.6 million foreigners employed in regular jobs and paying taxes and social insurance (Butterwege 2005). By 1990, Germany had the largest foreign population in Europe (Chin 2007).

German industry "reaped the benefits of a fully flexible and temporary workforce" (Chin 2007:45) through the recruitment of migrants. Unions, too, subscribed to the economic benefits "of full employment and continued economic growth" (IG Metall 1966) resulting from organized migration. But, as a survey commissioned by the IG Metall (1964) and repeated newspaper reports revealed, the integration of such a large number of foreign workers into the production process was not without tensions on the shop floor (Chin 2007: 59). It presented German unions with extraordinary challenges, both in industrywide collective bargaining and at the local workplace with its governing mechanisms of works councils and codetermination. Unions had to overcome language barriers in recruiting foreigners to their membership and address the concerns raised by migrant worker activists on inclusion.

By the mid-1960s unions were debating ways of integrating foreign workers into representational structures in the union and at the workplace. One of the demands advanced by the unions for the reform of the Works Constitution Act of 1952 was to permit non-Germans to run for positions on the Works Council. When the German Parliament passed the revised Act in 1972, it included such a provision along with a passage (art. 80, par. 7) that it is the obligation of each works council "to promote the integration of foreign workers at the workplace and further an understanding between them and German workers. Furthermore, the works council should make application for measures to combat racism and xenophobia at the workplace." When the first elections to works councils were held in 1972 based on the revised law, 3,850 (metalworking industry: 1,445) foreign workers were elected[3] (Karahasan 2011).

The *Gastarbeiter* program was not designed to recruit immigrants, but, rather, to recruit individual temporary workers to come to Germany without their families. For their part, these workers came to make money and mostly to use that money to fulfill their aspirations at home. They did not intend to settle in Germany. However, in many cases their contracts were renewed for a second or third period, or they started a business, extending their stay. These unforeseen developments combined with a markedly different economic situation to usher in the second phase of migration.

Phase Two: Settling-in after the Boom Economy

The onset of the 1973 recession, the so-called oil crisis, prompted the German government to cancel its recruitment program. Formally, this policy change raised a potential difficulty only for migrant workers from countries outside of the European Economic Community (EEC)[4] who now had to either return home or apply for a residence permit if they wished to stay and move their family to West Germany. But for those migrant workers who had employment and had come from EEC countries, this development brought with it the opportunity to bring their families and live in West Germany. During this phase, migration to Germany did not grow, as chronic economic difficulties, characterized by high unemployment, made for fewer work opportunities, especially for migrants.

Still, the foreign population grew in Germany even though the number of migrant workers coming to Germany decreased considerably. Foreign workers for the first time were confronted with job losses in the wake of economic downturns. The number of unemployed foreign workers rose markedly and many of them found themselves unable to find new jobs in industry. By 1985 the number of foreigners holding regular jobs with social insurance benefits was down to 1.6 million (Butterwegge 2005). Out of necessity, many of them began seeking other forms of (self-)employment or became more willing to accept employment under nonunion contracts.

This second phase of migration was also characterized by the arrival of family members. It transformed the migrant population from individual male workers intent on making money to send home into migrant communities requiring regular housing, schools, shopping facilities, and other community services. Previously, the issue of integration was concentrated primarily in the workplace, but in this phase it became a contested communal and social issue as well.

The German populous at large did not respond positively to this development, being continuously reminded by politicians that "Germany was not a country of immigration." Indeed, "the guest worker program presumed a basic rejection of permanent immigration, making access to German citizenship an irrelevant issue." (Chin 2007: 22) Strict requirements made attaining permanent residency and citizenship quite difficult until citizenship laws were revised in 2000. For their part, many migrants reacted defensively to the uncertainty regarding their status, wavering on learning and using the German language, a situation that enhanced their social isolation. Efforts at pushing for more constructive policies on migration, such as those proposed by the official federal office for foreigners (Kühn 1979), were met with insufficient political support and not implemented.

Although attitudes of many German trade union members certainly reflected much of the general discomfort among the German population, union activists made concerted efforts to open organizational channels for the involvement of foreign members and to mobilize support for union policies backing constructive approaches to migration and the integration of foreigners. Still, in the overall climate of uncertainty and divisiveness such efforts, while successful in many parts of the union movement, had limited impact outside the workplace environment.

To be sure, the unions came out strongly in their condemnation of the rash of attacks on foreigners during the early 1980s, but there were also pronouncements from the DGB headquarters offering contradictory messages. At times the unions intensified their efforts to represent migrants, while characterizing migrant workers as "reserve labor," meaning that German workers should have a better opportunity or more of a right to a particular job. Meanwhile, faced with declining membership and the loss of industrial jobs, many union leaders actively sought foreign workers support. Interesting migrants in trade union membership became an imperative. Moreover, as attacks on foreigners increased and the government tightened its migrant worker policies, and even sought to send many workers back to their country of origin, the DGB responded with support for a whole range of concerns critical to migrant worker well-being (Kühne 2000: 49). These included opposing the limitation of family reunion rights, endorsing the right to stay in Germany without being required to have a work permit, limiting the causes for expulsion, petitioning for migrant workers to have local election voting rights, fighting for legislation against ethnic discrimination, and launching an initiative seeking naturalization and dual nationality[5] for migrant workers.

Despite renewed union efforts in support of migrant workers, the overall climate of exclusion and separation remained threatening. It became more explosive in the late 1980s as the number of refugees from dictatorships, civil wars, and other conflicts increased. When the political changes began to occur in the Soviet Union and in its satellite states in Eastern Europe—including East Germany—the stage was set for a new phase of migration policy and new challenges for the German trade unions.

Phase Three: Postunification Migrant Worker Context

Previous migration trends quickly changed in the early 1990s with the end of Soviet influence and control in the East. The arrival of migrants increased substantially and grew in complexity. Although the presence of migrants who actually settled in Germany was undeniable, making Germany in fact a country of immigration, many regarded the early 1990s and the advent of German unification to represent "the spreading of a prevailing mood of xenophobia" (Seifert 2012: 1). Indeed, the early 1990s were a period in which violent attacks killing migrants occurred in several localities (East and West) in which the number of asylum seekers peaked. During this time, the German constitution was revised to include restricting conditions for the granting of asylum (Seifert 2012). On these issues, trade unionists spoke out and developed ties at the local level to refugee councils, organizations of foreigners, and antiracism initiatives (Kühne 2000: 53).

The 1990s increase of migrants included citizens from the former Soviet bloc countries and the former Soviet republics. According to official statistics for the first half of the decade, more than 1 million migrants came to Germany each year (Statistisches Bundesamt 2013). By far the most significant number of lawful migrants included persons of German heritage from the former Soviet bloc (*Spätaussiedler*) who enjoyed a relatively privileged status. Other migrants, mostly from Eastern Europe, arrived on specially created temporary work permits. Over time, more came as contract laborers hired through agencies and firms in their own country.

During this period the impact of globalization on labor markets was increasingly being felt in Germany, especially after the previously hermetically sealed border between East and West disappeared. Different migrant workplace patterns began emerging, as seasonal, temporary, contractor, and self-employed workers increased tremendously. These types of "atypical" work, coupled with their likely assignment to lesser-skilled factory and construction-based positions, cemented the statistically confirmed pay gap between foreign and German workers. Union contracts ensured equal pay for equal work for migrant workers. But in the growing segments of the economy where there was no union or works council presence, and with there being no minimum wage, large parts of the workforce—women, youth, and certainly foreign workers—had to settle for considerably lower wages.

The issue was further complicated after 2004 when eight countries from Eastern Europe (new member states) joined the European Union. The German unions met this enlargement by actively supporting a seven-year ban on the freedom of movement of persons from these countries, a policy designed to allay the fears of heightened competition and job loss among its members. These actions, however, did little to lessen the presence of foreign workers in Germany and partially caused the degrading conditions of employment which nonunion migrants faced.

The Current Context of Worker Migration in Germany

In the historical context of West German development since World War II, union successes in integrating migrants at the workplace (works councils) and in their own organizational structures were impressive. But according to more recent reports from the unions even those advances may be in question today. Statistical reports covering the period 2010 to 2012 from both ver.di and IG Metall indicate there has been more of a decline in migrant worker membership than in German workers. Interviews with trade union officials whose responsibilities include the incorporation of migrant workers into works council and union leadership positions reveal very modest, if any, growth since 2000.

A disturbing IG Metall (2011a) report confirmed what we learned through interviews and case studies. It found that foreign workers are structurally disadvantaged in the German metalworking and electrical engineering industry, and are severely underrepresented in employment relationships requiring a high level of qualifications. Moreover, they are in relative terms much more likely to be in limited-term or temporary employment than their German coworkers. The unions from the service sector have been trying to deal with such problems for even longer, being the first to demand a legal minimum wage that would improve the lot of all low-wage workers regardless of their citizenship. Initially, the German industrial unions argued from a position of strength and against state intervention into their constitutionally protected rights of coalition and collective bargaining. But the mounting pressures from restructuring, flexibilization, and outsourcing coupled with the massive spread of agencies for temporary employment has led them to take up the fight in their own industries and to publicly support other unions campaigning for a national minimum wage.

Complicating this mixed picture, workers from the new member states, starting in 2012, enjoy the basic right of free movement within the EU and can thus enter the German labor market. Extremist political parties and organizations on the Right have attempted to gain political traction by opposing this, raising the specter of a massive influx of migrant ("foreign") workers bent on "stealing German jobs" by undercutting standards. In their rhetoric, all migrants, be they EU citizens seeking work, refugees, or asylum seekers (who are forbidden to work) are lumped as one "dangerous" group. The DGB and its affiliates have responded to such attacks on migrants with a wide-range of policy measures, including advancing antidiscrimination legislation, developing German language trainings to prepare migrant workers for German society, and vehemently opposing political violence directed at foreign workers.

Still, union efforts to protect migrants have come up short in the face of the societal challenges posed by the integration issue. Despite their numerous activities, the German unions have not been able to significantly build on their historic and progressive migrant worker achievements by expanding their activities and influence beyond the realm of the workplace. To be sure, membership decline has certainly restrained their capacity to campaign effectively for the integration of migrant workers into civil society. But, there is concern that conceptual and strategic problems are operative in union policy as well.

Early evidence of this was brought out by an internal investigation launched by the DGB. Following reports in the late 1990s of a significant number of votes for right extreme political parties by union members, the DGB created a high-level Commission on Right Extremism. Its report, published in 2000, concluded that opinions and attitudes of union members mirrored those of the nonunion population. Because unions do not exist in a vacuum, it was not surprising but still disturbing that xenophobic and racist attitudes were just as virulent within the membership as in the general population. The report acknowledged the existence of right-wing attitudes among the members, and it suggested the possibility that union acceptance of the argument that Germany must be more competitive (*Standort Deutschland*) played into the hands of the far right by providing arguments for the marginalization of foreigners.

By contrast, the authors of a later study on right extremist attitudes among union members argued in their initial hypothesis that union members have a definable "trade union belief system," which does not mirror the political views of the general population. Workers become members because they hold particular beliefs and values associated with trade unionism. But, under the threat of unemployment, workplace restructuring and job uncertainty, this consciousness necessarily reflects contradictory attitudes and beliefs.

Although the survey itself turned up no evidence of the existence of a trade union belief system in the membership, it did find that union officials and activists generally embraced a common understanding of "unionism." In particular, unionism constitutes principles such as equality, solidarity, internationalism as well as codetermination and participation. The study found that these principles could operate as "immunizers" against right extremism.

However, the increasing economic and political challenges facing unions have weakened their ability to fulfill the role as immunizers. Under these circumstances the development of far right trade union attitudes occurs as workers' sense of individual and collective powerlessness grows, limiting the influence of the achievements of the German model. Union weakness opens the union belief system to far right attitudes because its programmatic assurances of protection and collective solidarity seem hollow when unions fail to counter employer chal-lenges and prevent the dismantling of sociopolitical achievements (Fichter 2008).

More recent research (2012) has shown how the institutions and practices of workplace labor relations affect relationships between German and migrant workers. All three cases investigated, two in the metalworking sector (IG Metall) and one in chemicals (IG BCE), were representative of the status of migrant workers in the workforce throughout Germany: "foreigners are more likely to work as unskilled and semi-skilled manual workers than those with German citi-zenship" (Schmidt and Müller 2012: 7; for a statistical reference, see IAB 2009: 289). The authors found that relationships among German and migrant workers were based on a system of "pragmatic cooperation" that functions on the princi-ple of "internal universalism." That is, all persons at the workplace are colleagues shed of their diverse social identities and the externalization of social differences and conflicts:

> The threshold between the world of work and the private sphere limits not only the societal importance of 'pragmatic cooperation'-type rela-tions, it also eases the requirements of cooperation within the work-place. Difference gets externalized. Not only resentments but cultural differences in general are regarded as a private matter, which does not belong to the world of work. (Schmidt and Müller 2012: 16)

Interestingly, the authors encountered different approaches to "internal uni-versalism," which they interpreted as being associated with different unions. Whereas a "strict" internal universalism represented by the exclusive use of Ger-man language for publications, training, and announcements was used in the two metalworking factories, a less strict approach based on managing diversity and using multilingual means of communication was found in the chemical fac-tory (Schmidt and Müller 2012: 20). In each case, written material was provided for distribution by the responsible union. The different positions of these two unions are also reflected in the IG BCE training agreement to strengthen diver-sity management with the employers' association BAVC for their members with a migration background (BAVC and IG BCE 2008: online). For its part, the IG Metall launched a broadly based Respekt! campaign to improve the training and employment chances of young migrants and youth with migration backgrounds (IG Metall 2011b).

Schmidt and Müller (2012)point out the importance of understanding that the construction of "pragmatic cooperation" and "internal universalism" is not to be taken for granted. Rather they emerge "from a combination of societal differentiation and the German model of industrial relations." German soci-ety is not strong on developing common social values across different ethnic, cultural and racial backgrounds, they argue, and indeed, is more prone to foster-ing differences.

> Because the German model of industrial relations does not differentiate in principle between persons of different origin, the 'employee model' of interest constitution predominates at workplaces: Employees articu-late their interests as employees rather than as members of different ethnic or cultural communities. (Schmidt and Müller 2012: 21)

Schmidt and Müller (2012: 23) emphasize that the model is functioning well in the three representative cases they researched; however, they argue that it is limited to the workplace and indeed, "seems to be quite blind to real existing structural ethnic inequality." And they point out that over the past decade, core elements of the model—union membership and works council coverage, have been declining (Ellguth and Kohaut 2012), raising questions as to the future via-bility of the model even in the workplace.

Trade Union Involvement Reflects Struggle with the Migrant Worker Question

Our understanding of German trade unions' relationship to migrant workers has been mixed. The country overall, and this includes many union members, has had a difficult time accepting that migrant workers will remain in Germany. German institutions have not made the adequate cultural, educational, and other adjust-ments needed to accommodate the significant numbers of non-German work-ers and their families that now live in the country. Meanwhile, migrant workers have been often indifferent to integration, frustrated by discrimination, and for many reasons resistant to assimilation. Third and fourth generation migrants are often less "arrived" and socially integrated than their ancestors.

In the face of persistent criticism of its policies on migration, the federal gov-ernment of Chancellor Angela Merkel's conservative-liberal coalition invited a wide range of civil society organizations, including the unions, to a summit meeting in 2006 on integration. The following year it rolled out with consider-able fanfare its National Integration Plan (NIP) which consisted mostly of good-sounding intentions, colorful pamphlets, and discussions. The unions criticized the NIP for being primarily aimed at "eliminating the presumed deficits of the migrants" instead of emphasizing the advantages of migration and focusing on improving migrants' chances of participation (DGB 2008). The response from many migrant organizations, most prominently the Turkish community, was a rejection of offers to participate. The two years of the plan's existence (from 2006 to 2008) showed little in the way of real improvements. Some of its proposed measures have even met with formal rejection by the chancellor herself. Instead of curbing societal hostility to migrants, and especially in the wake of the 2008 economic crisis, the NIP failed to discourage the noticeable rise in worrisome racial tensions and formal scapegoating by even parts of the "respectable" intelligentsia.

The space for trade unions to build on their past successes in integrating migrants at the workplace to achieve a greater measure of integration in the political sphere and in civil society is limited. The government's reticence to do more, opposition from employers, the massive increase in insecurity and precariousness, are all real barriers to integrating migrants and overcoming xenophobia in Germany. In the face of these challenges, union support for a change requires more rigorous action, and we have not discerned a concerted, comprehensive and strategic approach by union leadership to tackling this issue. Our research has yielded a limited number of cases that reflect this uncertain environment. Certainly, the case of the dock workers in Kiel demonstrates that when a trade union decides to integrate their non-German colleagues into the leadership of their union (IG Metall) and assists in strengthening their minority members' (Turkish) capacities in civil society, it can be done. Likewise, we see an unmistakable determination of ver.di officials in Hamburg, despite the law's constraints, to assist an undocumented domestic worker in her struggle to fight against wage theft and other inappropriate treatment by her wealthy employer. In doing so, these trade union officials built coalitions with migrant worker groups that appear to be ad hoc but hopefully consist of relationships that can be revisited and strengthened in the future.

We include a series of interviews of non-German workers who as second generation migrants succeeded in rising to very important high-level jobs in IG Chemie, Papier und Keramik (now IG BCE) and IG Metall. Their explanations of their success, while for the most part a function of remarkable individual drive, also speak to the supportive organizational environment within the unions that has and will continue to make such advancement possible.

We also learned of an approach to the migrant worker issue that was European-based and highly controversial among the affected unions. This was the IG BAU construction union case where an attempt was made to create a European-wide parallel construction workers union. But this approach failed to gain the support and recognition outside of Germany needed to address its agenda.

The Kiel Case (IG Metall)

The IG Metall has a migration office at its national headquarters. Its tasks include supporting and lobbying the target groups as well as helping members with migration backgrounds to get involved in union representational structures and in contributing more to union work. Even with a mandate to do so, only about 20 percent of the 164 regional administration offices have a migration committee. Given these developments, the migration and integration work of the IG Metall office for the Kiel/Neumünster region in northern Germany is quite special. Our perspective of the situation in Kiel is based on interviews with trade unionists, migrants, and nonmigrants, and documented information such as annual reports, member journals, and academic works.

Opportunities for migrant integration in Kiel were created by national migrant committee initiatives undertaken by the IG Metall in 1983. The regional IG Metall office responsible for the northern German coast (*Küste*) followed up on this by implementing a number of programs over the following years. Under the direction of Wolfgang Mädel of the Kiel region, a vigorous Migration Committee was established where Turkish workers shared the leadership with local works council members. Activities included language seminars, assisting seniors with their retirement issues, organization of training seminars for foreign colleagues, and the provision of support to foreign colleagues with respect to various legal issues. The committee also organizes yearly celebrations of the union's diversity ("Oriental Night"). Cultural respect by the German leaders was very important to successful integration. Interviews with German and Turkish leaders explained that "honoring" by the Germans of Turkish cultural and sports associations contributed to the closeness between unions, German and Turkish workers, and their families. The IG Metall chair of this region in the 1990s, Wolfgang Mädel, shared leadership of the integration efforts with the Turkish chair of the Migration Committee.

The long-term success of integration efforts in the Kiel region is visible in a number of ways. Migrant workers are a firmly established component of the presidium of the IG Metall Kiel as delegates at the district level and in the works councils. Since the mid-1990s, the IG Metall delegates of the Kiel Administration Office have been selected based on a delegate key, which determines that the delegating companies must send a number of migrant delegates that correspond to the proportion of migrant employees. This is a voluntary obligation in other workplaces, but mandatory in Kiel. For works council elections there is a consensus to ensure that Turkish workers are well positioned on the IG Metall slate. Migrant worker children's education and advancement in Kiel has been a central focus of the Migration Committee from the very beginning. Almost all of the children of the current migrant members of the current committee have higher-level school or vocational certifications and hold good jobs.

Responsibility for these successes seems to lie primarily with the dedication of both migrants and German union members to the union work promoting integration. As Hans-Ulrich Stangen—a former works council member—emphasized in a 2010 interview, the politically left-wing attitudes of many of the active members contributed to the strong support on the part of German workers for the interests of the guest workers. The spirit of internationalism, the struggle against capitalist constraints—from which guest workers suffered the most, and humanitarian motives, caused Stangen and others to stand up on behalf of their colleagues from other countries. Finally, the homogeneity of the Turkish migrant families who settled in Kiel and their interest in advancing themselves was and is a factor, too, in facilitating integration.

This Kiel case, then, has many elements of integration success, including the clear support of the national and regional IG Metall offices, and focused, sincere, and consistent local union leadership. The latter may have been the most significant factor, but these other union structural and political contributions also shaped the valuable political and social integration practices observed in Kiel.

ver.di Au Pair Case, Ana S. (Undocumented)

Hamburg's regional ver.di office engaged in an unusual practice to assist a local au pair who was mistreated and cheated out of her wages. In doing so, this trade union coordinated its efforts with local migrant worker groups and created a formal contact point location where migrant workers could seek similar help. Part of this case's importance is that ver.di officials were willing to confront the dark side of a migrant worker's work, the informal economy, which negatively controls and severely affects the tens of thousands of mostly female workers who have no work permit.[6]

Germany, like many industrialized countries, seeks to satisfy its needs for inexpensive and flexible service workers to do the work that Germans will not by turning somewhat of a blind eye to the employment of irregular, paperless migrants. The society's "informal" need to acquire such workers is not matched by its interest in protecting them. In fact, these workers' "illegal status" interferes with their ability to achieve justice in their often unprotected work places. Lacking a proper residence or work permit creates an excessive and frightened dependency on the ostensible employer. The immigration laws often dictate summary expulsion for the complaining, mistreated, paperless migrant worker. A sense of hopelessness often characterizes the paperless worker who finds herself in the situation where ver.di leaders in Hamburg stepped forward.

But there is more than despair to this situation. EU law clearly protects the right of undocumented workers to be paid, even where there is no contract, and the wage rate, if disputed, is often the customary one for that type of work in that country. German law supports this notion, yet permits—but does not require—a labor court judge, hearing these cases, to report the undocumented nature of the worker before the court to the police.

Following her work permit expiration, Ana S.'s employer worked her excessively, by any country's standards, and, after being helped by migrant organizations, she joined ver.di and began to fight her unpaid wages case. There were many twists and turns, but ver.di's actions (and perhaps its political skills) assisted Ana in maneuvering through the courts and avoiding police involvement to attain a favorable settlement. This settlement may have created a limited precedent for labor courts to deal with undocumented workers without turning them over to the police. Ana S. remains as a domestic worker in Germany, illegally, like so many thousands of others. She has little to no chance of gaining citizenship, but Germany needs her labor, and that, in real ways, provides her with a sense of safety and security.

ver.di's actions in this case will not add significantly to its membership rolls, but it does evidence a moral stance that enhances its standing in the migrant worker community in Hamburg. Domestic workers are among the most abused throughout the developed and developing worlds, and it is of considerable importance when powerful trade unions take action that says, "they are one of us."

ver.di's success, while laudable, was not a solo effort. Interviews with actual participants in this lengthy struggle for Ana report that significant support and effort was contributed by left-wing and feminist trade union members as well as migrant worker groups. These coalition partners took notice of the globalized expansion of irregular domestic employment, and the need for trade union organizations to become more deeply involved in this overlooked part of the labor market.

The informal economy will not have its abuses solved in this way, to be sure, but the case of Ana S., an example of civic integration by this union for this worker, may well make wealthy Hamburg domestic worker employers think twice before behaving as this employer did. In addition, the push by ver.di, after taking up Ana S.'s case, in starting its migrant worker "drop in Center" (MigAr) in 2008, to assist migrants in the low-wage sector with wage, abuse, health and safety issues, as well as other legal problems, constitutes an institutional shift in German trade union integration policies. Several hundred migrant worker problems have been reviewed at the MigAr. Taking note of this development the DGB in 2010 resolved that the work place and political reality of persons without regular residence permit status was a task of German trade unions and the DGB.

IG BCE and IG Metall Interviews

Would interviews with high-ranking trade unionists with migrant family backgrounds help us better understand trade union integration of migrant workers? Hoping to learn how different migrants made it to high level union positions, our research team interviewed Giovanni Pollice, department head of Migration, IG BCE in Hanover;[7] Nihat Öztürk, the first chairperson of the IG Metall

Administration Office Düsseldorf/Neuss in North Rhine–Westphalia; and Francesco Grioli, a secretary at the headquarters of IG BCE in Hanover. The first two interviewees are of the second generation of migrants, while Grioli is of the third generation. Discussions with these trade union leaders informed us that their rise to high level positions came about from very strong personal initiative, mastery of the German language, considerable internal union support, and great respect from their migrant worker colleagues.

Pollice's rise began in the most conservative southern regions of Germany, but his workplace problem solving and leadership skills were quickly embraced by his union's regional leadership. He served as a shop steward and on the works council of his company while still in his twenties. He continued to gain the respect and confidence of trade unionists, within and without IG Chemie, and went on to work for years at the DGB before returning to the Migration Department of his now merged union. He became its head in the late 1990s.

Along the way, Pollice received special assistance from a grade school teacher ("who taught me German on his own time"), numerous union and works council officials, and never saw his migrant status as interfering with his union career. Pollice emphasized that IG BCE has pursued the support and fostering of migrants very seriously. The substance of his interview revealed an individual who has experienced a very positive trade union integration experience, and his union, given its leader and stories like this one, certainly take integration into its leadership structure quite seriously.

The conversation with Grioli, also of IG BCE, and being of the 3rd generation, revealed other explanations about integration. He worked at one of the largest chemical plants in Germany, the Hoechst AG plant in Frankfurt Main, along with 30,000 other workers. In the late 1990s migrants were so fully integrated into the workplace that the union decided to end its practice of submitting a separate migrant slate in the works council elections. Grioli was a youth activist first, not focused much on migrant workers' status in the plant. He never felt himself to be "a foreigner" who needed to stand up "for the interests of his fellow countrymen." But it is possible, notes Grioli, that others viewed him as a "migrant" and used him accordingly.

By 1998, he was off to IG BCE headquarters, where he found more people than he expected with migration backgrounds included in the vocational training sector and as officials. Grioli acknowledged that this reality at headquarters has changed as migrant worker concerns not central to trade union work—such as membership declines and the inability to attract youth—have become more pressing.

Nihat Öztürk, of IG Metall in Düsseldorf, born in Turkey, began his German work career just before the migrant worker restrictions were imposed in 1973. He worked with his father at a plant in Bavaria, where all the workers were migrants, and the only Germans were supervisors. He became an organizer in the mid-1970s, joining the IG Metall after attending a multilanguage training event. After successfully completing his studies at a university, he was hired by the DGB in the late 1980s. His work took him back to the IG Metall by the mid-1990s.

Similar to the Italian leaders from IG BCE, Öztürk reported that he has not been preoccupied with his migrant status. Nevertheless, he offered rich insights to the struggles over the migrant worker question. In Öztürk's view, the DGB supported the policies of the German government (migrants were to be "integrated for a limited time only") for many years and refused to accept the reality that Germany had become a land of immigration. In many ways, what he described was still German social policy well through the 1990s, and some would argue—with the failure of integration—continues until this day.

These stories explain that well educated and persevering migrant workers have opportunities to rise inside the leadership fabric of Germany's trade unions. The percentages that succeed do not convince us that this "opportunity to rise" is available to all or most. Only a small fraction of migrant workers have attained significant positions of leadership in German trade unions, and this aspect of internal trade union integration is still undeveloped.

The IG BAU Case

In 2004 the German construction workers' union IG Bauen-Agrar-Umwelt (IG BAU) established what they hoped would become a transnational union to organize and represent hyper-mobile posted workers across Europe and in a wide range of sectors.[8] The European Migrant Workers Union (EMWU), however, failed to meet its targets to attract a substantial membership and support from other existing unions. From our research we believe that this case reflects the difficulty many German unions have in assisting migrant workers.

IG BAU sought to bring unorganized Eastern European (mostly) construction workers into a European wide union that would protect the construction industry labor market from nonstandard wage rates. It reached across several nations' boundaries but was not successful in incorporating these non-German construction workers into their own EMWU or into the German union.

EMWU had some success in integrating migrants into society. It created a space for a relatively hard-to-organize group within the structure of IG BAU and provided advice and legal services. EMWU also provided support and advice to vulnerable central Eastern European workers, usually by pressing claims for back wages. It provided these services from bases in Warsaw and Frankfurt and hired staff who spoke the languages of most migrant construction workers (Polish and Romanian).

However, the organizing model created by IG BAU proved to be unsustainable. This was primarily due to its service-heaviness. It was simply not possible to attract and retain enough members facing severe problems at work to pay for the service. EMWU spent six to seven times what it earned in member dues. Furthermore, the broader trade union movement did not support EMWU due to worries about jurisdictional conflict. The trade union movement overall also lacked IG BAU's sense of immediate crisis. This applied as much to construction unions in other countries as to other German unions. Finally, EMWU faltered due to the contradictions of IG BAU's overall strategy, one of organizing migrant workers while favoring legislation to restrict their access to the labor market and working with the labor inspectorate to enforce these rules.[9]

In this sense, the IG BAU case explains that the EU's and Germany's trade unions are not yet able to meet the civic and union-based integration needs of migrant construction workers. IG BAU's efforts started just before the government's launch of the National Integration Plan, but these initiatives do not appear to have worked effectively in any mutual fashion to institutionalize migrant worker integration.

Concluding Observations

Our research of trade union policy in migrant integration in Germany has produced important insights on successes and shortcomings, all of which are explainable in the context of union organizational and institutional strength. In this environment, German unions have seen no need for social movement approaches when dealing with the integration of migrants at the workplace, in the union, and even to an extent in the community. Since the end of World War II, we have observed a consistent struggle on the part of German unions, but also within German unions, on behalf of workplace and wage equality, legislative initiatives coupled with strong, internal antidiscrimination policies, and language and other trainings that promote meaningful opportunity to migrants. At times, migrant workers have become regional and even national trade union leaders due, in part, to unions' efforts to promote civic and internal integration. It is at the local and plant levels that integration in the world of work does or does not take place, and there we have found convincing and impressive evidence of integration. Is this evidence equally apparent throughout the country? Probably not, as union membership and leadership as well as the communities of migrant workers (and their families) vary across locations. Sectoral factors may also contribute to integration disparities. This is evidenced by the growing gap between wage levels and working conditions in industries with strong union and works council representation and those without.

Despite this positive evidence of inclusion, of a history of countering widespread antipathy toward migrants and even more explicit antiforeigner behavior, the overall scale of union integration efforts appears to be halting. Widespread internal restructuring and membership losses have curtailed integration policies within the DGB. Added to this is the poor record most unions have had for years in recruiting and organizing young workers, a growing number of whom have migration backgrounds. The government's mixed messages concerning migrant workers' well-being, vacillating between support and disinterest, has played a role in these developments.[10] One wonders, but cannot confirm, whether the worrisome extreme right attitudes of a sizeable segment of trade union members interferes with making more progress in the integration of migrant workers. Giving it a higher internal union priority, as for example in a new public-private campaign in Berlin, would be a powerful signal in this respect.

Migrant workers came to Germany and played a key role in its industrial rebirth. Many of them returned to their homes, because of the country's failure to integrate these migrant into German society. Germany's trade unions have done a much better job, but still, by the oral histories and other research undertaken, much more needs to be done. In the current climate of the post-2008 financial crisis, this will be quite difficult. Societal and trade union reluctance, the now lengthy passage of time, and the impacts of economic downturn in Europe, present major barriers to further civic and trade union integration. Successful advancement of trade union integration policy will continue to be a task for the next generation of union leaders, but they will have a base to build on.

Part III

COMPARISONS AND POLICY IMPLICATIONS

OPPORTUNITY AND CHOICE FOR UNIONS ORGANIZING IMMIGRANT WORKERS

A Comparison across Countries and Industries

Gabriella Alberti, Jane Holgate, and Lowell Turner

Previous chapters have provided a detailed analysis of the cases examined in this comparative study. We have seen cases in which unions and other organizations based in civil society have mobilized immigrant workers to challenge the considerable exploitation that many of them face in both the workplace and society. In this chapter we deepen the analysis to consider campaigns across all the countries involved in the study and across industries within national contexts. Addressing similarities and differences across and within France, Germany, the United Kingdom, and the United States, our aim is to shed light on campaign strengths and weaknesses, successes and failures, cause and effect, and wider patterns as immigrants and their allies in the labor movement work toward promoting a better life for those operating at the margins of labor markets.[1]

We started our comparative crossnational research with the question, "In what ways are trade unions in Europe and the U.S. trying to integrate immigrant workers into their structures, and what are the results of their efforts?" We were interested in the extent to which these were coherent strategic approaches made by national unions or whether they were ad hoc attempts made at local levels. Related questions included: Does the scale (national/local/workplace) at which campaigns occur matter and if so, how? Does strategic coherence facilitate organizing efforts and innovation? While these questions were ever present as we talked to immigrants and union organizers in our field research, we were acutely aware that the macroeconomic picture could not be ignored: globalization and the crisis of capitalism have a major impact on the lives of immigrant workers.

In a context of economic crisis, most immigrant workers find themselves in the ranks of what authors have identified as the precarious workforce or the "precariat," to indicate the growing numbers who face employment, job, and social insecurity while lacking access to workplace rights and channels for representation (Standing 2011). We considered union action to challenge the vulnerable and marginalized position of migrants in the labor market and local communities. We found the picture differed considerably across the countries and it was here that historical understandings of immigration policy and attitudes toward immigrants were important in national contexts—something that few studies of unions and immigrant workers have covered (for exceptions, see Greene, Kirton, and Wrench 2005; Penninx and Roosblad 2000; Wrench 1997).

Unions are not immune from wider social, economic, and cultural influences and these are reflected in their behavior toward immigrant workers. Many observers have emphasized the traditionally white male character of trade unions in the Global North and ways in which unions have adopted restrictionist practices to protect the interests of native-born workers; in our research we focused on the specific barriers faced by immigrant workers in today's fragmented labor markets, and how these barriers might be overcome.

Our interest in workplace and civic integration also led us to explore the ways that workers' lives intersect between home and work, and how ethnic as well as occupational identities mattered to the approaches taken to bring immigrants into the labor movement (Fine 2005; Milkman 2006). Across case studies, industries, and countries, labor's willingness to engage in wider coalitions with nontraditional actors and community-based groups, such as worker centers, social movement groupings, and other nongovernmental organizations (NGOs), appeared to have major effects on the possibility for vulnerable immigrants to fight for their own rights. This in turn appeared as a critical factor influencing the relative success of the campaigns studied.

Union efforts to organize immigrant workers thus afford a window into broader efforts aimed at labor movement revitalization in a context of international labor market restructuring. The focus on immigrant workers allows us to rethink institutional transformation, moving beyond viewing unions as relatively closed institutions and instead considering what it means for the union movement to adopt a social movement approach that includes the wider lived experience of workers' lives.

Methods: A Cross-Case Comparative Analysis

Most of the literature on union revitalization has been country specific and has assumed the nation state as the unit of analysis in comparative research

(Fairbrother and Yates 2003; Kelly and Frege 2004; Penninx and Roosblad 2000). The literature on changes in union strategies and tactics brought about by the diffusion of union organizing from the United States to Australasia, Britain and Ireland enriched the methodological approach on union revitalization (Gall 2009a, 2009b). For instance the collection of essays on the future of organizing (Gall 2009b) has the merit of considering national, subnational, and supranational sector-based case studies (i.e., cleaning and steel) and of including challenges in relation to specific categories such as migrants, youth, and "insecure workers." However, in an attempt to identify best practice Gall's collection does not systematically compare the outcome achieved by unions at these different levels, nor does it include an explicit comparative assessment of the uneven diffusion of the model. Our methodological approach on trade union renewal in the field of migrant workers organizing is different, matching pairs among different union strategies across industries within the same country, as well as across countries. Furthermore, while this previous research refrained from drawing recommendations due to diversity of factors, we consider crossnational, intranational, and international case comparisons to assess the wider picture.

By considering industry rather than country as a unit of analysis, globalized industrial sectors provided useful comparisons to identify common economic and social patterns across countries, as well as differences in outcomes in the same locality (e.g., between the Justice for Cleaners campaign and a campaign in the hotels sector, both in London). We also compared national union policies, integration models, and different educational policies to incorporate immigrants according to each country's specific history of immigration.

The national framework of industrial relations, including the traditional positions of unions toward immigrant workers and the associated integration profile, obviously influences the choices made by union leaders, both for organizing immigrants and for union policy positions, including decisions to support or oppose the regularization of undocumented workers. The ways in which unions have dealt with immigration reform has also emerged as a field of strategic mobilization per se, as in the case of the French *sans papiers* campaign.

Because of its very nature, however, the study of transnational labor immigration and union engagement with immigrant workers also offers the opportunity to identify common patterns across countries, thus superseding the limits of national framework approaches while still taking the latter seriously. The national context remains a necessary starting point to analyze social facts within historical and juridical boundaries, as demonstrated by the decisive influence of national policies on the regulation of immigration and on (what is left of) the regulation of the labor market and industrial relations in each of our case studies.

Recognizing the importance of the national context does not exclude the possibility either that unions might try to mobilize workers across national and industrial boundaries, or by contrast organize primarily at the community level. Scaling down organizing strategies by searching for alliances in local communities or at regional levels can allow unions to reach out to immigrant workers more effectively (as reflected, for example, in the "community union" strategies of Unite in the United Kingdom or the US AFL-CIO's collaboration with immigrant-based worker centers). Community approaches at a smaller geographical scale offer opportunities for a renewal of union structures and policies. In addition, going beyond the national scale involves consideration of how unions may engage in forms of cross-border organizing, where the transnational rather than the local or national levels appears as a strategic locus to unite highly mobile, unprotected workers. Thus while different union strategies can be combined within a "multi-scalar approach" (Anderson, Hamilton, and Wills 2010) a transnational strategy, as illustrated by the IG Bau's (Germany's Industrial Union for Construction and Agriculture) attempt to build a European Migrant Workers Union (EMWU), introduces new challenges for union organizational renewal in efforts to incorporate immigrant workers (Lillie and Greer 2007).

A methodological contribution of this study thus lies in the claim that the unit of analysis in comparative industrial relations research cannot be confined to the nation state, especially when labor unions confront transient and precarious workforces. National systems of industrial relations, and specifically their intersection with immigration policies in each country, crucially influence the successful integration of immigrant workers in unions and civil society. Yet other factors, such as the characteristics of an industry or immigration regime, must be taken into account in order to assess union strategies in the workplace and beyond.

The following analysis uses in-depth original case studies based on the field research of our country research teams, matching pairs both across and within nations, as well as a broader, systematic comparative analysis.[2] For analytical purposes, we draw on a range of literature, including comparative political economy and sociology, labor geography, institutional analysis, and social movements.

Globalization, Immigration, and Changing Union Strategies

As economic globalization has driven millions of people to move from their home country (IOM 2011), immigrant labor has become a growing concern for unions. According to the 2011 World Migration Report produced by the International Organization for Migration the number of international migrants around the world has gone up from up from 191 million in 2005 to 214 million people in

2010 (IOM 2011: 49). From 1945 through the end of the twentieth century, most unions in the Global North followed their national governments in policies to restrict or even prevent immigrant workers from taking jobs that "belonged" to workers in the host country. Now that many basic functions in the world's global cities, such as cleaning and catering (as well as agricultural work in rural areas), rely on immigrant labor, such strategies on the part of unions are less sustainable.

At the turn of this century, Penninx and Roosblad (2000) identified three options for unions in relation to immigrant workers: to resist immigration (seen as increasingly unrealistic), to collaborate with employers in the recruitment of immigrants, or to address the specific issues facing immigrants in the workplace and labor market. In many cases, unions have reconsidered past protectionist stances, which sought to restrict the work done by immigrants or to bar access to certain jobs or even entry into the country. Economic reality, globalization, and the decline in union power and influence, including in some cases drastic reductions in union membership, have driven unions to consider new approaches to the challenges of immigrant labor. Although private service sector jobs have typically had low rates of unionization, the fact that many of these jobs cannot leave the country offers a strategic advantage to unions in an era of "offshoring." The place-bound nature of these jobs and the impossibility for capital to relocate internationally in search of new spatial fixes (Silver 2003) has meant that unions could focus organizing efforts in places grounded in local communities. And many of these jobs—in hospitality, retail, and building services, for example— are heavily populated by immigrant workers.

A historical analysis of attitudes toward immigrant labor provides a useful reminder of the ways in which unions in the four countries have changed their stance over time. The "integration profiles" endorsed by different unions are clearly influenced by national models of integration of immigrants (for instance the French assimilationist model based on the republican tradition of universal citizenship rights and the UK multicultural approach emphasizing the ethnic identification of migrants with their national group) (Wrench 2007). For much of the postwar period, union views were typically protectionist, supporting government positions on immigration controls. For example, prior to 1969 the UK's Trades Union Congress supported immigration controls, and it was not until 1973 that the confederation changed direction with opposition to the restrictive 1971 Immigration Act. Organized labor in the United States in the 1920s had supported a national origins system to curb the immigration of unskilled workers from eastern, central, and southern Europe, and by the late 1980s labor was still supporting strong border controls and sanctions against employers who hired undocumented workers. In postwar West Germany, unions, as social partners, negotiated with government for recruitment of foreign workers based on labor standards similar to those faced by German workers (same working conditions and equal pay). But this position shifted during the recession of the early 1970s, as many Germans, including union officials, saw immigrant workers as taking the jobs of German workers in a context of rising unemployment.

Union attitudes changed at critical turning points during the 1960s and 1970s because of internal strategic choices or pressure triggered by the mobilization of immigrant workers themselves. For instance, in the United Kingdom, immigrant worker strikes in the 1970s forced unions to open the doors and offer support (see chapter 4). In the context of the May 1968 mobilization in France, the active participation of immigrants in labor strikes forced unions to improve their acceptance and integration policies (chapter 5). In Germany (chapter 6), the participation of so-called guest workers in wildcat strikes of the early 1970s forced both unions and companies to shift toward strategies of cooptation if not full inclusion. Over the past 20 years in some countries shifts in union policy toward migrant workers have occurred in correspondence with the emergence of union-led organizing opportunities in the industries employing immigrants, combined with migrants' spontaneous organization. In waves of mobilization that began in France in 2008, the CGT and other unions campaigned for the regularization of *sans papiers* workers. In the United States (chapter 3), a dramatic policy change by the AFL-CIO in 2000, targeting immigrant workers for organizing campaigns, was driven by unions such as SEIU and HERE who had found considerable enthusiasm for unionization among largely Latino workforces in building services and hotels.

Between 2008 and 2011, when our case studies were conducted and we were witnessing renewed integration attempts, anti-immigrant rhetoric was again on the rise in all four countries. In France, for example, where substantial majorities had supported both immigrant schoolchildren in 2005–2006 and the *sans papiers* movement in 2008–2010, 20 percent of the population voted for the anti-immigrant Front National in 2011 local elections and 18 percent supported the party's candidate Marine Le Pen in the 2012 presidential election.

The expansion of migration through Europe as a consequence of EU enlargement triggered controversy everywhere, including Germany, with nativist discourses influencing workers' attitude toward immigrants as well as trade union policies. The discourse "Germany for the Germans" (expressed increasingly in political discourse as the eurozone crisis developed) clearly recalls the "British jobs for British workers" slogan that appeared outside the Lindsey oil refinery in Lincolnshire on January 28, 2009. Hundreds of protesters demonstrated against the company's decision to bring in its own lower paid Italian and Portuguese workers, perceived by some as "stealing" local jobs. The economic crisis has also fanned racism—with the scapegoating of immigrants both with and without papers, as well as black and minority ethnic workers in general—and served to discourage union-led immigrant integration in all countries. Intensified nativism in our Tennessee cases highlights the challenges for unions facing local resistance to immigrant integration.

New challenges have thus appeared as trade unions confront the social consequences of the economic crisis, including precarious working conditions and growing racial tensions in society. These challenges call into question traditional approaches to the integration of immigrant workers.

French and German Integration Profiles: A Crossnational Comparison

The French and the UK models of immigrant integration are traditionally contrasted as representing the "assimilationist" and "multiculturalist" approach to the civic and political integration of noncitizens. However, our analysis of the impact of the national integration profile on unions' attitudes toward immigrants highlighted that even between two "assimilationist" countries such as France and Germany critical elements of comparison have emerged. German trade union emphasis on acquiring language skills as a precondition for equal rights for immigrants reflects an understanding of integration that differs from that of recent French union campaigns. In the *sans papiers* campaigns, membership in the workforce or "labor citizenship" was enough for French unions to promote equal social rights and benefits for immigrant workers. In the German case, knowledge of the language is viewed as a sign of civic integration, meant to precede entitlement to labor rights and full integration into workplace and society.

These differing approaches may explain why in France we found more instances of local union engagement with recently arrived, precarious, and undocumented immigrants—without the expectation that these workers would be fully integrated in the national culture and society as a condition for full acceptance by the union. By contrast, in Germany national union leadership programs and integration policies involved mainly second and third generation or relatively settled immigrants, whose level of integration is higher than the recently arrived. Most of the organizing attempts recorded in the German case studies involved workers of Italian or Turkish background, two relatively old immigrant communities of the former *Gastarbeiter* in Germany.

Though French unions appeared more flexible than German unions in integrating recently arrived migrants, we do not mean to romanticize the French model of integration. The template that links immigrants' civic and human rights to their position in the workforce (as in the CGT-led campaign for status regularization) contains a number of problems. The notion that immigrants are entitled to be regularized only as they become active members of the workforce mirrors the principle of dependency between work contract and residence permit at the core of most immigration regimes across Europe and the United States. Making the right to stay dependent on employment is in contradiction with the current flexible global labor market. Various authors have highlighted the role of government policies in augmenting the exploitation of immigrant workers through barriers to entry and obstacles to citizenship (e.g., Anderson 2010; Gammage 2008). Linking immigrant rights to the workplace is problematic in so far as work becomes increasingly intermittent and precarious (CoVe 2008; Rogers, Anderson, and Clark 2009). One might understand immigrant worker demands for regularization as arising from the French assimilation approach, whereby immigrants ask to be included in the national framework of citizenship in order to secure rights. Yet the *sans papiers'* demand for regularization was also a pragmatic response to a precarious situation in which noncitizens were particularly vulnerable in relations to employers. Demands for regularization offer a way to escape the forms of dependency created by regulatory frameworks and have proven successful in the context of the *sans papiers* campaign.

Historical positions have ebbed and flowed according to the views of political parties in government and the impact of anti-immigration rhetoric in periods of economic difficulties. However, the reality is that each country now has a significant immigrant population and unions are faced with a choice of either organizing or ignoring this growing section of the labor market. In thinking about how to organize and integrate immigrant workers, unions face not only cultural but also structural and organizational challenges. Policy pronouncements from the union movements in the four countries investigated for this research are now generally favorable toward immigrants, but actual practice has been patchy and piecemeal. Our findings show that national differences are in many cases less important than social, economic, and cultural differences that play out at a smaller scale than the nation state.

Success and Failure in the United Kingdom: The Importance of Local Communities

Moving from a cross-country to a cross-industry comparative approach, we consider two British campaigns, one involving cleaners and the other hotel workers—both of which took place in London. These examples are useful to identify both limits and opportunities for unions in immigrant-rich sectors of urban economies. A critical factor is the scale at which unions (in this case Unite) tried to build unity among fragmented workforces. More broadly, the strategies employed in these cases can be understood as union responses to the patterns of labor market segmentation.

The cleaning industry in London, as elsewhere, is dominated by multinational contractors serving large corporations, which are themselves global companies. The union must negotiate with cleaning companies to set terms of employment, but in this case Unite decided to upscale its tactics to put pressure on the cleaning contractors' clients through "blaming and shaming," in public demonstrations at high-profile buildings in the city. Following strategic approaches developed by the US-based SEIU in their Justice for Janitors campaigns, the aim was to target building owners rather than cleaning companies, because owners control the money available for contractors to spend on labor (Alzaga 2011; Wills 2008). Another point of leverage was that owners of buildings and the companies that occupy them have higher public profiles, and they prefer to be known for corporate social responsibility rather than for the exploitation of vulnerable workers. In Unite's Justice for Cleaners campaign, the plan was to move from workplace organizing to London as a whole. While it made sense to create a zonal approach to target big companies (often banks) in close proximity, this approach also helped to create a collective identity among cleaners, as part of something bigger, and provided safety in numbers.

Although Unite was not successful in achieving city- or industrywide agreements, significant victories were delivered at companies such as Barclays and Merrill Lynch in the City of London and at the Canary Wharf financial district, as some companies agreed to pay the London Living Wage.

If we compare the structure of the cleaning sector with that of the hotel industry we find a similar system of layers and "scales of organizing" that must be negotiated to bring collective representation to workers in this industry. For the hotel sector, the building owner is at the top of the hierarchy, building management at each particular hotel a scale down, and finally the various agencies supplying and managing manpower (partly corresponding to the contractor cleaning companies) at the bottom. In the hotel workers campaign, Unite and London Citizens tackled the main multinational management company (the hotel brand) rather than the contractors or the building owners, attacking the most visible segment of the hierarchy and the one perhaps most vulnerable to public pressure.

As part of an industrywide strategy, and in partnership with the UNITE HERE local in Los Angeles, campaign organizers in London selected the Hyatt as a "global employer" in their campaign targeting a small number of establishments in different areas of the city. This strategy carried the advantage of targeting the company's reputation, as with tactics employed in the Justice for Cleaners campaign (Holgate 2009a). Although Hyatt management was put under pressure by public demonstrations during the campaign, the strategy was not sufficient to unite the workers at particular establishments to build a strong base for union recognition. Compared to building services and the context faced by Justice for Cleaners, the structure of the hotel industry is complicated by a further level of subcontracting that includes different companies managing various hotel departments (food and beverage, housekeeping, etc.) (Figure 7.1). This contractual fragmentation generated confusion and broke cohesiveness among workers with regard to the "real employer" and the proper focus of the campaign (Alberti 2010).

Thus in the hotel sector, the presence of multiple staffing agencies and complex scales of governance has resulted in more labor market segmentation than in the cleaning industry. If the workforce is further fragmented along migration and ethnic lines, as expressed in the tension between newly arrived white Eastern Europeans and older black and ethnic minorities in London (comparable to divisions between Latinos and African Americans sometimes observed in union organizing efforts in the United States), then the impact of neoliberal restructuring in the service sector produces more obstacles to workplace organizing. The combination of migrant and subcontracted labor makes even stronger the case for zonal agreements across workplaces to recreate unity out of fragmentation where different contractors recruit different ethnic groups of workers.

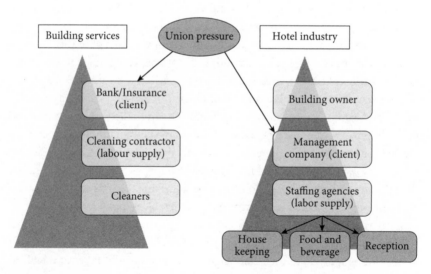

FIGURE 7.1 Union strategies and industry structure: Hotel and building services

Indeed a core element of the more successful Justice for Cleaners campaign was to promote zonal agreements to regularize working conditions across locations (Wills 2008). The basic idea is an old one: that it makes less sense to organize workers in just one company than across companies in a geographical area, because a new set of standards that applies to only a fraction of the market will soon lose contracts to cheaper companies. On the contrary, the objective is to raise standards across the board (as with living wage ordinances applied within geographical areas in the United States), to free employers from labor cost competition. A geographical approach to union organizing appears more effective for immigrant service workers than campaigns targeted at one company, allowing for greater pressure on employers within certain market segments—despite workers' high mobility and dispersion across work sites.

In the hotel campaign, the workforce's contractual fragmentation and high turnover undercut the union's effort to unite migrant workers against their respective employers, contributing to campaign failure. Unions in sectors such as hospitality still have to find strategies to unravel the complexities of the subcontracting chain, which involve more localized and diverse agencies compared to the global cleaning companies in building services. A sense of commonality is essential in uniting different groups of migrant workers via economic status (class position), alongside immigration status as well as minority ethnic group identities.

Organizing and Building Solidarity across Intersecting Identities

The issue of identity and the way it has played out in many of the case studies is of great significance. We were interested in the extent to which worker identities were taken into account by unions when organizing among immigrant workers. To what extent, we asked, were immigrants considered "just workers"—or were the specificities of an immigrant worker a factor in union approaches to organizing among particular groups of workers? In many ways, the separation of home and work is not possible in the lived experience of immigrant workers. Distinctive ethnic and immigrant identities are created (and learned), and immigrants often have to contend with the consequences and negative connotations of becoming workers who are also immigrants.

An important issue for unions in this period of globalization is not only to rebuild power to challenge exploitation but to overcome workforce divisions by bringing together the different parts of increasingly fragmented labor markets, where immigrants are often found in the lower segments. Issues raised in an organizing approach include whether to mobilize based on equal or special treatment. Here we found very different approaches in each of the countries, closely linked to historical and ideological views on the origins of national populations.

Overall, we found more successful examples of unions building collective strength where the practice was to engage "immigrant as immigrants" and not just as workers. For example, in the carwash campaign in Los Angeles, a broad understanding of oppression opened up the framing of the campaign and allowed organizers to talk about workers' rights alongside immigrant and social rights—acknowledging the intersection of these aspects of immigrant identities. In the CLEAN campaign (with clear resonance to Unite in the United Kingdom) there were two different ways of framing the approach according to the contexts in which workers were organized. On the one hand, a union space framed the issues around immigrant workers as workers, no matter their immigration status. On the other hand, a community space allowed for a representation of immigrant worker issues in a context of aspirations for political recognition in the larger society. Dual framing allowed for recognition of overlapping discrimination and exploitation faced in both workplace and society.

Comparing cases in the United Kingdom and the United States, British unions appeared limited by the heritage and structures of occupational and industrial-based unionism, while paradoxically U.S. unions seemed more open to immigrant worker concerns due to an overall weaker union presence that has forced unions to engage outside the traditional industrial relations arena. We found that unions in the United Kingdom were more likely to organize "immigrants as workers" rather than focusing particularly on their immigrant status. The UK's "immigrants as workers" approach showed elements in common with the German cases, reflecting how postcolonial immigrants and ethnic minorities have been treated in both countries as relatively settled (rather than as transitional or circular migrants) and integrated into traditional structures based in the workplace. Since 2004 the issue of "new migrant workers" in the United Kingdom has become more central to union policy and discourse. The consequences of EU enlargement and the increasingly temporary and transient nature of intra-EU migration (Holgate 2012) has required unions to think about new approaches toward a labor market stratification that concentrates immigrant workers in sectors such as cleaning, catering, and caring.[3]

In the UK case studies, all three unions set up special projects to deal with immigrant worker issues. Unison received funding from the Union Modernisation Fund (UMF)[4] to establish a Migrant Workers Participation Project, staffed by a three-person unit within its national office. Unite received similar funding to set up a Migrant Workers Support Unit, and GMB created a local Polish sub-branch in Southampton to accommodate the growing number of Polish workers in the region.[5]

In the study of Unite's Migrant Workers Support Unit (MWSU), our findings illustrate a politically distinctive union choice. Established in 2007 for a duration of two years, the MWSU was part of Unite's national organizing department. The unit consisted of a series of tailored services for immigrant workers such as a help line with interpreters for members with language difficulties and the development of advocacy activities to influence the government's immigration policy. The main concern of the MWSU was to offer services and educational training to match immigrant members' requirements. One interviewee also emphasized that the unit adopted Unite's general principle that "the whole point of a union is to have freedom of association and to bargain collectively no matter where you are from." Thus, on the one hand, the MWSU raised the question of immigrants' specific problems as immigrants; on the other, it did so within the union's universalistic philosophy of treating all "workers as workers." The weak link in this relationship was that the policy and structure of the union did not provide channels for an effective collaboration between the MWSU and Unite's traditional industrial branches.

In sum, one could argue that looking at the UK approach to immigrant identities, their incorporation into unions happens most often indirectly, that is as a result of organizing efforts in sectors that are immigrant-rich, with features such as flexibility, turnover, and low pay. This organizing focus shows that the real challenge for unions is not simply organizing immigrant labor but the nature of precarious work more generally. Whether or not the "precariat" constitutes a "class-in-the-making" (Standing 2011), the concept should not be used as an umbrella to blur the important differences that emerge even within immigrant workforces.

Multiple forms of precarious working and living conditions cut across different social groups, continuously reaffirming and complicating differences among them: between women and men, immigrants and indigenous workers, settled immigrants and newer arrivals, racial and ethnic groups, workers with and without legal work papers. Focusing on specific industrial sectors in which immigrants happen to be found carries the risk that unions lose track of the specific needs of such workers—from language to legal advice to immigration problems. If structures and services are not tailored to the needs of immigrant workers, the latter may end up marginalized from the wider union. At the same time, our research demonstrates the need for strong connections between any separate structures and existing union channels focusing on workplace issues. One of the reasons for the failure of the hotel workers campaign was indeed that services related to immigrant workers were effectively externalized to the temporary unit set up to deal with their concerns, which in turn did not play a role in the industry-based effort.

As we saw in other cases, the rigid distinction between industry-based organizing and immigrant-tailored services can be overcome through union collaboration with other groups in the community. In Germany, for example, the IG BAU experience setting up the transnational EMWU showed how crucial it is to have specialized staff with language skills to provide support to vulnerable workers (in this case from central and eastern Europe). Although the double ambition of organizing workers across sectors and across countries matched the reality of higher mobility for posted workers in the EU, the ambitious IG BAU transnational effort lacked institutional and political buy-in from other unions and thus became unsustainable. Acting as a migrant unit to provide more tailored help to mobile and temporary workers, the EMWU could not retain enough members to cover expenses. The lack of support from the broader labor movement—based in part on worries about jurisdictional conflicts—also helped to undermine the union effort. The EMWU can perhaps be seen as a heroic but failed attempt to transform the way that unions do business in a global labor market, where capital has the upper hand and the ability to innovate at a much faster pace than labor.

Strategic Choice, Institutional Transformation

In chapter 2, Tapia, Turner, and Roca-Servat considered unions as countermovements to challenge the arbitrary power of employers whose ability to exploit workers appears, in some instances and for some groups of workers, to be transporting us back to the early days of industrialization. Here we consider the ways in which unions have begun to address the institutional transformations that may be necessary to recruit, organize, and integrate new groups of workers. The first point to note is that existing organizational frameworks, be these unions or other organizations, do not fit neatly with the complex experiences and social demands of immigrant labor in our studies. Research on immigrant social networks has shown the importance of intraethnic support networks and ways in which immigrant community organizations can assist with issues beyond the workplace: in dealings with bureaucracy, housing, work permits, and other issues (Datta et al. 2007; Hagan 1998; Holgate 2011; Holgate, Keles, Kumarappan, and Pollert 2012; Ryan, Sales, Tilki, and Siara 2008; Wahlbeck 1998).

There is also a growing body of research on new forms of collective representation, where unions have been unable or unwilling to combat the isolation of low-paid, vulnerable workers (Ellem 2003; Fine 2005; Turner and Cornfield 2007). Holgate and Wills, for example (Holgate 2009c; Holgate and Wills 2007; Wills 2012), have written extensively about London Citizens, a broad-based community coalition that has campaigned for a living wage and for the regularization of immigrant workers, sometimes without much union involvement. And

Janice Fine (2005) has analyzed in great detail the emergence of immigrant-based worker centers in the United States.

It is not by chance that our campaign studies have highlighted a combination of tactics, scale, and organizational models to empower and organize low-paid immigrants. Unions are opening up to community and other nontraditional industrial relations actors in the process of engaging immigrants. A major challenge remains the engagement in genuine reciprocal "community unionism" and effective cross-pollination whereby both labor and community groups learn from each other and exchange tactics and methods to improve immigrants' conditions. In our LIUNA case in the United States, for example, a fruitful relation between labor, a community organization, and a worker center developed in which the union—in processes of "hybridization"—functioned as a medium for immigrant integration in the community. It protects day labor from police harassment, negotiates sensible solutions to community tensions caused by housing issues, and addresses migration issues (Fine 2011a). The LIUNA case is important in this regard for highlighting the impact of stricter immigration policies in the United States and the need for unions to sustain long-term organizing, improve street presence and civic protection initiatives, and further collaborate with worker centers. And this case demonstrates how the selection of partners in a coalition-building strategy directly influenced the issues that the union engaged.

For union strategy, how relations with local community organizations are handled and strategic demands selected is indeed of the utmost importance. The problem we identified in the Tennessee Tyson poultry workers case was not only the failure to build broad community support but a questionable decision by the union bargaining committee. Rather than simply adding a religious day off for Muslim workers in response to the demands of the many Somali workers at the plant, the union agreed to substitute the Muslim holiday for the traditional U.S. Labor Day (Cornfield 2009b). What could possibly have been better designed to evoke backlash among the predominantly non-Muslim local Tennessee population? Conservative activists in the "community" then went to war against the agreement, and the union and company were forced to change course.

Tensions between different types of organizations reflect different political cultures and strategies as well as the very nature of the demands at stake. In all four countries we found divisions of labor between the different organizations involved, partly reflecting their different approach to immigrant organizing and integration. In the United Kingdom, for example, collaboration between Unite and London Citizens reflected contrasting approaches to immigrant integration and organizing models. In reality, the two organizations operated for the most part independently, and sustained collaboration lasted only a couple of years before weakening in the face of differing ideologies and approaches to organizing. In the Los Angeles carwash campaign, the workers brigade addressed issues close to the work sphere and political integration, while the health and safety committee focused on issues of sociocultural integration. In France, unions focused exclusively on the workplace while immigrant advocacy and human rights groups addressed issues such as housing and education. In Germany, unions focused on workplace and social needs of foreign-born workers, including language training, in union strongholds, leaving the needs of immigrants in non-union workplaces to be addressed (if at all) by NGOs. The division and distribution of tasks between different organizations is to be expected, and may be more or less constructive in building cohesive campaigns and effective labor-community alliances.

The French *sans papiers* campaign offers important insights for managing community and labor relations within wider coalitions. The relationship between actors in the Collectif des Onze (C11, including five labor confederations and six NGOs) and the trajectory of the unions into the collective help explain why this collaboration was particularly fruitful. The fact that from 1984 to 2008 the focus of immigrant rights was outside the workplace, aimed at wider social issues, left unions eager to build coalition with community groups and broaden the agenda into social issues such as regularization—once the successful immigrant schoolchildren campaign aroused public support. The CGT intervened with good timing, making the most of an opportunity structure that allowed coherence and momentum for the *sans papiers* movement. The strategic move by unions within the coalition linked immigrants' societal security and protection obtained through legal status back to the workplace. The demand for regularization was meant to provide a legal status to afford protection for the promotion of workplace interests. More broadly, the strength of the *sans papiers* campaigns lay in the capacity to diversify targets and claims with demands that addressed not only wages and working conditions but also urged employers and local governments to support work permit applications of individual workers. The role of the unions—and coalition—in supporting community initiatives provided a breakthrough for the civic integration of immigrant workers.

The internal institutional transformation required by unions is in many ways cultural as well as structural. The different spaces of the union (where all workers are workers) and that of the community (where workers claim membership in the broader community of citizens) raises the need to maintain these spaces of empowerment as separate while effectively combining them. Rather than simply favoring amalgamation between labor and community groups, our research shows that unions may well benefit from the relative autonomy of the groups involved as well as that of the workers themselves. There is much to be

gained from both differences and commonalities in issues, identities, and solidarities emerging from an increasingly diverse workforce. Productive intersections are possible when unions engage with local groups as well as broader social
movements.

Immigrant Workers and Social Movement Unionism

Addressing the interests of immigrant workers provides opportunities for trade
unions to work in coalition with other social justice organizations, in ways that
have been described as "social movement unionism" (Turner 2007). In a context
of declining membership and bargaining power, union confederations and member unions across the different countries appeared eager to adopt inclusive policies toward immigrant workers. Some unions engaged in wider campaigns with
grassroots organizations in the urban milieu, employing strategies typically used
by activist NGOs. Thus we ask: In what ways have the various campaigns used
(or not used) social movement strategies, such as social justice framing, grassroots mobilization, and community involvement to organize immigrant workers? What difference has this made, and what were the outcomes and lessons from
such efforts? Why do the German cases differ in this regard from social move-
ment-type cases found in the United Kingdom, the United States, and France?

To start with our most dramatic example, the French *sans papiers* movement
of 2008–2010 included widespread direct action tactics including a series of
strikes and occupations at restaurants, building sites, and other workplaces with
low-wage immigrant workforces. The union privileged the workplace as the primary site of struggle, viewing "labor citizenship" (membership in the workforce)
as the main channel for access to civil and political rights. In the course of the
campaign, however, the CGT moved beyond the workplace to a wider human
rights discourse in support of undocumented workers. Expansion into the Collectif des Onze facilitated a wider agenda and an expansion of social movement
tactics. For public impact, the coalition successfully implemented high-profile
direct action tactics, culminating in an encampment at the Bastille in May–June
2010, as well as media attention and social justice framing. The strikes made marginalized workers visible, spotlighting the abuse of undocumented migrants at
work and more invisible groups such as temporary and domestic workers. Poll-
ing showed that up to 60 percent of the French public supported the demands of
the striking undocumented workers demonstrating the success of the campaign
in raising awareness of the rights of *sans papiers* workers.

A moral argument about protecting vulnerable workers through the use of
blaming and shaming tactics was similarly employed as part of the "comprehensive

campaigns" found in other country cases, such as Justice for Cleaners in the United Kingdom. Unite and Unison, however, did not develop a social movement approach comparable to the strategic orientation of the French *sans papiers* effort. British unions have built few sustained relationships with social movement and community-based actors. London Citizens played a crucial role in the Justice for Cleaners campaign but without a close relationship with Unite, hindering the expansion of the coalition into a more composite one such as the French C11. Although the French case included a productive combination of rank-and-file mobilization and social movement unionism, a more narrow industrial/occupational approach by most British unions helps explain why a community organization such as London Citizens played only an ancillary role in organizing efforts. As illustrated by the London hotel campaign, the mobilization aspect in the end was effectively contracted out to the wider community, whereby efforts were focused on obtaining support from local political and business figures rather than developing strong links with grassroots groups (Alberti 210).

By contrast, the capacity of unions to combine social and political rights by endorsing social justice framing emerged clearly in the case of the car wash campaign in Los Angeles. This campaign's comprehensive social movement strategy included a mix of confrontational "persuasion" strategies vis-à-vis employers, including litigation, administrative complaints, and social mobilization in collaboration with worker centers—a much richer combination, for example, than one based largely on lobbying and negotiation such as "the politics of incentive" endorsed by Unite and LC in the hotel sector. The carwash campaign encouraged a sense of entitlement and active involvement by workers on the ground. Collaboration between labor and community actors offered a "third space" for multiple forms of immigrant worker integration (Roca-Servat 2011), in processes facilitated by cross-pollination between different political cultures and strategies. By contrast, the development of social movement unionism was limited in the United Kingdom, despite a blending of organizing tactics and organizational cultures in some of our case studies (Unite and London Citizens in the hospitality and cleaning sectors; Unison and the Filipino community in the care workers campaign).

The carwash campaign provides a positive example of combined organizing strategies led by the Carwash Workers Organizing Committee (CWOC) of the United Steelworkers (USW), to bolster the engagement of workers through leadership development. The Carwash Workers' Leadership Brigade provided immigrants with the opportunity to learn fundamental principles of leadership and community organizing. Training included public speaking and media interview skills, communication with coworkers, running a successful meeting, working with community groups and faith-based organizations, and relations with employers (Osmer 2009).

At the same time the carwash campaign depended on support from a wide constellation of grassroots and advocacy groups, including the Los Angeles Workers Advocates Coalition (LAWAC) and Coalition of Low Wage and Immigrant Workers Advocates (CLIWA). This support network translated into political influence and a new Carwash Worker Law, to enforce standards in the carwash industry in California (Roca-Servat 2011). In this case, public legislation was used to galvanize the efforts of social and labor movement actors and to complement workplace-based tactics.

Our British and German case studies, by contrast, did not produce examples of unions or community groups promoting new legislation to implement workers' rights. Both the carwash and LIUNA cases in the United States show that unions can combine individual empowerment strategies and high-profile campaigns aimed at local or national governments, when such efforts are supported by a wide coalition in the community. Although collaboration between unions and community-based worker centers in the United States may not lead to immediate membership gains for the union, such common effort appears effective in building sustainable coalitions and workforce mobilization. In very different contexts and despite obvious limitations, both the LA carwash campaign and the French *sans papiers* movement brought collective representation to invisible and marginal workers, breaking with existing patterns to demonstrate that organizing is possible even in informal and nonunion sectors of the economy.

A research finding that stands out is the absence of cases of social movement mobilization on behalf of immigrant workers by German unions, to parallel "best practice" findings in the United States, France, and the United Kingdom (for more on this, see chapter 2). Where German unions have integrated immigrants into their ranks and developed them as leaders, this has happened mainly where unions are already strong, through works councils participation and local union branches, often working hand-in-hand. Union efforts to integrate immigrant workers (from first generation on down) has thus followed a traditional workplace, industrial model of organizing, rather than a social movement approach that could reach out to the large numbers of immigrant and precarious workers lacking in representation. Unions such as the Metalworkers and Chemical Workers, in their strongholds, have developed impressive educational programs to bring immigrant workers into active membership and works council participation. The capacity of German trade unions to integrate immigrants into the fabric of existing unions is distinctive for the mediation of deeply embedded structures of representation, such as the works councils, rooted in the workplace. The problem facing German unions is the rapid growth of low-wage, immigrant-rich, precarious workforces, especially in private sector services, where unions are weak and works councils rare. It is hard to see how such workers can be organized in the absence of a coalition-based, social justice-oriented campaign, a capacity that German unions have for the most part not yet developed (Turner 2009)).

All our case studies, with more and less successful outcomes, contain lessons for unions seeking innovative structures and strategies in today's fragmented labor markets. For union renewal, a key difference emerged between ad hoc projects (such as temporary bodies like the British Migrant Workers Unit), more embedded and durable structures (such as the Migration committee of IG Metall [German Metalworkers Union]), and comprehensive strategies (as in sustained union collaboration with worker centers in the United States). The relatively limited outcomes of ad hoc projects point to the need for a longer term industry-based strategy, not limited to the workplace, especially in sectors immersed in processes of economic restructuring. Still, industry-based approaches to union growth may well benefit from new strategies that go beyond a traditional focus on job-based membership as a precondition for active incorporation. Innovative forms of "contingent membership," independent of long-term standard employment, may better apply to contemporary conditions of labor mobility and precarious nature of employment. Thus the German strength is also a problem: well-developed processes for the integration of immigrant workers in regional and national union structures affected mainly permanent employees, especially relatively settled and already somewhat socially and culturally integrated immigrants.

Despite all national differences, the fact that across countries most recent immigrants work in the same low-paid, fragmented, and globalized sectors (cleaning, hospitality, care work, transport, construction, routine manufacturing such as food processing) has common implications for union strategies. As employers play off groups of workers against each other and government policies foster further divisions and fragmentation in the workforce, unions face multiple challenges in efforts to bring workers together in collective representation. A sense of unity can be fostered across different occupational identities, emphasizing the precarious nature of "immigrant jobs" across industries, in combination with the specific vulnerability of the migrant condition.

Low-wage work is characterized by measurable remuneration and its direct impact on workers' living standards; in addition, our findings highlight qualitative changes in employment relations. These include job security, length of contract, entitlement to benefits, and dependency on a particular employer or work contract for immigrants to obtain residency rights. Intersections between precarious work, immigrant labor, and racism make union strategies to integrate immigrant workers both difficult and important. One challenge for unions is to combine the fight for mobility rights with that for decent wages and work standards. The battle for equality can thus be understood at multiple levels, where campaigns for regularization go hand-in-hand with the unionization of immigrant workers. As the French *sans papiers* movement reminds us, if unions cannot bring rights to the most vulnerable, precarious work could eventually become the norm for all workers.

In Conclusion

Key findings of our comparative analysis include:

Traditional union strategies of restriction or neglect of immigrant workers are, in contemporary labor markets, no longer sustainable. The domestic face of globalization in the Global North takes shape in growing immigrant-based workforces, especially at the low end, and we see no indication that such processes are reversible. Many of the jobs that immigrants occupy are both weakly organized and not leaving the country, in industries such as building services, retail sales, customer service, hospitality, domestic care, transportation, and construction. To the extent that so many workers have so little in the way of rights or representation, the rights and standards of all workers are threatened—even in the most unionized industries.

Attitudes toward immigrant workers on the part of union confederations and many national and local unions in the United States, Germany, the United Kingdom, and France have changed significantly over the past two decades. Movement from restriction toward inclusion began as early as the 1970s and has accelerated in the 2000s, despite the 2008 economic crisis. Driving forces for change include union membership decline and the need for new members; recognition on the part of union leaders at both national and local levels that immigrant workforces are not going away and must be incorporated if labor movements are to regain lost influence; a recognition also that the precarious nature of the work done by many immigrant workers negatively affects the labor standard of every worker; and not least, the pressure from immigrant workers themselves for rights, representation, and inclusion, at the workplace and inside unions.

Increasingly, if haltingly, unions are recognizing the significance of the growth of precarious workforces, up to 25 percent or more of the total labor force in our four countries. Defining criteria for such workers include the absence of any kind of employment security as well as weak or nonexistent workplace rights and channels for representation. Labor market fragmentation and the growth of precarious workforces are key factors promoting growing inequality in the United States, Germany, and the United Kingdom—attenuated in France by minimum wage indexation. Precarious workforces are largely populated by foreign-born workers (and often their native-born children and grandchildren); bringing rights and representation to immigrant workers is thus a major challenge facing unions in efforts aimed at reducing inequality and stabilizing labor markets.

Unions face overlapping but distinct challenges in efforts to include immigrant workers in labor movements seeking revitalization. One such challenge is to integrate immigrant workers into existing organizational structures at workplaces where union representation is already well established. For this task, German unions such as IG Metall and IG BCE (Industrial Union of Mining, Chemicals and Energy) have led the way—with education and leadership training for immigrant workers in union strongholds. A more difficult challenge is to bring rights and representation to "greenfields," to sectors and firms where immigrant workers, and the precarious workforces in which they are situated, lack meaningful protections. Because the obstacles are great, successful campaigns typically require a social movement or mobilization approach, with tactics ranging from grassroots activism to coalition building and corporate campaigns—especially if they are to involve the recently arrived, more invisible and isolated immigrants. Here we have found "best practice" cases in the three of our case study countries, but not in Germany.

Factors accounting for expanded integration within strongholds include pressure from immigrant workers themselves (those lucky enough to find employment in such workplaces) as well as a strategic commitment on the part of key union leaders.

Factors underpinning campaign success where unions are weak or absent—in sectors such as hospitality, retail, customer service, domestic care, food processing—include a zonal/industrial scope rather than a focus on single firms; strategic targeting of key owners or employers to unravel subcontracting chains; the recognition and acceptance of ethnic identities, including a focus on the complex needs of immigrant workers as immigrants as well as members of the workforce; institutional change within unions to accompany strategic reorientation, for example with separate structures for the incorporation of ethnically or nationally distinct immigrant groups; a close linkage of such campaigns or structures to mainstream union channels; community and public support developed in active coalition building with immigrant advocacy and other social justice groups; and an appropriate, coordinated division of labor between unions and other campaign-supporting organizations.

Successful union campaigns to integrate immigrant workers depend on sustained—if very challenging—efforts to overcome workforce divisions: between native born and immigrant, different ethnic and racial groups, more and less settled immigrant workers, in more and less precarious circumstances. Our research shows that with social-justice framing and comprehensive campaigns, the mobilization of immigrant workers offers one path to labor movement revitalization.

THE COUNTERMOVEMENT
NEEDS A MOVEMENT
(AND A COUNTERSTRATEGY)

Janice Fine and Jane Holgate

Trade unions need organization for their power and movement for their vitality, but they need both power and vitality to advance their social purpose.

—Flanders 1972: 31

Fundamentally, we believe that the cases presented in this book attest to the powerful synergy that can occur when the labor movement and immigrant rights movements get together. For reasons we will explore further in a moment, our view is that the revitalization of the labor movement is intertwined with immigrant worker movement-building and vice versa.

We do not underestimate the profound historical, structural, and ideological differences between the American, British, French, and German states and their respective labor movements. However, we do perceive a set of immigrant worker organizing and migration policy challenges that are common to all of them. In this chapter we explore these mutual dilemmas drawing on examples from the case studies presented in this volume. We do this to offer our ideas about the strategic implications of these puzzles for unions and for immigrant worker organizations and then reflect on what the different organizing approaches teach us about the conditions under which partnerships between unions and immigrant worker organizations work best.

We begin from the proposition that one of the deepest commonalities between all four countries is the economic restructuring that has taken place since the end of the 1980s. The concomitant changes in employment relations that have followed has left unions of liberal market economies and coordinated market economies alike in a weaker position. Another commonality is that the recruitment of immigrant workers to fill positions more cheaply means that unions will not rebound unless they build alliances with immigrant worker organizations (and others campaigning around issues of social justice) and prioritize bringing immigrant workers and other groups into the labor movement *as active constituents*.

Yet migration has always presented difficult choices for unions both in traditional countries of immigration like the United States and France (and the United Kingdom with regard to citizens of Commonwealth countries) and in countries with less of a tradition like Germany. Although these labor movements have not historically focused on drawing immigrant workers into their organizations (and have on occasion vigorously opposed such integration), today the pendulum has swung more in favor of organizing this group of workers. There have been celebrated exceptions like the United Farm Workers and the Service Employees International Union but our point is that the organization and integration of immigrant workers is not widespread. As some unions have become more militant and willing to confront the economic restructuring that is a hallmark of neoliberalism, there is much greater interest and focus on organizing and recruiting immigrant workers as union participants.

The chapter draws on the comparative analysis provided in chapters 2 through 6 of this volume to think through the implications of the research for the future organizing and inclusion of immigrant workers in labor unions. This is done in the context of the increased movement of labor due to globalization and the neoliberal-inspired global economic crisis. The latter issue is of considerable concern as we see growing hostility to immigrant workers when indigenous workers feel threatened and in fear of losing their livelihoods (often encouraged by political parties and governments seeking to shift the blame for their failing economic policies). In addressing these issues we argue that national differences are still relevant and have a significant effect on the perceptions toward immigrants. We also argue that the similarities in terms of union organizing are much greater in and across nations and there are significant opportunities to create a countermovement involving immigrant workers.

Unbundling the Firm, "Un-governing" the Market

Despite national differences, as Frege and Kelly (2003) observed in their examination of unions in a comparable set of countries, all have been confronted with similar challenges including the internationalization of financial and product markets; decentralization of neocorporatist and industry-level collective bargaining; and changing structures of employment. Although the actual impact of globalization on national economies is often overstated (Hirst, Thompson, and Bromley 2009), advanced industrial economies *have* undergone a *fragmentation* of employment relations through strategies of subcontracting, third party management, franchising, temping, and independent contracting in major sectors including manufacturing, construction, retail, hospitality, food services, and health care (Bernhardt, Milkman, and Theodore 2009; Carré et al. 2000; Van Wezel Stone et al. 2009, Weil 2010, 2011; Zatz 2008). These strategies, some of which had long existed in the secondary labor market, have resulted in a more attenuated relationship between employees and firms and they have made effective industrial organization much harder to achieve. Labor costs (e.g., unemployment insurance, workers compensation, payroll taxes) and legal liabilities (workplace injuries or hiring of undocumented migrants) are shifted from large employers and on to smaller firms or labor brokers and temporary employment agencies. Often the employer of record is further down on the "industrial food chain" where profit margins are tighter and pressure to lower costs is very strong.

While we are all familiar with these arrangements in sectors like the garment industry for example, where workers were often hired by small contractors who assemble and sew clothing for manufacturers and retailers, more and more we see these same arrangements occurring in other sectors, for example in the warehouses of multi-national retailers where the employer of record is often a temporary employment agency—or the worker is paid as if she is self-employed. As Weil (2010: 20) describes it in the U.S. context: "From the post World War II period through the 1980s, the critical employment relationship was between large businesses and workers in major sectors of the economy. Increasingly, however the employment relationship has shifted away from those large employers who continue to play critical roles in shaping competition in the market-and towards a complex network of smaller employers. These lower level employers typically operate in more competitive markets than those of the firms that shifted employment to them." These dynamics that had long characterized the secondary labor market—where migrants were often employed—have now migrated *decisively* into the primary labor market, shortening the experiential distance between immigrant workers and the native and naturalized, including unionized workers. This fundamental shift in labor market structure requires unions to reconsider how they operate in the growing secondary labor markets as the global workforce becomes increasingly precarious.

State regulation of the employment relationship has not kept pace with the fissuring of the employment relationship resulting in weakened labor standards enforcement, antiquated collective bargaining regimes and outdated union rules and structures. When we speak of labor union decline as a secular trend across the United States, France, Germany, and the United Kingdom we do so understanding that decline looks different in each country due to divergent structures of industrial relations between them (see Hyman and Ferner [1994] for discussion from a European point of view). In the United States and the United Kingdom, the most important indicator of a weak labor movement is membership decline, while in France and Germany it is more about reduction of bargaining coverage or deterioration of structures of interest representation, such as workplace unionism or works councils (Frege and Kelly 2003). Common to all is a declining level of worker identification with the labor movement and with it, labor's capacity for large-scale collective action.

With private sector unionization rates in the single digits in the United States and in the low double digits in the United Kingdom, it is difficult to justify that unions must oppose migration in order to defend their labor standards. Yet the main focus for labor unions in the United States and Europe remains their core constituencies—the "already" members whose numbers have been shrinking since the 1980's. Although our case studies show innovation and progress, unions are still grappling with migration policy and immigrant worker organizing and how to bring those who have never been members into the fold. These issues are not new and debates in this area have been going on for over a century (see Avci and McDonald 2000; Fine and Tichenor 2009; Haus 1995; Wrench 2000). However, the conversations have become even more salient due to the considerable increase in migration across the globe over the past thirty years (Holgate 2011; Watts 2002; Wrench 2000) and the widespread economic crisis, which is having devastating effects on the society's poorest and most vulnerable members (Sakiko Fukuda-Parr 2008).

Unions and Migration: Balancing the Tensions

A clear observation from the case studies in all four countries is that immigrant workers both *need* and *want* to join unions. Alongside this, there is a greater openness toward immigrant workers from the various labor movements which, in some cases, translates into organizing. At the same time this convergence of views is taking place at a moment of crisis for labor. Low union densities, and the overwhelming task of servicing current members who are facing unprecedented attacks on terms and conditions as well as redundancies and layoffs, means that unions are struggling to survive and convince workers of their relevance. The dialectic is that at the very time labor unions are most wanted and needed they are also faced with extraordinary attacks and are naturally being pulled by their members to focus inward rather than outward. In these circumstances tensions around organization and integration of immigrant workers are to be expected—some of these are external to the labor movement and others are internal.

The external factors are a reflection of what is occurring in wider society. Nation states and political parties are highly influential in contributing to the way issues, like migration, are perceived by their citizens and members and it is often difficult to divorce views on migration from historical events such as that during the post–World War II period when unprecedented economic growth occurred on both sides of the Atlantic. Within less than a decade, the economies of Western Europe expanded so rapidly that many countries were experiencing labor shortages. As such, from roughly 1960 to 1973, a system of temporary immigrant labor evolved between some of the countries of northwest Europe, including France and Germany and some of those bordering the Mediterranean Sea as labor suppliers. According to Penninx and Roosblad (2000), the temporary nature of these programs made labor recruitment more acceptable for the unions because it would not undermine their bargaining power and also seemed consistent with the preferences of the migrants themselves, who in the first phase mostly did go to work temporarily and then return home. Within a few years however, it became clear that the majority of temporary workers had begun to settle permanently in the receiving countries and had become a structural part of the western European labor markets (Penninx and Roosblad 2000).

Between 1968 and 1973, national governments—largely with the support of the trade union movements—responded by developing mechanisms for tightening immigration legislation. In some instances they developed entry policies where workers had to apply for temporary residence permits prior to their arrival and employers were required to get employment permits and were limited in the total number for which they could apply. In the United Kingdom there were increasing restrictions on the entry of British citizens from overseas territories. In response to the 1972 oil crisis and recession that ensued, most national governments adopted restrictive policies that banned recruitment and stopped the issuance of temporary residence or work permits—policies that unions endorsed but did not initiate.

Beginning with the Treaty of Rome in 1957, European integration and enlargement has greatly altered the immigration terrain by guaranteeing the right of free movement of capital, goods, services, and labor between member states. EU law gives the right to any citizen to work in any member state but when enlargement occurs and new states become members, it also gives existing member states the right to adopt "transitional arrangements," which restrict the free movement of new members' workers for several years (Menz 2008). The 1997 Amsterdam Treaty formalized a commitment on the part of the European Union to create a common Asylum and Migration Policy but in practice the EU has had great difficulty getting its members to commit to a common set of policies. An integrated European migration policy has been limited by the ability of countries to opt-out of various programs (or phase them in over an extended period) and they mostly leave aside national policies toward non-EU labor migrants.

This free movement of labor and the opt-out arrangements have allowed some governments and political parties to exploit migration policy for their own ends and use it to play up to popular anti-immigrant sentiments. In Germany, one-third of all protests in the first half of the 1990s were related to the immigration issue, a proportion far higher than activity related to labor and unemployment issues, the environment, or war and peace (Koopmans et al. 2005). Economic crisis, high unemployment, and fear that one's own living standards are falling are often breeding grounds for negative views to immigrants and an increase in racism and discrimination—and the 2008 economic crisis is no different (Gauci 2011). One example, which typifies the way in which these sentiments are easily aroused, was in the construction industry in the United Kingdom. Here "posted workers have been targets of bitter resentment as was seen in the dispute at the Lindsey Oil refinery in the United Kingdom in 2009 (Summers 2009). In 1996, the EU adopted the Posted Workers Directive (PWD) as part of the provision of services framework of the European Community Treaty, which was intended to ensure that EU workers are covered by basic labor standards protections in the Union's member country in which they are performing work. The PWD requires that pay and working conditions in effect for a member state are applicable to both native laborers and those from other EU states who are posted to work there. However, this directive, meant to improve labor mobility in Europe, has already led to European Court of Justice cases, as it often undermines local labor standards and plays in favor of the company.[1]

As such, tensions arise because companies based in countries with lower pay rates still bring their workforces with them to perform jobs at wages cheaper than domestic labor (EIRO 2007).

In 2009 in Britain we saw how unionized workers responded to this issue. Picking up on Prime Minister Gordon's Brown phrase which was uttered in a different context, unionized construction workers at refineries, angry at plans by oil companies to employ Portuguese and Italian workers, demanded "British jobs for British workers" as they went on strike in protest. Although it is a basic trade union response to protect the terms and conditions of its workers, the wildcat strikes organized by these rank-and-file construction workers picked up on anti-immigrant sentiments about "foreigners taking our jobs," thus shifting the focus of the dispute from a class issue to a race issue.

As Solomos and Wrench (1993: 1) have observed: "In contemporary European societies the question of racism, linked to the politicization of migration, is a major issue in social and political debate. Developments in a number of European societies have highlighted the volatility of this phenomenon and the ease with which racist and extreme-right political movements can mobilize around the question of immigration and opposition to cultural pluralism." In

August 2012 in Greece—one of the most crisis ridden countries in Europe—the government began one of the country's biggest ever crackdowns on suspected illegal immigrants when they deployed 4,500 police in Athens, detaining more than 7,000 immigrants in less than seventy-two hours (Smith 2012). Most trade unions have strong policies on racism and discrimination, yet trade union members are not immune from such racist and xenophobic sentiments, which can lead to internal tensions around organizing immigrant workers. According to a report about German union members' views by Fichter (2008), far right attitudes are similar to the population as a whole, but there are considerable differences within the membership. In particular, unionized skilled workers and middle managers are significantly more inclined to exhibit extremist attitudes than non-unionists. In their analysis of the contentious politics of immigration in Europe, Koopmans et al. (2005: 4) argue that globalization has played a role in the rise of nationalist anti-immigrant mobilization: "In our age of economic globalization and worldwide pressures toward cultural blending and homogenization . . . many people experience a loss of identity and control over their destinies. . . . At the same time, there so far is nothing beyond the nation state that can serve as a new anchor for collective identities and can renew the sense of control. Our age of globalization is therefore also a time of nationalism."

In the case studies presented in this volume, we have highlighted some of the best practice in and policies toward union/community organizing of immigrant workers. We also found points of internal tensions within some union bodies as they try to manage the different demands of their membership. These differ considerably between the countries and are, once again, derived from differing (state) ideological approaches to nonindigenous citizens. In the European cases, union bodies have tended not to fight or campaign publically for the regularization of undocumented immigrant workers, perhaps because of concerns about seeming to support illegality, but also with the knowledge that such a stance may not be popular with the membership. Historically, such was the case in France, but in 2008 this changed and there has been considerable union support for the *sans papiers* movement. Even so, tensions emerged in the CGT when other groups of workers (unemployed and isolated) were not included in the campaigns—highlighting the problem of a specific focus and resource allocation toward organizing immigrant workers. Similarly, despite UK unions having a tradition of self-organizing among minority groups, protests arose when the GMB union established a temporary sub-branch for Polish immigrant workers in the south of England. Union members complained that this was divisive and that immigrant workers should be placed in standard GMB structures.

In Germany, the construction unions have taken a tough line with regard to illegal working as they argue this has a significant impact on their members. They have adopted supportive measures for immigrant workers, such as removal of the requirement to hold a master or journeyman certificate to be self-employed. At the same time, the IG BAU (Industrial Union of Construction and Agriculture) has been co-operating with the state, customs, and the construction industry to inform on cases of illegal employment, leaving the union open to criticism from sections of the media and left-leaning political parties. Conversely, as has been demonstrated by the case studies, there are also the beginnings of positive examples of individual German union practices (even if they are as yet small scale). For example, the IG Metal Kiel Administrative Office requires that union delegations at the district and works council levels correspond to the proportion of immigrant employees and ver.di leaders in Hamburg became involved in a campaign to defend the right of an undocumented au pair to collect her back wages and to be allowed to stay in the country. In taking on this case and allying with immigrant worker and feminist organizations, ver.di also helped to challenge the immigration laws that have often resulted in workers who complain about poor treatment being deported. Although it is difficult to extrapolate a trend from these examples, they do show that some unions are at least starting to think about wider engagement with immigrant workers and other social movement actors.

In the United States, at the top of the movement, the national AFL-CIO has strongly supported amnesty for the undocumented immigrants since 2000 and several national unions have aggressively targeted them for organizing, but at the local and regional union levels, leadership attitudes toward undocumented immigrants vary. In 2006, the Laborers International Union of North America (LIUNA) launched an organizing campaign in the residential construction industry in the Southwest. Through their research they learned that 95 percent of the workforce—and not just those workers who were employed by small subcontractors, was made up of undocumented Latino immigrants. Some in leadership felt the union's focus on Latino immigrants was also likely to be resisted by some local union leaders. The national union decided to avoid the culture clash by running the campaign entirely outside of the traditional structure. None of the LIUNA locals, regions, or district councils in the targeted markets participated in the campaign and the national union planned to set up new union locals to accommodate the residential members. Members of the national organizing team leased their own office space and had no interaction with the local union infrastructure. Organizers on the ground were instructed not to go to the locals for help and in the few instances when they did, they did not receive it (Fine 2011a). As one union staffer described the situation in LIUNA, "Terry [the national union president, Terry O'Sullivan] has always had to play a careful role because geographically around the country we have very different views. We have places where our laborers can't organize the construction site, don't speak the language of the workers, the contractor is non-union and has threatened the workers not to talk to the union and our folks have no recourse but to end up calling ICE (the federal immigration authorities). . . . We have other places where the majority are immigrants or second generation and very active in immigration reform politics" (Fine 2011a: 23).

Organizing Challenges

One of the most fundamental challenges faced by the labor movement is trying to organize in the macroeconomic climate in the contemporary context of neoliberalism. The current economic crisis is hitting workers in a way that has not been seen since the depression of the 1930s and the scale of attacks on workers' pay and their terms and conditions are unprecedented in modern times. Despite this, we do not discount the agency of workers in countering these assaults. As Hyman (2007; 198) has pointed out: "whether, and how, unions respond to external and internal challenges is also conditioned by what may be termed organisational capacity. This can be understood as the ability to assess opportunities for intervention; to anticipate, rather than merely react to, changing circumstances; to frame coherent policies; and to implement these effectively." Unions do have the potential to create a countermovement to challenge the arbitrary power of employers, but paradoxically, the more that institutional channels of worker representation are destroyed and employers resist power sharing, the more likely it is, at times of crisis that alternative means of expression are found.

The Arab Spring of 2012 is one example of how people were prepared to fight back despite the seemingly all-powerful repressiveness of globalization, capital, and authoritarian governments (Manhire 2012). Other examples include the mobilization of workers and communities of the state of Wisconsin in 2011, when the governor decided to withdraw collective bargaining rights from state employees (Borsos 2012) and the Occupy movement (Hardt and Negri 2011). But what is missing, and which poses a considerable challenge for labor, is the development and adaptation of clear models of organizing that reach beyond traditional union constituencies. As our case studies show, there is potential, but the campaigns and approaches we studied are small scale and there is a need both to upscale and to develop organizing models able to be rolled out at regional and national levels. As of 2013, this coordinated approach is lacking.

We have already mentioned the way in which many immigrant workers are to be found in sectors that are difficult to organize—often nonunion, low paid, multiemployer, transient, and geographically dispersed. Contrast this with a large established single employer workplace, and you can see the cost benefit analysis from a union organizer perspective. Yet our case studies demonstrate that these hard to organize sectors can be organized, but this requires unions to rethink their organizing models and practices as well as the way in which campaigns are framed.

Most American labor market, social insurance, employment and labor laws are premised on assumptions about structures of employment that have drastically changed. These laws assume long-term, stable employment at employers who built the provision of equitable wages, employee benefits, and on-the-job training into the cost of doing business. The Wagner Act (National Labor Relations Act [NLRA]) of 1935 was constructed with these assumptions in mind, and American unions became coterminous with the model of full-time employees at large firms, secret ballot elections, and the exclusive representation it set forth. The 1947 Taft-Hartley Act barred secondary boycotts, which has made it more difficult to address the challenge of organizing supply chains in which subcontractors, although the nominal employer, are not where the real power lies. Existing labor law also bans independent contractors from unionizing. In the context of "unstable" firms and "unstable" workers, most unions have not yet refined other strategies and forms of representation that broadly apply in today's private sector. They need the kind of union membership that helps them fill in the benefits and training that is not available to them at their place of work and it needs to be flexible and fully portable between employers. For example, the greatest membership growth at SEIU in recent years has resulted from the organization of home health-care workers who work for private agencies or individuals but are paid by the government for their services. Some of its largest victories in recent years (70,000 homecare workers in California, 40,000 childcare workers in Illinois) have come about through organizing this enormously diffuse workforce in campaigns that have necessitated organizing not only the workers, but in effect organizing employers so that there would be an employer-side entity that could be bargained with.

In addition to new models, over time, labor appears to have lost its ability to project itself as standing for the whole—speaking on behalf of all workers—not just union members as it once was perceived to be doing. In the United States, in particular, there has been a concerted and increasingly successful political effort to target public sector unions and to portray them as self-serving and only concerned with protecting their members' interests. The dominant narrative about teachers' unions in the media and popular culture for example is that they are the major barrier to education reform and improvement of inner-city school systems. Even in Wisconsin, after so much collective action, the labor movement's effort to recall the governor was decisively defeated when it was brought to a popular vote.

In Germany where union membership is still higher and trade unionism is based on a social partnership model, unions are, despite a fracturing of this model over the past generation, still very much wedded to an institutional form of industrial relations (Greer 2008). This institutional embeddedness meant that, barring a few exceptions unions have not developed the social movement approach adopted by some unions in other parts of the world and are therefore more inward than outward looking. It is also evident that German unions are somewhat behind the unions in other parts of the world in their approaches to organizing immigrant workers outside of collective bargaining structures and works councils.

The challenge is then to think how workers' issues can be reframed to reflect their lived experiences as workers and as citizens, recognizing how these two parts of people's lives are so very much interlinked, and particularly so for immigrant workers. By analyzing our cases studies we find that although workplaces issues are still of primary concern to labor unions, a framing of issues in terms of social justice had much greater appeal as most immigrant workers' concerns stretched way beyond that of pay and conditions. For example, the Los Angeles carwash campaign successfully incorporated social and political rights into their organizing strategy, but this was done through a strong community-labor alliance involving over 100 different organizations. Some unions have gotten much better at building these community relationships, but it is still a major challenge for unions to build and sustain reciprocal relationships.

In contrast to "solidarity coalitions" in which community groups are mobilized tactically to provide support for union organizing efforts, or where unions are mobilized to give contributions of money or labor to community efforts, community unionism implies relationships that are more based upon mutual self-interest and accountability. Community organizations and unions work together to improve conditions in the labor market through joint economic and political action. These organizations are explicit partnerships between a community organization and a union. But just as lobsters have one claw that is larger than the other, these partnerships often seem to have a dominant claw as well (Fine 2005). Unions, with their higher level of resources and greater degree of institutionalization and power, often become that dominant claw.

An internal tension for unions surfaces while working in coalition with non-union bodies who might have different approaches to organizing. This was particularly the case in the United Kingdom where unions and Telco/London Citizens failed to understand each other's culture and tactics resulting in a breaking down of the relationship (Holgate 2009c). This was also the case with the very promising partnership between New Labor, a worker center in New Jersey affiliated with the National Day Laborer Organizing Network (NDLON) and LIUNA.

From an organizational structure and cultural perspective, there was strong dissonance that undermined the partnership. Hoping for active participation on the part of New Labor members in the decision-making process, the worker center felt the union process was too top-down with the important decisions having to be made by the regional vice president. In terms of the deliberative process, the laborers very structured agendas for each union board meeting and formal procedures seemed to stifle the participation of worker center representatives (Fine 2011a).

The difficulty lies in union adaptation to different ways of working. For example, the community and nongovernmental (NGO) sectors are often much quicker to react, having much more nimble and less restrictive structures that are unhindered by bureaucracy. This can cause difficulties for unions who feel bound to put all decisions through hierarchical committees, which restricts their ability to respond quickly to events. But also, as the larger and more powerful, and better-resourced civil society organizations, labor unions have a tendency to dominate coalitions making it difficult for other voices to be heard. Although often not intentional, unions can inflict a cultural hegemony or particular modus operandi rather than recognizing that they are just one of many actors in the coalition and that skills, knowledge, and experiences of other actors may be equally valid. This form of collaborative working is challenging and can be difficult but the sum of the parts has the ability to build greater power to effect change, as was shown in the case studies of the French unions and the *sans papiers* movement and the carwash campaign in L.A.

What Works Well? The Strategic Implications of Our Findings

The findings from our research lead us to believe that there are a whole range of strategic implications for both unions and other organizations concerned with the organization of immigrant workers—and more widely, the growth and revitalization of the labor movement. There will always be a need to be sensitive to social, economic, and cultural differences in differing localities and communities. But we argue that there are numerous issues to be considered, which are applicable in most organizing situations. The following is what we have observed in the country cases that seem to contribute to union willingness to engage with immigrant workers and immigration issues:

The way in which unions frame their issues is of real importance. This matters, because the way unions are perceived, affects whether people join and become active, or not. In the recent past, unions have primarily marketed themselves as "your friend at work," there to help negotiate your wages, terms, and conditions and to support you if you have a problem with your employer. Yet union power to collectively bargain has been drastically curtailed as union membership has declined and employers have gained the whip hand in the employment relationship. Many workers recognize this weakness and factor this in when deciding to unionize.

Our questions are thus: Is a social movement form of unionism becoming more attractive to workers as they recognize that the issues facing them are much greater that what happens in their individual workplace? Is there a strange paradox emerging whereby workers recognize their weakness in the workplace but at the same time recognize they have a strength in a wider collectivity? Do workers feel less able to win on the bread and butter issues, but see the big picture and feel the necessity to scale up their activity to act alongside others in society? Is it that the issues in the workplace and outside of the workplace are so interlinked that workers feel that it is not possible to deal with them as discrete and separate issues (work-related issues, personal/society issues)? Perhaps these questions are too big to answer fully here, but we can nevertheless draw on the case studies to gain an understanding of the issues of concern to workers involved in the campaigns and the way in which these were framed.

The messages in the Justice for Cleaners campaign in the United Kingdom, the *sans papiers* movement in France and the CLEAN carwash campaign in the United States, each used the language of social justice to construct a narrative around which to organize. According to Dechaufour 2010: 2): "the demands of this movement [*sans papiers*] are based on a human rights speech, and it is first and above all as citizens that they ask for their regularization . . . the leaders of the movement identify themselves as citizens of the world more than employees." During the Justice for Cleaners campaign, unions—working with the London Citizens community coalition—tapped into social justice concerns about paying workers less than a living wage by framing the issue in terms of a moral right. "This ability to make use of social networks and link them together for a general concern for the 'common good' provides a simple narrative that taps into messages of morality (in the case of faith communities) or social justice (in the case of non faith communities)" (Holgate forthcoming)

Institutional self-interest. In the cases of UNITE in the United Kingdom and LIUNA, the United Steelworkers (USW), and the Retail, Wholesale, and Department Store Union in the United States, the unions have developed an interest in organizing immigrant workers out of a realization that it cannot organize or reorganize the sector unless it organizes immigrant workers. There is a willingness to admit weakness—and to acknowledge that membership is in crisis in general or in the sector in which the union has traditionally been strong and a sense that existing models are not working. There is also a rejection of the idea that the best way to protect the sector for unions is to keep immigrant workers out.

Beyond self-interest. empathy and leadership: In most of the case narratives, a union leader has expressed some form of personal identification with immigrant workers, recognized in the collective action these workers have taken the roots of their own unions, and played an important role in persuading her organization and mobilizing its resources on their behalf. Sometimes the process begins locally with a concrete action by one local or region that percolates up, but just as often it begins at the national level and diffuses down. But this leadership support and endorsement of campaigns is highly significant.

Direct contact between union leaders, members, and immigrant workers. When union leaders and members move beyond an abstract consideration of the issues or observing immigrant workers from a distance, and come into direct relationship with them, the experience is transformative for all parties. Hearing workers' stories directly, getting to know them as human beings, and taking collective action together is the yeast from which solidarity rises. This was evident in a number of our case studies such as IG Metal leaders making a policy decision to instigate procedures to integrate immigrant workers by ensuring they had opportunities to get elected and play a greater role in the union and also in France where CGT leaders played a central role in the decision of the unions to actively take part in the *sans papiers* movement. However, merely advocating for immigrant workers without bringing them into relationship with union members does not lead to the same opportunity.

Openness to experimentation, willingness to risk failure. Also common to almost every case study we found unions that were willing to initiate action even if they were not certain of the outcome and willing to try out different strategies—and to fail. Most organizers who are honest will say that they have learned much more from their failures than their successes. During a period in which few private sector unions are succeeding, some unions are willing to accept that immigrant worker organizing efforts will require patience, long lead in times and tweaking of campaigns before they bear fruit.

Interest in organizing drives support for policy and administrative changes. In the United States and the United Kingdom, as some unions became more involved in efforts to organize immigrant workers they—along with their federations, AFL-CIO and TUC—became more actively engaged on the policy front in support of legalization efforts. These policy statements and national level campaigns contribute to changing culture among workers as people become more educated about the issues. Taking part in, or control of, public debate helps to shifts the emphasis from media and political attacks on immigrant workers to defending their human rights.

Campaigning for policy changes is where most successful collaboration with community organizations and greatest victories have come. Partnerships between worker centers and unions have not yet resulted in many worker center participants becoming union members but they have had successes working together in political partnership around federal immigration reform, administrative action, and opposition to anti-immigrant legislation at the federal, state, and local levels. Similarly, the campaign for a living wage in the United Kingdom by Telco/London Citizens has shifted the debate about the minimum wage even though it has not resulted in significant union membership increases.

Partnership with a community organization that is powerful in its own right leads to more equal partnerships. The stronger the worker center, immigrant rights, or community organization, the more equal the coalition effort will be. When the coalition effort is more equal, both partners are more likely to remain involved and to maximize and leverage their resources. We can see this in the carwash campaign in Los Angeles where the worker centers were well established and the United Steelworkers accepted their strategic judgments, as well as with the current joint home-care campaign between the National Domestic Workers Alliance (NDWA) and several national unions in which NDWA has brought new attention to caregiver issues and created coalitions in thirty-one states. For worker centers and other NGOs this means that it is important for them to be clear about the value they bring to the partnership and not to lose their independent identities, to keep building their own capacities and to communicate honestly with their union partners about what is going well and what is not. Furthermore, as Amanda Tattersall (2010) noted on her work on labor/community coalitions, positive sum coalitions of union and community organization provide greater sources of power for unions. This needs to be "power with" rather than "power over" any community partners. As Tattersall (2010: 161) concludes: "in contrast with the way community organization provide support for union goals, positive-sum coalitions enable unions and community organizations to jointly craft issues and campaigns that work to build each other while also meeting each other's direct interests. We have seen that when coalitions operate in a way that generates reciprocity of decision-making and a mutuality of interest, organizations are much more likely to share power, resources, and skills for the long haul."

Offering educational opportunities and legal advice to immigrant workers. Several of the cases involved unions helping immigrant workers file legal cases particularly with regard to wage theft in the United States, Germany, and the United Kingdom, and supporting their immigration cases in France. In the United Kingdom, the use of education and training provided through the government-funded UnionLearn (via the TUC) was instrumental in providing opportunities to reach out to immigrant workers by providing English-language training through union learning centers. Community-based initiatives around union learning helped to show that unions were more than providing help for workplace problems—they could help workers find jobs and improve their prospects for promotion to higher skilled jobs. These concrete services helped unions build relationships with immigrant workers although given concerns over maintaining funding and resources there were issues of the extent to which these projects were sustainable and we saw this in the United Kingdom, France, and Germany case studies. There has also been a long "servicing versus organizing" debate in the United States labor movement, but in worker centers there is less black and white thinking about it. Providing concrete services has often been seen as a critical pathway to recruitment and organizing rather than a distraction and there is more foundation funding available for this type of activity in the United States than in many parts of Europe.

Uniting against a common enemy. In the United Kingdom, labor's changing relationship with its own workers of color and its subsequent embrace of more liberal policy was also a strategic shift brought about by alterations in its relationship to the state as well as the labor market. Thatcherism devastated British trade unions by its end effectively cutting membership in half and it was followed by the rise of the New Labour government that worked to reduce the influence of unions on the party and whose embrace of a neoliberal economic strategy for the country further weakened unions. A deteriorating relationship with the state, which was marked by the collapse of traditional bargaining institutions and the loss of influence under Conservative and Labour governments, combined with radical labor market changes. With the decline of traditional industries and the rise of the service sector, organizing became an imperative and organizing immigrants and workers of color came to be increasingly viewed as the future of the labor movement. In the United Kingdom and France unions and immigrant worker organizations also became allied in the struggle against the rise of right-wing parties—British National Party and Le Pen's Front National. For example, Unison, the public service union, launched an education project to ensure Polish workers registered to vote and were able to take part in EU elections for Members of the European Parliament. As these elections are by proportional representation, a low turnout can often favor marginal candidates such as the far right British National Party. These political campaigns around voter registration help to demonstrate that unions are more than about mere workplace representation—their concerns reach out into the community and are concerned with the lives of immigrant workers outside of the workplace. Challenging racism and xenophobia was central to this.

During the 2000s, the emergence of the Front National led the CGT and other French union confederations to speak out forcefully in support of immigrants' rights. The CGT has strongly opposed the Front National, putting forth the argument that the party's anti-immigrant agenda was part of a larger program that would undermine solidarity and increase inequality. "The National Front continues to add new categories of enemies," a CGT statement argued in July 2004. "Immigrants and everything that comes from the outside are considered a threat to France's identity. It is normal for labor to counter these ideas with great vigor."

More attention is needed to the scalar dimension of union organizing. Labor geographers have been at the forefront of thinking through and imagining the way in which unions need to consider the appropriate scalar strategies when mounting campaigns (Anderson, Hamilton, and Wills 1998, 2010; Herod 2001; Rainnie, Herod, and McGrath Champ 2007). But beyond the campaigns themselves unions perhaps need to give greater thought on how their internal structures affect the way in which groups of workers currently outside of unions—and in our case this applies to immigrant workers—are able to involve themselves in union activity. How do they become an integral part of union practice and democracy? To what extent do the different scales of union activity (local, national, international) talk to each other and interact when formulating policy and practice around the organization and inclusion of immigrant workers and what impact does this have on the sustainability of campaigns. In what ways do union structures impede or add to the social, spatial, and cultural isolation of immigrants? Our research finds that a greater understanding of the lived experiences of immigrant workers and the additional complications for life as an immigrant worker requires unions to look internally at the way they operate but also to look externally to figure out how different spaces may be utilized. By this we mean that internally the culture of unions can be perceived as alienating to outsiders, while externally—as our case studies show—community space was a much more comfortable and welcoming environment in which to organize. In addition, there was overall a disconnect between what was happening at the local scale—and most of our case studies were, indeed, at a very local scales—and the national or internal union scale. Most unions had good policies on racism, xenophobia, and immigrant employment but this was somehow abstract from the activity at local level. Where there was connect at these different scales campaign activity was either more successful or had greater sustainability.

Another observation from our case studies shows a disconnect between what is happening at the national/federation, regional/state, and locals levels of unions in approaches to organizing immigrant workers. The LIUNA case provides an interesting example of a national union, making a deliberate decision to launch a national campaign to organize the residential construction industry that has high concentrations of undocumented workers, and at the same time making a decision not to involve LIUNA locals. This was done in order to avoid conflict with local union leaders, which may have made sense politically for the national union but not in terms of building relationships at the local level—which is the most essential locus for changing attitudes and altering union practices. What these examples show is that unions are often confronted with difficult strategic decisions about their scalar strategies to overcome potential problems if they are to move the union forward on dealing with organizing among marginalized groups—particularly those of immigrant workers.

The example also raises another development—the extent to which immigrant worker organizations are upscaling their activity by beginning to federate—moving from the local to the national. Fine (2011b: 615) reports that there has been a growing trend among worker centers toward federation, "in which strong individual centres have joined existing national networks or formed new ones which have, in turn, helped to establish new organizations or affiliate new ones." This upscaling activity has considerable benefits for both policy and practice. For example, since 2007, the Restaurant Opportunities Center New York (ROC-NY), Domestic Workers United and the NY Taxi Workers Alliance, like NDLON before them, have all begun to create national structures and develop guidelines for the establishment of new organizations or to affiliate existing organizations and to coordinate activity at the local, state, and national levels. However, while this is a huge step forward we still find a disconnect or a gap between the national level work of some unions and the day-to-day practice of union locals, where we did not find many instances of union locals organizing and integrating immigrant workers into their own structures or local campaigns.

Although unions have a great deal of expertise in labor and employment laws, many have not yet developed the skills or knowledge of immigration law to be able to address issues of illegality and protection of undocumented members. As a result, they sometimes assume they cannot organize undocumented workers, cannot help them if they are fired by employers during a union drive, or cannot help them if their employers are notified that they may be undocumented. Given that there are so many undocumented workers employed in the United States and the EU, it would contradict the goal of raising labor standards for all in low-wage sectors to take the position that undocumented workers cannot join unions. This is an area of law that is complex and still evolving but national federations and some national unions are gaining expertise. In general, those unions most actively involved in organizing immigrant workers take the position that if workers have been hired by employers then they can and should be organized and it is not the business of the union to verify immigration status. If, as is often the case, employers attempt to derail a union drive by asking workers to show proof of their authorization to work in the United States, unions can file an unfair labor practice with the National Labor Relations Board or appeal to the Social Security Administration (SSA) to suspend this reverification proce-dure. In the United States, E-verify is the federal government's largely voluntary (but not for those receiving federal funds) Internet-based system that allows an employer to determine the eligibility of employees to work in the United States. If a "no-match" is found between the social security number given by a worker and the number on record at the SSA, the employee receives notification from the federal government as does the employer. Since a successful lawsuit was brought by the AFL-CIO in 2006, there is no requirement that employers, upon receipt of these letters require verification documentation from their employees or terminate their employment. E-verify has been opposed by immigrant, civil rights, and civil liberties organizations as well as the AFL-CIO both on privacy grounds as well as because of its high rate of false negatives. Those unions that are actively organizing the low wage immigrant workforce take the position that as long as workers are providing numbers, it is not the union's business to police their authenticity—especially in light of the fact that current immigration poli-cies have made it too difficult for workers to gain legal authorization to work in the United States.

Concluding Remarks

In all four countries of our study—despite their many structural, cultural, and political differences—there is a clear shift at the national union and national federation levels toward supporting more liberalized admission policies, stronger civil and employment rights for immigrant workers, regularization opportuni-ties for the undocumented, speaking out forcefully against the xenophobic plat-forms of far right parties, and greater openness on the part of national unions and federations to organizing immigrant workers. For their parts, immigrant workers have demonstrated an interest in trade unionism and an appreciation for what an alliance with unions can do for them. However, while national union policies have swung strongly in favor of defending, organizing, and represent-ing immigrant workers, they have done so during an extremely dark period for unionism.

Private sector labor organizations have not been able to keep pace with the creative destruction and disorganization that has been wrought by twenty-first-century global capitalism and its impact on employment relations. Membership and density figures and industrial power in all countries have been declining. Unions may never have been more "proimmigrant" than they are now but they may never have been less capable of transforming those proimmigrant sentiments into better wages and working conditions and union contracts for immigrant workers. The very forces that have inclined unions more favorably toward immigrant workers have also largely stayed their hands. Nevertheless, the fact that unions and immigrant workers are now fighting on the same side of the barricade is an enormously positive step and would seem to be a prerequisite for building power sufficient to regovern the market.

To conclude; writing in the early 1970s, Allan Flanders, a well-respected British industrial relations academic, was predicting the decline in power and influence of trade unions. His reasoning, beyond that of the changing labor market and economic and political environments, was that union decline "had its counterpart in an absence of movement." He asked, "where were the new objectives directed toward a further fulfillment of the unions' social purpose, which could alone have generated a genuine movement to capture interest and arouse enthusiasm?" (Flanders 1972; 32). Perhaps, given the global economic crisis and the way in which austerity is impacting all but the most well-off in society, it is now time for unions to return to their social movement origins.

INTEGRATIVE ORGANIZING IN POLARIZED TIMES

Toward Dynamic Trade Unionism
in the Global North

Daniel B. Cornfield

Mobilizing against Inequality provides a new roadmap for labor in the Global North to pursue its historic mission of realizing an inclusive and democratic society. The roadmap is based on this edited collection's inventory and analysis of the many innovative, contemporary cases of labor organizing in France, Germany, the United Kingdom, and the United States. The roadmap is a timely contribution to an enduring theme in a diversified and polarized world region. In the Global North, rising inequality has accompanied neoliberal deregulation and austerity policies, the transition to a service economy, and union decline. Persisting and emerging forms of social exclusion have accompanied increasing immigration, and heightening social tensions periodically erupt into urban riots. In this context of rising inequality, unions have arisen to organize a growing precariat of ethnic and racial minorities, youth, and immigrants.

This concluding chapter provides a synthesis of the cases of immigrant labor organizing presented in this book and highlights the temporal patterns—the historical and macroeconomic timing—of the cases. From the synthesis I also derive a dynamic model of trade unionism for addressing social inequality in the Global North.

Immigration, Restructuring, and Social Inequality

Immigrant labor organizing in the Global North addresses increasing and persistent social inequality that accompanies neoliberal deregulation, union decline, and seismic restructuring of national economies. Since the 1970s, the national economies of France, Germany, the United Kingdom, and the United States have restructured and shifted toward service provision (Brady 2009: 145–164). By the early twenty-first century, a majority of these national labor forces have become employed in services (see table 9.1). In 2010, approximately 70 percent to over 80 percent of the national labor forces of the four countries discussed here were employed in what the International Labour Organization refers to as "services." By contrast, no more than 28 percent of these national labor forces were employed in "industry" in 2010.[1] Economic restructuring has proceeded the farthest in the United Kingdom and the United States among the four nations. By 2010, the percentage employed in services in these two countries exceeded that of France and Germany[2] by approximately 5–11 percent (see table 9.1).

Labor union memberships have declined as economic restructuring eroded traditional union membership bases in manufacturing (Brady 2009; Cornfield and McCammon 2003; Frege and Kelly 2004; Turner and Cornfield 2007). As shown in table 9.2, union density—the percentage of all wage and salary earners who belong to labor unions—declined in all four nations between 1970 and 2010.

Income inequality has persisted or increased with economic restructuring and union decline in Europe and the United States (Gangl 2005; see also the

TABLE 9.1 Percentage of employment in industry and services, 1980–2010

	Percentage in industry				Percentage in services			
	1980	1990	2000	2010	1980	1990	2000	2010
France	35.5	29.6	26.3	22.2	56.2	64.8	69.6	74.5
Germany	n.a.	40.3[1]	33.5	28.4	n.a.	55.5[1]	63.8	70.0
United Kingdom	37.2	32.3	25.1	19.1	58.9	64.9	73.1	78.9
United States	30.8	26.4	23.2	16.7	65.7	70.7	74.3	81.2

[1] Data are for 1991.

Source: International Labour Organization, *Key Indicators of the Labor Market*, 2012, http://kilm.ilo.org/kilmnet/.

TABLE 9.2 Union density, 1970–2010

	1970	1980	1990	2000	2010
France	21.7	18.3	9.9	8.0	7.6[1]
Germany	32.0	34.9	31.2	24.6	18.6
United Kingdom	44.8	50.7	39.3	30.5	27.5[2]
United States	27.4	22.3	15.5	12.8	11.4

[1] 2008.
[2] 2009.

Source: ICTWSS: Database on Institutional Characteristics of Trade Unions, Wage Setting, State Intervention and Social Pacts, 1960–2010, May 2011, http://www.uva-aias.net/207.

November 2012 special issue of *Work and Occupations* on "Precarious Work in Polarizing Times"). In several European nations and the United States, economic restructuring has led to expansions of both high-skill and low-skill jobs or "job polarization." Crossnational comparative research on change in skill hierarchies in the 1995–2007 period indicate that job polarization has accompanied economic restructuring in the four countries (Fernandez-Macías 2012; Kalleberg 2011). Fernandez-Macías (2012) attributes job polarization mainly to expansions of employment in precarious, low-wage, nonstandard jobs and to modest increases in high-wage jobs.

Union decline undermines national income redistributive efforts. Brady's (2009: 94–120) study of crossnational variations in poverty rates among multiple European nations, Australia, and the United States between 1969 and 2002 shows that poverty rates are highest when weakened labor movements lack the political strength to pursue expansions of national welfare states.

Persistent or increasing income inequality has accompanied economic restructuring and union decline in all four countries. The Gini coefficient, a leading indicator of income inequality, ranges from 0 (equality) to 1.000 (inequality). The Gini coefficients of Germany, the United Kingdom, and the United States increased between 1979 and the mid-to-late 2000s, indicating increasing income inequality within these nations during this period. The Gini coefficient for France was relatively stable and remained the lowest of those of the other nations (see table 9.3).

Immigrants increasingly arrive in a polarizing Global North. Between 1995 and 2009, the percentage of foreign-born population of the four nations grew and converged around 12 percent (see table 9.4).

As they enter the polarized service economies of the Global North, immigrants are often employed in marginal informal sectors. Many are employed in precarious, low-wage, nonstandard jobs in services, construction, and agriculture (Andriessen et al. 2012; Cornfield 2006; Donato et al. 2008; Lehmer and Ludsteck 2011; Portes and Rumbaut 2006). Furthermore, increasing immigration is not

TABLE 9.3   Gini coefficients, 1979–2010

	1979	1989	2000	2007	2010
France	.293	.287	.278	.280[1]	n.a.
Germany	.263[2]	.258	.266	.290	n.a.
United Kingdom	.267	.336[3]	.346[4]	.344[5]	n.a.
United States	.299	.335[3]	.367	.378	.373

[1] 2005. [2] 1978. [3] 1991. [4] 1999. [5] 2004.

Source: Luxembourg Income Study Database, http://www.lisdatacenter.org/lis-ikf-webapp/app/search-ikf-figures.

TABLE 9.4 Percentage of foreign-born population, 1995–2009

	1995	2000	2005	2009
France	n.a.	10.1	11.0	11.6
Germany	11.5	12.5	12.6	12.9
United Kingdom	6.9	7.9	9.4	11.3
United States	9.9	11.0	13.0	12.7

Source: OECD Factbook, 2011–2012: Economic, Environmental and Social Statistics, http://www.oecd-ilibrary.org/
sites/factbook-2011-en/02/02/01/index.html?contentType=/ns/Chapter,/ns/StatisticalPublication&itemId=/
content/chapter/factbook-2011-13-en&containerItemId=/content/serial/18147364&accessItemIds=&mime
Type=text/html.

associated with declining unionization and increasing poverty in Europe and the United States. Brady (2007; 2009: 173–177) found no associations between levels of immigration and unionization, and between levels of immigration and poverty rates, among eighteen Western nations over the 1969–2002 period. This suggests that patterns of immigrant occupational segregation in the precarious, low-wage economic sector result from discrimination, human capital deficits, self-selection into ethnic enclave subeconomies, and insufficient union protection in these sectors (Kanas, van Tubergen, and van der Lippe 2009; Kanas et al. 2012; Lehmer and Ludsteck 2011; Pichler 2011; Portes and Rumbaut 2006; Ram, Edwards, and Jones 2007; Rustenbach 2010).

The rise of an economically marginalized immigrant workforce compels the revitalizing European and U.S. labor movements to organize immigrant workers. In this time of heightened social inequality, labor movements are playing a vital role in helping immigrants to become fully incorporated—economically, politically, and socially. Unions, however, have kept their distance from the antiprecarity movement of youth, freelance knowledge workers, and low-wage service workers that has emerged in both Europe and the United States, reflected in the Occupy movements, especially in the United States and the United Kingdom (Lee and Kofman 2012). If immigrant labor organizing is a strategic act of labor revitalization that is inspired and compelled by economic restructuring and heightened social inequality, this expression of labor solidarity is facilitated by shifts in macroeconomic conditions.

Labor Mobilization and Unrest during Booms and Busts

Contemporary immigrant labor organization is the latest epoch in the post–World War II effort to organize the growing public and private service sectors in Europe and the United States. During the 1960s, European labor movements especially aligned themselves with the peace, civil rights, and women's movements to organize white-collar workers, professionals such as teachers, and low-wage service workers (Turner 2003). A tragic marker of the era, Martin Luther King's assassination in 1968 occurred during a union rally of African American sanitation workers who were striking for union recognition from the city of Memphis, Tennessee.

Today's immigrant labor organizing in Europe and the United States confronts, like the earlier era of service-sector labor organizing, challenges from employers, as well as labor-solidarity challenges. In the 1960s and 1970s, managerial challenges for service-sector unionization took the form of the privatization of public services, office automation, and employer resistance during organizing drives. The recent attack on public sector unionism in the United States—with the focus on Wisconsin and Ohio—is a continuation of employer resistance to public-sector unionization. Labor-solidarity challenges in the 1960s centered on divisions by race, ethnicity, and gender.

Currently, managerial challenges to immigrant labor organizing in the low-wage, private service sector take the form of automation of service transactions such as online retail in the self-service economy, off-shoring, geographical dispersion of home-care services, independent contracting arrangements, employer-customer alliances against service providers such as taxi cab drivers, and employer resistance during organizing drives. Contemporary labor-solidarity challenges focus on immigrant-native relations, religious intolerance such as Islamophobia, and divisions by ethnicity and race.

As was demonstrated throughout this volume, contemporary labor movements in Europe and the United States—like their predecessors in the 1960s—are surmounting these obstacles to immigrant labor organizing by mounting creative, socially integrative campaigns and initiatives (see also Cornfield and McCammon 2003; Erne 2008; Frege and Kelly 2004). Labor mobilizations are facilitated by shifting macroeconomic conditions. Labor union mobilization and membership growth have tended to occur during growth periods of the business cycle when opportunities for economic gain abound and workers have little fear of employer reprisal. By contrast, labor mobilizations tend not to be launched during recessionary periods of the business cycle because, with little employment opportunity, workers fear employer reprisal (Commons et al. 1918: 10–11; Cornfield and Fletcher 2001; Hourwich 1912: 30–31). Furthermore, severe challenges to labor solidarity that take the form of deteriorating immigrant-native relations, such as urban riots, tend to occur during recessionary periods of the business cycle.

Shifting macroeconomic conditions in the four nations are captured in the 1990–2011 trends in unemployment rates in table 9.5. Growth periods are indicated by relatively low unemployment rates and recessionary periods are indicated by relatively high unemployment rates. It is important to note the unique nation-specific trends and crossnational differences in the patterning of the business cycle as indicated by the trends in the unemployment rates (see table 9.5). In any one year, the four national economies may be experiencing different macroeconomic conditions. For example, 2006 was a full-employment year in the United States (unemployment rate = 4.6) and the UK (unemployment rate = 5.5) but it was a recessionary year in Germany (unemployment rate = 10.3).

U.S. and European labor movements have undertaken important socially integrative mobilizations in immigrant incorporation and in organizing service workers. As the cases in this volume show, these mobilizations tend to occur during full-employment periods of the business cycle, periodically appearing in the wake of major urban unrest that reveals disaffection among ethnic and racial minority youth in a previous period of economic recession.

TABLE 9.5 Unemployment rates, 1990–2011

	United States	France	Germany	United Kingdom
1990	5.6	8.0	5.0	7.1
1991	6.8	8.2	5.6	8.9
1992	7.5	9.1	6.7	10.0
1993	6.9	10.2	8.0	10.4
1994	6.1	10.8	8.5	9.5
1995	5.6	10.2	8.2	8.7
1996	5.4	10.7	9.0	8.1
1997	4.9	10.8	9.9	7.0
1998	4.5	10.4	9.3	6.3
1999	4.2	10.1	8.5	6.0
2000	4.0	8.6	7.8	5.5
2001	4.7	7.8	7.9	5.1
2002	5.8	8.0	8.6	5.2
2003	6.0	8.6	9.3	5.0
2004	5.5	9.0	10.3	4.8
2005	5.1	9.0	11.2	4.9
2006	4.6	8.9	10.3	5.5
2007	4.6	8.1	8.7	5.4
2008	5.8	7.5	7.6	5.7
2009	9.3	9.2	7.8	7.7
2010	9.6	9.5	7.1	7.9
2011	8.9	9.4	6.0	8.1

Source: U.S. Bureau of Labor Statistics, "International Labor Comparisons," http://www.bls.gov/fls/#laborforce.

United States

In the United States, urban labor-community coalitions have appeared after violent expressions of inter-ethnic and inter-racial tensions in recessionary years. Of the major urban immigrant gateways from the Global South to the United States, Miami and Los Angeles have been the sites of significant inter-ethnic and inter-racial riots that have been followed by the appearance of inclusive labor-community coalitions in immigrant labor organizing.

In the recessionary and presidential election year of 1980 that concluded President Jimmy Carter's one-term presidency, produced President Ronald Reagan, and ushered in the neoliberal moment, multiethnic Miami erupted into a major riot. With the news that an "all-white jury in Tampa acquitted four white police officers charged with beating to death Arthur McDuffie, a black insurance executive," a three-day riot broke out in May in the predominantly African American, Miami neighborhood of Liberty City that resulted in eighteen deaths and $80,000,000 in property damage (Thomas 1981).

The Miami riot was reportedly contextualized by a race gap in unemployment, a long history of black-white racial tensions, an urban population of whom over half were Hispanic and one-fourth were black, and mounting inter-ethnic rivalry between African Americans and Latinos (Porter and Dunn 1984: 185). Nationally, the unemployment rate had climbed to 7.1 percent, among the highest annual unemployment rates since the 1950s (U.S. Bureau of Labor Statistics 2012a). In Liberty City, the unemployment rate had increased from 6 percent to 17.8 percent between 1968 and 1978 (Porter and Dunn 1984: 190). What is more, riot accounts suggest that inter-ethnic and inter-racial tensions were exacerbated by perceptions of a disproportionate allocation by the federal and local governments of economic development resources toward whites and Cubans over African Americans, African American underrepresentation in local government, and the dramatic arrival and increase in the number of Cuban refugees in Miami with the Mariel boatlift (Miami Police Department 1980; Porter and Dunn 1984; Thomas 1981).

During the ensuing period of economic growth of the 1980s and 1990s, and through the recession of the early 1990s, labor unions and worker centers have pursued multiple socially integrative initiatives in South Florida. These initiatives include SEIU's organizing drives among health-care workers and janitors, the South Florida Jobs with Justice movement, and the Miami Workers Center (2011), which was established in 1999 in the African American community and has since expanded its outreach "to build the collective power of low-income African American and Latino communities" (for more on this, see chapter 3 in this volume; see also Nissen and Russo 2007: 154).

In the recessionary and presidential election year of 1992, which concluded the one-term presidency of George H. Bush and produced what would become the two-term, surplus-generating presidency of Bill Clinton, multiethnic Los Angeles, in late April–early May, erupted in a major riot that was the "costliest" unrest "in U.S. history" (The Staff of the *Los Angeles Times* 1992: 130). The riot followed the announcement of the acquittal of four white policemen in the videotaped and globally viewed beating of African American motorist Rodney King. The three-day riot started in the predominantly African American, South Central Los Angeles neighborhood, spread to neighboring Korean, Latino, and white neighborhoods, claimed sixty lives, and resulted in $1 billion in insured losses (Baldassare 1994; The Staff of the *Los Angeles Times* 1992: 130). Riot reports attributed the riot to underlying causes much like those identified by the Kerner Commission of the urban riots during the 1960s and those of the 1980 Miami riot: mounting social and economic exclusion of African Americans, increasing inter-ethnic rivalry among native and immigrant minority groups, and racialized perceptions of police abuse (California State Assembly 1992).

Over the next decade and a half, as the nation entered into what might be called a "post-Los Angeles" era of immigrant labor organizing, Los Angeles labor helped to forge a nationally significant, "black-brown" labor-community coalition. The formation of the coalition was based in a series of successful organizing campaigns among low-wage, private- and public-sector service workers, construction workers, and factory workers (see Greenhouse 2001; Hauptmeier and Turner 2007; Milkman 2006). Politically, the formation of the coalition culminated in the 2005 election of former teachers union and SEIU activist Antonio Villaraigosa as the first Latino Los Angeles mayor in over a century (Broder 2005a, 2005b; Sonenshein 1993; Willon 2009). The following year, another full-employment year (see table 9.5), Los Angeles labor, along with the Catholic Church and Spanish-language radio, spearheaded the nationwide, immigrant worker May Day rally that involved some 4,000,000 protestors in over 160 cities. The May Day rally is thought to have been the largest protest rally in U.S. history and to have contributed to the defeat of the Border Protection, Antiterrorism and Illegal Immigration Control Act (H.R. 4437) in the U.S. House of Representatives (Voss and Bloemraad 2011). The act would have increased federal investment in border security and cooperation between federal and local law enforcement agencies and stiffened penalties for employers who hired illegal migrants.

Post–Los Angeles labor mobilizations of the economically robust mid-2000s were national in scope and took place in urban and rural places. The AFL-CIO's 2003 Immigrant Workers Freedom Ride happened during the mild recession of the early 2000s, providing what would become the intercity itinerary of the 2006

May Day rally (Voss and Bloemraad 2011). The fractious formation of Change to Win occurred in the full-employment year of 2005 (see table 9.5) with a socially inclusive commitment to organize the physically anchored service sector of predominantly immigrant, minority, and women low-wage workers. The 2008 United Food and Commercial Workers (UFCW) organizing victory among the multiethnic workforce at the huge Smithfield hog slaughtering plant in rural North Carolina occurred just before the onset of the Great Recession and culminated a fifteen-year organizing campaign and nationwide Smithfield consumer boycott.

The five U.S. cases of immigrant labor organizing in this volume are post–Los Angeles mobilizations that were initiated during the economically robust 1990s and mid-2000s and either endured or dissipated in the Great Recession of the late 2000s. Together, the five cases depict a panorama of mobilizations that vary by organizational strategy, workplace employment relationship, the ethnicity/race and religion of the workers, and spatial context that typifies post–Los Angeles immigrant labor organizing in the United States. The LIUNA case shows the pioneering transformation of a construction union into a diversified advocate for immigrant workers in multiple regions of dense immigrant settlement through its continuing dual affiliation with Change to Win and the AFL-CIO. LIUNA conducts organizing campaigns in coalition with national and local progressive community allies among a wide range of immigrant workers, including poultry workers and day laborers, and serves as a national policy advocate for immigrant rights (Fine 2011a).

The cases of Arizona roofers and Los Angeles carwash workers are mobilizations of urban labor-community coalitions that were conducted by local and national labor organizations with progressive community allies (Roca-Servat 2011). The Arizona roofers campaign was distinctive in its strong bicultural approach to organizing the predominantly Latino workforce of documented and undocumented workers, the successes of which galvanized organizing drives among other building trades. The Los Angeles carwash campaign adopted a bicultural approach to organizing the predominantly Latino workforce, and served to strengthen the tie between the United Steelworkers and progressive Los Angeles labor. As the nation emerged from the Great Recession—the national unemployment rate decreased steadily from 9.6 percent in 2010 to 7.8 percent through November 2012 (see table 9.5 and U.S. Bureau of Labor Statistics 2012b), the union succeeded in signing three historic contracts in the carwash industry in 2011 and 2012.

The Tennessee cases of Nashville taxi cab drivers and rural poultry processing workers are mobilizations of Muslim Somali refugees (Cornfield 2011).

Having formed a local, urban labor-community coalition, the Somali-led multi-ethnic independent Nashville Metro Taxi Drivers Alliance went on strike for improvements in working and employment conditions for these independent contractors. With the onset of the Great Recession, mounting Islamophobia in the region (Suleyman 2012), and the post-2010 improvement in macroeconomic conditions, the drivers movement demobilized and the Somali and (Christian) Ethiopian drivers went on to form their own separate taxi cab companies in 2012. Turning to the case of rural Tennessee poultry workers, the multiethnic UFCW-affiliated RWDSU local union, responding to the worship needs of the substantial minority of Muslim Somali production workers, signed a historic agreement in 2007 with Tyson. The agreement made the Muslim holiday of Eid al-Fitr one of the plantwide paid holidays, the first instance in U.S. labor history of a contractual provision for a Muslim holiday. The subsequent deterioration in both macroeconomic conditions and immigrant-native relations in the region prompted a national right-wing media assault on the historic holiday agreement, compelling the union and company to renegotiate and rewrite the contract respecifying the Muslim holiday as an optional paid personal day. Mention of the holiday nonetheless remained in the contract, having endured the Great Recession and Islamophobia.

United Kingdom

The English riots of August 2011, occurred during a recession that had been officially declared in 2009 (for more on this, see chapter 4 by Maite Tapia). As demonstrated in table 9.5, 2011 was the year of highest unemployment of the previous fourteen years in the United Kingdom. Characterized as "arguably the worst bout of civil unrest in a generation" (*Guardian* and London School of Economics 2011: 1), the four-day riots were sparked by the fatal police shooting of a black man, Mark Duggan, in the North London neighborhood of Tottenham. It spread to other poor neighborhoods in London and to several other English cities, resulting in more than £300,000,000 in riot-related insurance claims. Reports on the riots attribute them to a similar litany of underlying causes as those given to the French and U.S. riots described in this chapter: social and economic exclusion of poor youth of majority and minority ethnic backgrounds and a deterioration in police-community relations. The predominantly ten to twenty-four-year old English rioters were also said to be alienated from a British society they characterized as unequal and unjust and angered over national austerity measures that curtailed youth services and the education maintenance allowance. Riot reports suggest that the English rioters, approximately 40 percent of whom were black, were more ethnically diverse than the French and U.S. rioters (*Guardian* and

London School of Economics 2011), suggesting a complex of ethnic and racial as well as class- and age-based underlying causal factors.

The apparent class and ethnic and racial complexity of the English riots is not inconsistent with the complexity in contemporary British approaches to immigrant labor organizing, characterized by Maite Tapia as "multicultural" rather than restrictive and assimilationist. Following World War II, British labor moved toward a multicultural approach to immigrant organizing. This coincided with the increase in immigration from the Global South by the 1970s and from Eastern Europe in the 1990s coupled with racialized industrial conflict in the early 1970s and the rise of the right-wing British National Party.

In 2007, the British TUC established a Commission on Vulnerable Employment to examine the status of Britain's 2,000,000 precariously employed workers, many of whom are immigrants. The commission has prompted a shift in approach away from the migrant worker and toward the exploitative employer, that is "workers are workers, regardless of their nationality," as Tapia put it. Inroads in immigrant labor organizing have been achieved especially through educational channels, such as offering English-language instruction, and in collaboration with community groups.

The UK case studies presented in chapter 4 show that British approaches to immigrant labor organizing range between "separatist" and "integrative" organizing strategies. Four of these "key campaigns" occurred during the period of economic growth of the early and mid-2000s (see table 9.5). These include the 2001–2010 Justice for Cleaners campaign, a labor-community mobilization of The East London Citizens Organization and the TGWU/Unite among a predominantly immigrant workforce. The union established a cleaners' branch and recruited some 2,000 union members. Next came the 2006 establishment of the GMB's migrant workers' branch in Southampton. The 500-member branch comprised mainly Polish, other Eastern European, and Pakistani workers and provided education, training, and English instruction. Then the 2007 Unison Filipino care workers campaign in which Unison successfully lobbied Parliament to allow Filipino care workers to remain employed in Britain. Many of these workers joined the union. Finally, the 2007–2009 hotel workers campaign, a labor-community mobilization of the T&G and London Citizens among the precariously employed, predominantly immigrant workforce of the large hotels. This campaign failed due to heavy management resistance and the inability of the union to achieve solidarity among different immigrant worker groups. The demobilization of this campaign also may be attributable to its extension into the recessionary period of the late 2000s. The fifth case is the 2009 anti-British National Party (BNP) political campaign conducted by Unison to encourage Polish immigrants to vote against the BNP in the European elections. According to Tapia, this historic campaign "can be considered a first attempt of Unison to reach out to the Polish community in the UK, going beyond the workplace and moving towards a more community-inclusive model."

In sum, the British cases, when juxtaposed to the English riots in 2011, reveal a socially complex low-wage service sector workforce and diverse and dynamic portfolio of approaches to immigrant labor organizing. In the wake of the riots, British labor is moving toward new socially integrative models of community unionism.

France

French unions are having an important socially integrative impact on undocumented workers—the *sans papiers*. In chapter 5, Lowell Turner characterized the French *sans papiers* movement of the 2008–2010 as "a dramatic breakthrough for union participation in battles for the rights of immigrant workers." The movement constitutes a breakthrough for several reasons. In the French Republican tradition, the workplace-centered French labor movement has typically not recognized workers' ethnic identities in its organizing drives and has remained distinct from civil rights movements, such as the immigrant rights movement. What is more, the French labor movement is an ideologically fragmented movement, as indicated by its multiple, constituent national labor federations. The emergence in late 2009 of the Collectif des Onze—a group of five labor federations and six NGOs bargaining with the state for the "regularization" of predominantly North and West African undocumented immigrant workers—constituted an unprecedented expression of solidarity among labor federations and between the labor and human rights movements.

Although the French business cycle is more stable than those of the other nations depicted in table 9.5, the timing of the emergence of the *sans papiers* movement is not dissimilar from that of post-Miami and post-Los Angeles immigrant labor organizing in the United States. The CGT labor federation launched the *sans papiers* movement in 2008, the year of the lowest French unemployment rate in a two-decade period (see table 9.5). The movement gained further traction with the subsequent founding of the Collectif des Onze.

Furthermore, the 2008 launch of the *sans papiers* movement occurred some three years after the two-week eruption of violent riots in urban centers of immigrant settlement throughout France in October–November 2005 (*New York Times* 2005). The riots occurred at a time of rising unemployment which followed an era of double-digit unemployment rates during most of the 1990s, a brief reprieve in the early 2000s, and the return of 9.0-level unemployment rates in the mid-2000s when the riots occurred (see table 9.5).

Contemporaneous reports of the French riots attributed them to the development of a disaffected urban underclass of ethnic minorities. According to one account in early November 2005, "The rioting began last week in [the working class Paris suburb of] Clichy-sous-Bois after two teenagers were electrocuted when they hid in an electrical substation from the police. Local youths, who believed the police had chased the boys into the enclosure, took to the streets, setting cars on fire in protest" (Smith 2005). The account cited social exclusion of ethnic minorities as an underlying cause of the riots: "France has been grappling for years with growing unrest among its second- and third-generation immigrants, mostly North African Arabs, who have faced decades of high unemployment and marginalization" (Smith 2005). Nor were the riots, the account claimed, an expression of Islam:

> Over the succeeding decades, North African and sub-Saharan immigrants replaced the working-class French who initially populated the neighborhoods. But jobs have dried up as the economy slowed—unemployment in some of the zones is as high as 30 percent—and the suburbs have become the French equivalent of America's inner cities.
>
> While labor immigration tightened in the 1980's, illegal immigration and asylum seekers have kept many of the neighborhoods growing. In 2003, France became the world's leading destination for asylum seekers, surpassing the United States . . .
>
> While the vast majority of the young people behind the nightly attacks are Muslim, experts and residents warned against seeing the violence through the prism of religion. The cultural divide between these second- and third-generation immigrants and the native French is deeper because they come from Muslim families, but to date the violence has had nothing to do with Islam. (Smith 2005)

Contemporaneous reports also stated that underclass disaffection partly derived from a deterioration in police-community relations (Smith 2005). An April 2005 report of the National Commission on Ethics in Security Services found that "a lack of training led to [police] behavior that was at best clumsy and at worst racist in those neighborhoods with large immigrant populations. It criticized the fact that French police officers have rarely been punished for misdeeds and lamented the lack of ethnic diversity in all branches of the police. That lack may be compounding the racial connotations of the civil unrest, with youths of North African descent pitted against a predominantly white police force" (Bennhold 2005).

The socially integrative mission of the *sans papiers* labor movement is all the more significant when seen against the backdrop of urban underclass disaffection in France. In the heavily regulated French economy, immigrant worker "regularization" is a meaningful mechanism of immigrant worker incorporation into the economy and society.

Germany

In 2011, on the occasion of the German government's celebration of the fiftieth anniversary of the German-Turkish recruitment agreement, "[m]any [German Turkish immigrants] in this young generation," claimed one account, "still feel as if they haven't arrived in Germany" (Popp et al 2011). What is more, German Turkish immigrants identify less with their "settlement country" than do their counterparts in France and the Netherlands (Ersanilli and Saharso 2011).

Little or no protest, however, accompanied the opening of Germany's largest mosque in Duisberg in 2008. Compared to the protested mosque openings in Berlin and Cologne earlier that year, the quiet opening of the Duisberg mosque was hailed as "unprecedented" and partly attributed to the mosque's broad function as a communitywide meeting center, its positive impact on local economic development and employment, and a welcoming approach taken by local native elected officials (Jenckner 2008). A signal of peaceful social integration of Germany's largest ethnic minority, the quiet Duisberg mosque opening occurred in an era in which the nation was nonetheless questioning the success of the "integration" of now second- and third-generations of Turkish Muslim immigrant families, many of whom are socially isolated, unemployed, and underemployed compared to natives and other immigrant groups (Elger 2009; Kanas et al. 2012; Lehmer and Ludsteck 2011). In 2010, the Duisburg mosque opening was revisited and supported by a rally of thousands of protesters that was organized by German trade unions and churches against a small far-right antimosque rally in Duisburg (Deutsche Welle 2010).

Germany has not experienced the urban riots associated with the social exclusion of ethnic and racial minorities that have occurred in France, the United Kingdom, and the United States. This may be partly attributable to the proactive campaigning and messaging against racism that the German labor movement has pursued in workplaces throughout Germany, as suggested in the chapter on Germany in this volume. Compared to the other labor movements, the German labor movement is especially well positioned to play this socially integrative role by virtue of its unique and profound integration into corporate decision making through the German system of codetermination and works councils (Turner 2009).

After the reunification, the German labor movement has increasingly, if haltingly and with regional variations, been concerned with migrant worker well-being. German unions have endorsed multiple immigrant rights, including family reunion rights, right to stay in Germany independently from a work permit, and voting rights in local elections as well as limiting the causes for expulsion and fighting for legislation against ethnic discrimination.

Our German cases (presented in chapter 6) suggest that German immigrant labor organizing has proceeded the farthest in the corporate manufacturing sector with codetermination compared to the informal service and construction sectors. The interviews with high-ranking immigrant labor officials imply, however, that immigrant inroads into labor officialdom have been limited.

In the case of IG Metall Kiel/Neumünster, native and Turkish workers convened on a local migration committee that promoted civic integration within the union. Beginning in the early 1990s, civic integration was achieved through ethnically diverse appointments in leadership and high-level works councils, language classes, legal assistance to immigrants, union training for immigrants, and immigrant-native collaboration in the workplace and union.

Next is ver.di's case of Ana S. The large German service-sector union was formed with a socially integrative commitment to immigrants, ethnic and racial minorities, youth, and women from a merger of several German unions in the nonrecessionary year of 2001 (see table 9.5). Ver.di conducted a two-prong approach to service-sector organizing in its start-up period. One prong was to diffuse codetermination by organizing works councils in the corporate retail sector (Turner 2009). The other was to organize undocumented, immigrant service workers, as in the high profile but largely symbolic, three-year case of Ana S. (Kiezfilme 2008; ver.di 2009).

Ana S. is an undocumented domestic worker in Hamburg whom ver.di, along with human rights and community organizations, helped to process and settle in 2009 her unprecedented claim for unpaid wages to which she was legally entitled but denied by her employer. As Ana S. put it in the film about her case:

> I thought that, without papers, I didn't stand a chance. It came as a complete surprise when they told me I could claim my rights even though I am an undocumented person.
>
> I always thought one can't do a thing without papers. At first I was very nervous too, but not anymore. I've become a lot more courageous. Now I say, I am only claiming what's mine. I don't expect anyone to give me anything for free. I am only claiming the wages for work I have already done. (Kiezfilme 2008)

Next is the 2004 case of IG Bauen-Agrar-Umwelt (IG BAU) transnational organizing of hyper-mobile posted construction workers. IG BAU collaborated with the European Migrant Workers Union in advocating from bases in Warsaw and

Frankfurt in Polish and Romanian for the predominantly Central and Eastern European migrant workers. The collaboration helped these migrant workers file claims for back wages. Yet the initiative did not translate into increasing memberships because of the unsustainability of the service-heavy organizing strategy. Small membership gains may also be attributable to the launching of the initiative during the recessionary period of double-digit unemployment of the mid-2000s (see table 9.5).

In sum, if the German labor movement's antiracism campaigns and inroads in immigrant integration in the formal sector have contributed to civil order, further inroads in immigrant integration will need to be made in the small-business, informal service and construction sectors. The latter sectors comprise a disproportionately large number of precariously employed immigrants who are largely excluded from the corporate system of codetermination and labor union protection. The German case studies in this book, along with Turner's (2009) analysis of ver.di's new organizing in the service sector, suggest that urban labor-community coalitions and community-based immigrant labor organizing outside of, and alongside of, the system of codetermination and works councils can further integrate Germany's immigrant service-sector workforce.

Toward a Dynamic Model of Trade Unionism

The cutting-edge cases of immigrant labor organizing in France, Germany, the United Kingdom, and the United States presented in this book occur at this polarized moment in the Global North. As they pursue the hope of realizing an inclusive democratic society, unions in a restructured Global North are creatively countering social inequality by organizing immigrant workers in low-wage jobs of a service sector which now employs a majority of these national labor forces. The terms and techniques of immigrant incorporation vary crossnationally, whether they are the pluralistic multiculturalism of the United Kingdom and the United States, French Republican regularization, or the social integration achieved through German codetermination. Such variations in approaches to immigrant labor organizing, and in their effectiveness, are attributable to a number of disparate factors. These include strength of national labor movements, cultural and political institutions and traditions, the presence and strength of right-wing political forces, immigrant-native differences in spatial residential and employment patterns, and the degree of social inequality and political unrest.

In conclusion, I assess the implications of the temporal patterning of immigrant labor organizing for furthering the development of a dynamic model of trade unionism in the Global North. Two relevant temporal patterns are common to the four nations covered in this volume. The first, a historical pattern, is that the chief labor organizing target—low-wage immigrant workers in the service and construction sectors—emerges as an economically and socially marginalized group from the contemporary moment of economic restructuring and increasing immigration in the Global North.

The second temporal pattern pertains to changing macroeconomic conditions. New organizing initiatives tend to be launched, and great inroads in immigrant labor organizing tend to be made, during the growth periods of the business cycle in between recessions. Some of these organizing initiatives even endure recessions and succeed with the return of better times. By contrast, if and when they take place, severe lapses in labor solidarity that take the form of violent urban riots tend to occur during recessionary moments of the business cycle.

The recessionary expressions of urban unrest in France, the United Kingdom, and the United States reveal a deep disaffection among immigrant, ethnic minority, and native, economically and socially marginalized youth and young adults. In these nations, the disaffection is toward police and what is perceived to be an unequal, unjust, and unwelcoming society. Although the disaffection has not been expressed in urban riots in Germany, social exclusion and disaffection among immigrants are revealed not only by social science research but also by national debates about the social integration of immigrants.

The temporal patterning of immigrant labor organizing has three implications for further development of a dynamic model of trade unionism in the Global North. First, labor unions should continue to confront urban disaffection of young adults by implementing trust-building organizing strategies, regardless of the business cycle. These community-based strategies meet the workers on their terms and in their spaces and take the form of worker centers and community unionism outside of, and alongside of, workplaces, as many of the cases discussed in this volume show. Trust-building strategies also take the form of labor-community coalitions that unite labor unions and a wide range of human rights advocates and middle-class consumers in organizing drives. Labor-community coalitions reinforce organizing drives not only by raising resources for the campaign but also by humanizing the interdependence between low-wage service providers and middle-class consumer allies whose own family well-being depends on that of their service providers.

Second, labor unions that organize low-wage service workers—immigrant, ethnic minority, and native alike—should collaborate with labor organizations of professional service workers in organizing and political initiatives, especially during growth periods of the business cycle, and throughout the political cycle of legislative lobbying and elections. Little or no research in the labor revitalization field has addressed any such collaboration that may exist. Specifically, these organized, professional service workers include salaried, human services professionals—for example teachers, librarians, counselors, social workers, nurses, and other allied health professionals—and freelance creative workers, including musicians and writers. Human services professionals and creative workers have long histories of occupational organizing as both independent professional associations and affiliated guild-like labor unions that conduct collective bargaining. Their labor and professional organizations are large, resourceful, and powerful and are often linked to the women's, civil rights, civil liberties, immigrant rights, environmental, LGBT, and other human rights movements. Most important, they are professionally committed to societal well-being, including the health, education, occupational training, and professional development of youth and young adults, and therefore to the same humanistic objectives and social welfare legislative agenda as that pursued by unions of low-wage service workers.

Third, labor unions should actively intervene during moments of civil unrest as intermediaries in search of a creative solution to the crisis. Little research has addressed labor's role in restoring a humanistic civil order, in preventing urban unrest, and in gaining the trust of both marginalized and mainstream communities and institutions.

The cutting-edge cases of labor organizing presented in this book inspire a dynamic model of trade unionism in the Global North. The dynamic model acknowledges the temporal patterning of labor mobilization, capitalizes on producer-consumer interdependence in a service economy, and avails itself of the overlapping social-legislative and political agendas of low-wage and professional service workers. With this model of trade unionism, the union's dynamic portfolio of initiatives in workplace and community organizing shifts as macroeconomic conditions change and social conditions may warrant. The dynamic model calls for organizing young, socially diverse, low-wage service workers in workplaces and communities, in coalition with progressive community allies and with organized professional service workers. Such a dynamic model of trade unionism offers a roadmap for labor in a restructured and socially diversified Global North to pursue its historic mission of realizing an inclusive democratic society.

Notes

FOREWORD

1. Susan J. Schurman and Adrienne E. Eaton, "Trade Unions Organizing Workers Informalized 'From Above': Case Studies from Cambodia, Colombia, South Africa, and Tunisia," Report to the Solidarity Center, 2013, 5.

2. OECD, International Migration Outlook 2012, http://dx.doi.org/10.1787/migr_outlook-2012-en.

3. Issues similar to those raised by the United Steelworkers (USW) and their community allies in Los Angeles in the carwash campaign have been advanced since the mid 2000s in New York City by the Retail, Wholesale, and Department Store Union (RWDSU) and their community and faith-based partners. RWDSU announced in late May 2013 that they signed the first ever carwash collective bargaining agreement in New York City. For more detail, see http://www.huffingtonpost.com/2013/05/28/car-wash-new-york-con tract_n_3348685.html, and http://www.maketheroad.org.

CHAPTER 1

1. This is also a reflection of the broadening of the field of industrial relations, a field of study that became quite narrow at least in the United States in the early postwar period. Scholars looked at specific events and outcomes within an industrial relations system, often detached from the broader political and economic context that was shaping and changing relations of power. Internationalists such as John Windmuller, Russell Lansbury, and Greg Bamber helped expand the perspective to situate industrial relations in a broader arena of international and comparative political economy (see Bamber and Lansbury 1987; Bamber, Lansbury, and Wailes 2011). A labor movement revitalization literature has emphasized labor's place in society: the linkage between workplace and social relationships, between labor and community, between actors representing the interests of workers and their families across a range of interrelated identities based on employment, occupation, ethnicity, gender, and sexual preference (Bronfenbrenner et al. 1998; Cornfield and McCammon 2003; Gall 2003; Turner and Cornfield 2007; Turner, Katz and Hurd 2001). Our focus on the workplace is central and essential, but we cannot make sense of things without the broader social context. Nor can unions mobilize the power necessary to reverse growing inequality without allies based beyond the workplace (Fletcher and Gapasin 2008; Getman 2010; Tattersall 2010; Van Dyke and McCammon 2010).

2. Research began in the United States in 2008 with grants from the Carnegie Corporation and Public Welfare Foundation. A larger grant from the Hans Böckler Foundation then allowed us to expand the work to three European political economies and develop a comparative analysis.

3. Coordinated at the ILR School at Cornell University by Lee Adler, Maite Tapia, and myself, project researchers have included Adler, Daniel Cornfield, Janice Fine, and Denisse Roca-Servat for the United States; Gabriella Alberti, Jane Holgate, and Tapia for the United Kingdom; Adler, Chiara Benassi, Emilija Mitrovic, Oliver Trede, Ian Greer, Zyama Ciupijus, and Nathan Lillie for Germany; and Mirvat Abd el ghani, Laetitia Dechaufour, Marion Quintin, and Turner for France.

4. Trade union commentators at the November workshop included Ana Avendaño (AFL-CIO), Wilf Sullivan (TUC), Francine Blanche (CGT), Peter Bremme (ver.di), Wolf Jürgen Röder, Petra Wecklik, and Bobby Winkler (IG Metall). Academic workshop commentators included Sébastien Chauvin, Michael Fichter, Steve French, and Otto Jacobi. Dialogue among us has been rich and sometimes contentious, and as subsequent chapters show, we make no claim to consensus on interpretation of our research findings.

5. A note on terminology: rather than quibbling about definitions and in the interest of variety, the following terms are used more or less interchangeably in this chapter: free-market capitalism, neoliberalism, market fundamentalism, global liberalization. This is not meant as an antimarket perspective; rather these terms are meant to point in a generic way toward the expansion of markets beyond the capacity of society to regulate them effectively (Polanyi 1944; Streeck 2009).

6. For data on inequality in the United States and its impact on economy and society, see, for example, Mishel, Bernstein, and Shierholz (2009); Wilkinson and Pickett (2009); Reich (2010); and Mishel et al. (2012). For crossnational comparative data, see OECD (2012) at www.oecd.org/els/social/inequality.

7. See Watt (2009) for a concise, insightful discussion of all the things that advocates of freer markets might think would cause a crisis, but did not. Thus high wages, rigid labor markets, unions, social welfare spending, too much regulation—none of these had anything at all to do with causing the financial collapse of 2008 that pushed the global economy into a period of sustained crisis.

8. For contrasting perspectives, cf. Hall and Soskice (2001) and Streeck (2009). Predecessors of the contemporary debates include Wilensky (1975); Schmitter and Lehmbruch (1979); and Steinmo, Thelen, and Longstreth (1992).

9. See OECD data, available at http://www.oecd.org/dataoecd/32/20/47723414.pdf. From 2000 to 2005, inequality grew faster in Germany than in any other OECD country; see http://www.oecd.org/dataoecd/45/25/41525346.pdf. See also Biewen and Juhasz 2010.

10. An earlier version of this introductory chapter was delivered as the Countess Markiewicz Memorial Lecture, for the Irish Industrial Relations Association, in November 2011.

11. Not everyone was so naive. Here is what Naomi Klein said in 2008: "rest assured: the ideology will come roaring back when the bailouts are done. The massive debt the public is accumulating to bail out the speculators will then become part of a global budget crisis that will be the rationalization for deep cuts to social programs, and for a renewed push to privatize what is left of the public sector."

12. A note on terminology: the term "immigrant worker" is used in this chapter to refer mainly to the foreign born, without positive or negative connotations. This usage is more common in the United States and France; the term "migrant worker" has become more common in the United Kingdom and now to refer across Europe to workers who move around within the European Union. In Germany, the term "foreign worker" (*Ausländer*) is still commonplace, even when referring to settled residents who are obviously not going "home." This is changing, in favor of reference to workers with a "migration-background" (*Migrationshintergrund*; Siebenhüter 2011). Terminology is just one of the complexities of crossnational comparative research; by default I fall back here on the generic term "immigrant worker," even as the term may be used in different ways in different countries—and this difference will also be reflected in various chapters of this book.

13. The TUC and DGB are umbrella federations that include most British and German unions. The AFL-CIO in the United States was also a unitary federation at the time of its policy change toward immigrant workers in 2000. (As the result of an internal split in 2005, the United States now has a second federation, Change to Win, whose policies

toward immigrant workers are nonetheless substantially the same.) The French labor movement is divided into contending confederations with a range of perspectives (see chapter 6).

CHAPTER 2

This chapter is a revised, expanded version of a paper originally presented at the conference "Across Boundaries" held at the London School of Economics, celebrating the fiftieth Anniversary of the *British Journal of Industrial Relations*, on December 12, 2011. In addition, an earlier version of this chapter, comparing trade union strategies in France and the United Kingdom appeared in the *British Journal of Industrial Relations* 51, 3 (2013), 601–622.

1. Precarious employment has been defined in many ways (see Rodgers and Rodgers 1989; Standing 2011; Vosko et al. 2008). The concept goes beyond particular forms of employment and includes different dimensions such as wage levels, access to benefits, legal and union protection, and employment security.

2. Even though collective bargaining coverage in France is very high (about 90%), union membership rates are very low (about 8%). Furthermore, a decentralized bargaining system has developed in which companies enjoy greater autonomy from collective agreements and labor legislation (Eurofound 2010).

3. The cases are presented in their contemporary contexts. Background for the postwar evolution of union strategies toward immigrant workers is presented in each of the country chapters in part II of this book.

4. This report is based on a survey of the cleaning industry. In reality, the percentage of immigrant workers is likely to be higher as companies such as hotels or schools that use large cleaning staff were not included in the sample.

5. TELCO was created in 1996 and is the founding chapter of the larger community organization London Citizens. Since then London Citizens has created other chapters: West London Citizens (2004), South London Citizens (2005), and North London Citizens (2010) (http://www.citizensuk.org).

6. The Justice for Cleaners case study was originally prepared in 2009 by Jane Holgate, one of the coauthors of this book, in the context of the broader crossnational research project. We have supplemented her findings with our own interviews and field research. The 2009 case report by Holgate is posted at http://www.mobilizing-against-inequality.info.

7. In addition to our interviews and field observations, the *sans papiers* case related here draws on Quintin 2009 and 2010; Dechaufour 2009; Le Queux and Sainsaulieu 2010; and Barron et al. 2011. Thanks also to Penny Schantz, AFL-CIO International Representative in Paris, whose contacts in the French labor movement helped launch the research in 2009; to Claude Didry, Annette Jobert, and Isabel da Costa at the research institute IDHE/CNRS at the École Normale Supérieure in Cachan, who provided a base for field research in 2009 and 2011; and to the Fondation Maison des Sciences de l'Homme, whose Maison Suger provided excellent research-friendly living quarters in Paris.

8. The CLEAN Carwash campaign case draws mainly on Roca-Servat (2011). In addition, we are grateful for the comments of Ana Avendaño with regard to this case at our workshop in November 2011 in Frankfurt. The case study report by Denisse Roca-Servat is posted in full at http://www.mobilizing-against-inequality.info.

9. See the announcement at http://www.cleancarwashla.org/index.cfm?action=article&articleID=f51c2693-cf61-4583-abf8-cf150e72293b.

10. These stories, and a full examination of the German case, are presented in chapter 6 of this book.

CHAPTER 3

We acknowledge RWDSU industry analyst Mathias Bolton for providing them with a copy of the original Tyson contract containing the Muslim holiday provision. In addition, we gratefully acknowledge the research and the additional case studies written by Denisse Roca-Servat and Janice Fine. Finally, we thank UFCW Vice President Pat O'Neill for his help in understanding his union's national efforts to assist their immigrant members.

1. The passage of the new AFL-CIO Immigrant Worker policy was the most significant, proimmigrant worker policy ever passed by the federation. It truly set a new national agenda and message, although its ability to implement this and other progressive statements about the rights of immigrant workers is quite limited and commensurate to the interests of its affiliates. Despite the 2005 split between unions affiliated with the AFL-CIO and the new federation, Change to Win, many of their supportive efforts, especially legislative and lobbying, at both the national and state levels, have been jointly undertaken.

2. Many friends of organized labor warned that these 1986 changes, enhancing employer sanctions, would result in considerable harm to immigrant workers, but the AFL-CIO's narrow vision at that time in these matters prevailed.

3. The Foreign-Born Population in the United States, U.S. Census Bureau, May 2012.

4. According to an ABC news report from August 2010: "For working people, wages remain stagnant. In fact, median weekly wages, when adjusted for inflation, fell slightly for both high school and college graduates from 2000 to 2009, according to a recent analysis by the *Economic Policy Institute*, a Washington think tank. For high school graduates, median inflation-adjusted wages were $626 per week in 2009, compared with $629 in 2000, according to the EPI analysis. That comes to $32,552 in 2009, down from $32,708 in 2000. For college graduates, weekly wages were $1,025 in 2009, compared with $1,030 in 2000, according to the study. Over the course of a year, that's $53,300 in 2009, down from $53,560 in 2000."

5. Consequently, the percentage of U.S. union members who were Latino or Hispanic increased from 7.6 percent to 12.4 percent between 1992 and 2010 (U.S. Bureau of Labor Statistics 1994, 2011).

6. An excellent example of the institutionalizing of the AFL-CIO's "progressive turn" may be seen in the efforts of its special assistant to the president Ana Avendaño's relentless efforts in May 2013 as a key player on the immigration reform legislative markup process in the U.S. Senate.

7. Regrettably, the number of affiliates that engage in focused migrant worker organizing remains with these few national affiliates, joined by CTW affiliates: LIUNA, UFCW, and its New York subaffiliate, RWDSU.

8. HERE was certainly the union initiator, but was successful, in part, due to the help of civil rights organizations, immigrant-rights advocacy groups, and worker centers.

9. The original CTW unions were SEIU, UNITE HERE, UFCW, UFW, LIUNA, UBC, and IBT, some of which have since reaffiliated with the AFL-CIO (Briggs 2001: ch. 6; Cornfield 2006, 2007; Parks 2003; Portes and Rumbaut 2006).

10. AFSCME's activities of organizing home health-care workers (low wage and often immigrants) in California, Illinois, Minnesota, and the successful organizing in New York of day-care workers (with both the AFT's affiliate in New York, the UFT, and AFSCME's affiliate, CSEA) are an exception to this statement.

11. We did find evidence of some internal change and an institutional commitment towards organizing in both the USW and Roofers.

12. What is also important about these developments is that during the past two decades more and more immigrant workers, with and without papers, are settling in interior portions of the United States that historically are rural and with sparse, earlier, nonwhite

migrants. These areas are usually without significant union presence, and civic as well as workplace integration is considerably more difficult for these workers and their families.

13. In July and early August 2012, following one of the longest strikes of that year, SEIU's representation of janitors in Houston, a historic organizing victory of mostly immigrant workers celebrated a decade earlier, resulted in a successful outcome, revealing the "staying power" of campaigns of immigrant workers that are truly developed "with and as a part of the immigrant community the union sought to organize."

14. This successful campaign, characterized by some as the largest successful organizing campaign since the late 1940s, not only placed nearly 100,000 home health-care workers under a union contract in California, but required numerous, highly complicated community, political, and other forms of organizing and coalition building over a period of nearly ten years.

15. AFSCME has launched a number of successful low wage/immigrant worker organizing efforts of home health-care workers in California, New Jersey, and Illinois, and has partnered with the American Federation of Teachers' affiliate, the United Federation of Teachers (UFT), to organize child-care workers in New York City and state.

16. Our research is incomplete on the national efforts of the American Federation of Teachers' work in these areas, but we did learn of the remarkable partnering of the UFT with the now defunct community-based NGO, ACORN, and CSEA, an AFSCME affiliate, to organize approximately 30,000 day-care workers, many of whom are first generation immigrants, in 2008–2009.

17. The hospitality industry main trade union, formerly HERE, was in Change to Win and SEIU for the period from approximately 2005 to 2009, and is now reaffiliated with the AFL-CIO. LIUNA, a CTW affiliate from 2005–2100, now holds joint membership/affiliation with the AFL-CIO.

18. The labor movement's relationship with the DWU is a shining example of the U.S. labor movement's serious commitment to enhancing the lives of some of our most vulnerable immigrants—domestic workers. Aside from the financial support and other expertise provided, unions in New York provided lobbying fire-power in 2010 that resulted in the first in the nation legislation that provided a workplace bill of rights to domestic workers. This was an astonishing development of societal incorporation and protection for these workers.

19. See note 3 in Foreword.

20. Labor movement support, ranging from the RWDSU to the Industrial Workers of the World, has been of considerable benefit to the Brandworkers organizing initiatives in New York City.

21. The complete case studies are available at http://www.mobilizing-against-inequality.info.

22. In 2012 the car wash campaign spread to the New York City area where there have been a number of organizing successes. Here, the union part of the organizing was directed by RWDSU. Side-by-side the union collaborated with community organizers lead by the community advocacy organizations—Make the Road New York and New York Communities for Change; see http://www.nytimes.com/2012/10/22/nyregion/webster-carwash-in-the-bronx-votes-to-unionize.html.

23. The entire case, a cultural and political tour de force, was originally published by Dr. Denisse Roca-Servat, earlier an organizer in this campaign, in the *Labor Studies Journal.* Full text is available at http://lsj.sagepub.com/content/35/3/343.

24. The COMET program is the name of a particular approach to union organizing often deployed by the building trades. In the context of this quote, the COMET program focuses more on organizing into the union nonunion workers, whereas the Roofers' approach was more to organize the workers by organizing the community where the workers live.

25. This material came from interviews conducted by Denisse Roca-Servat and Justice for Roofers campaign organizers Masavi Perea (August 2010) and Paula Arnquist (September 2010).

26. Interview conducted by Denisse Roca-Servat and former Roofers Local 135 secretary treasurer Masavi Perea (August 2010).

27. This quote seems to refer to this being the first attempt undertaken in this manner in a building trade work place.

28. LIUNA's work with NDLON resulted in a formal national Partnership Agreement in 2008 that was hailed by many progressives as a very important indicator that LIUNA was building real trust with immigrant worker representatives. It has, in part, but no major organizing or community successes have resulted from this development.

29. E-verify is a government created computer system, notorious for its inaccuracy and unreliability, that employers use more and more to "determine" a worker or prospective worker's immigration status and his or her eligibility to work.

30. ICE raids refer to the shocking rise in usage by the Obama administration in rounding up undocumented workers and their families, often separating workers from their families, and detaining those seized in desolate detention centers. Such government behaviors have, along with draconian state laws criminalizing their status, both driven immigrant workers and their families deeper underground and made questions of their status a bone of contention within parts of the LIUNA organization.

31. The strength of those in LIUNA who doubt that organizing immigrant workers makes sense is revealed in a particularly troubling Washington, DC, organizing story, available at http://www.washingtoncitypaper.com/articles/40036/concrete-bungle-how-immigration-divided-a-dc-union/.

32. Although mentioned in Ana Avendaño's foreword to this volume, there is value in repeating the AFL-CIO's dramatic undertaking with regard to the New York City Taxicab Drivers Alliance, in that union's words, captured from their website on June 3, 2013:

> On August 3rd 2011, the Executive Council of the AFL-CIO voted unanimously to welcome the Taxi Workers Alliance into the house of labor with a national Organizing Committee charter to unionize taxi drivers throughout the United States. As the 57th national union of the AFL-CIO, we are the first non-traditional workforce (non-employees) to be granted membership in over 60 years, and the first one in the history of independent contractors. It will mean greater power, influence and resources for the fight for justice, rights, respect and dignity for tens of thousands of taxi drivers.

33. See also AGREEMENT by and between TYSON FOODS, INC. Shelbyville, Tennessee and the RETAIL, WHOLESALE AND DEPARTMENT STORE UNION AFL-CIO, Effective November 15, 2007 to November 16, 2012, Article XII-HOLIDAYS, Section 1, p. 18.

34. We also learned in an interview with the United Food and Commercial Worker (UFCW) vice president, Pat O'Neill, in April 2013, that UFCW affiliates in Nebraska and Minnesota had also made contractual holiday adjustments reflecting their Muslim rank and file religious concerns.

35. And this is also true of the AFL-CIO's breakaway rival, Change to Win.

36. The New York City carwash organizing efforts have been undertaken by a coalition of community and union forces, the most prominent being Make the Road New York (MRNY) and the Retail, Wholesale, and Department Store Union (RWDSU). According By early 2013 6 different local car wash sites had voted for union representation (McAlevey 2013). At that time, there had yet to be a first contract signed at any of these car washes. That reality changed as the *Huffington Post* reported on May 29, 2013, that a first contract

had just been signed at one of the recently organized Queens, New York car wash facilities (Jamieson 2013).

The authors of this chapter believe that these coalition efforts offer a solid blueprint for the multiple ways that U.S. trade unions can significantly increase the workplace power and social integration of our nation's mostly immigrant informal and precarious workers.

CHAPTER 4

I thank my coeditors as well as Jane Holgate and Janice Fine for their insightful comments and feedback on earlier drafts. In addition, I am indebted to Neil Jameson and Matthew Bolton of London Citizens, to Paul Nowak, Liz Blackshaw, and Carl Roper from the TUC for letting me attend the Organizing Academy and giving me useful insights into the British labor movement, and to Steve French and Wilf Sullivan for their comments during the Frankfurt workshop in November 2011. Finally, the case studies mentioned in this chapter are based on the research conducted by Gabriella Alberti, Jane Holgate, and Maite Tapia. The GMB case study draws from our research as well as secondary sources such as Fraser (2006), Heyes (2009), and Karmowska and James (2012).

1. In 2011, Prime Minister David Cameron launched an attack on decades of multiculturalism in Britain, arguing that a doctrine of state multiculturalism is the cause of radicalism and can lead to terrorism. His speech was a radical departure from previous governments' policies. In a similar vein, the former French president Nicolas Sarkozy, Australia's former prime minister John Howard, former Spanish prime minister Jose Maria Aznar, and German chancellor Angela Merkel have all claimed that multicultural policies have failed to integrate immigrants (Townsend 2010; *Telegraph,* February 11, 2011).

2. Even though during the 1969 TUC Congress, rank-and-file trade union members challenged the immigration controls and supported government's plans in calling for positive action to combat discrimination, the TUC General Council prevented the motion receiving majority support, opposing therefore government plans for antidiscrimination legislation.

3. Although (black) migrant workers in the postwar period were clearly migrants, they were more commonly referred to in trade union terminology as black and Asian workers. Clearly second and third generations of these communities are not migrants and they are also referred to as black and Asian workers (more recently BME) workers.

4. The TGWU merged with Amicus in 2007 and is now known as Unite. Although some of this research was done before this merger and some after, I consistently refer to the union as TGWU/Unite.

5. Cases are summarized briefly here for purposes of analysis. Full case study reports are posted at http://www.mobilizing-against-inequality.info

6. TELCO was the founding chapter of London Citizens.

7. This case has been discussed in the crossnational comparison in chapter 2.

CHAPTER 5

Research and analysis for this chapter have benefitted from a generous research grant from the Hans-Böckler-Stiftung, as well as important institutional support from the ILR School at Cornell University and two French research institutes linked to CNRS: IDHE at the Ecole Normale Supérieure at Cachan, and LEST at the Université Aix-Marseille. Claude Didry and Annette Jobert at IDHE and Ariel Mendez and Paul Bouffartigue at LEST provided useful ideas, contacts, and feedback. Penny Schantz, AFL-CIO international representative based in Paris, offered advice and key contacts to help launch the field research in France in 2009 and again in 2011. Although I wrote this chapter and take responsibility for any errors of fact or shortcomings of analysis, Marion Quintin, Laetitia Dechaufour, and Mirvat El Abd el ghani provided indispensable contributions of field research, literature review, and case study reports. This chapter includes case study summaries. Full case study reports, as well as a review of the literature on French unions and immigrant workers, are available at http://www.mobilizing-against-inequality.info.

1. Waters run deep in the immigration literature on definitions of terms such as integration, incorporation, assimilation (see, for example, Plotke 1999). I prefer to avoid those debates and simply distinguish two types of "integration": "incorporation" takes into account ethnic, racial, and cultural identities explicitly and tends to bring in immigrant workers as groups; "assimilation" refers to individuals adopting and blending into the dominant cultural/legal framework.

2. On the expansion of a precarious workforce in France, including both foreign and French-born workers, see Béroud and Bouffartigue (2009a, 2009b) and Noiseux 2012.

3. See Fine and Tichenor (2012b, 545–552), on the postwar twists and turns of both French immigration policy and the shifting attitudes of French unions.

4. The French labor movement is divided into numerous contending confederations, rivals in ideology, membership recruitment, and workplace elections, but also often coalition partners in collective bargaining, mobilization efforts, and negotiations with government.

5. See Pezet (2012) on the housing crisis that gave unions an opening to break with restrictionist policies, in a context of public support for the interests of immigrant workers.

6. Note the parallel here to Pezet's (2012) analysis: in the earlier case, a housing crisis raised public awareness of conditions facing immigrants and provided a social and political context in which French unions could reach out to immigrant workers. In this case, the issue of immigrant schoolchildren played a similar role.

7. The division of labor in France is such that the national government sets immigration policy and establishes criteria for work permits, while local governments interpret the rulings in issuing (or denying) work papers to individual applicants.

8. See, for example, *Perspectives on Europe*, Autumn 2010, 40:2, 35–56: "Forum: How Are Europeans Made? Debating a National Models Approach to Immigrant Integration."

9. For a fascinating comparative study of internal processes of debate and reform in both the CFDT and CGT, although focused on an earlier period rather than current debates, see Ancelovici (2010).

10. Case study report researched and written by Marion Quintin and Lowell Turner. See also the background, analysis, and rich narrative of Act I by Cristina Nizzoli (2009), and of both Acts I and II in Barron et al. (2011). This case as well as Act II was also included for comparative purposes in chapter 2.

11. In the aftermath, over 3,000 of the striking workers had received legal work documents by early 2012, many more applications were still in process, monitored carefully on a case-by-case basis by Francine Blanche and colleagues in a "war room" packed with dossiers at CGT headquarters. Only three of the strikers had been deported, in each case based on other factors such as unrelated criminal charges, and in each of these cases Blanche claimed to be fighting for their return in legal proceedings (author interview with Francine Blanche, February 2012).

12. Full case study researched and written by Laetitia Dechaufour, available at http://www.mobilizing-against-inequality.info.

13. Full case study researched and written by Marion Quintin and Lowell Turner, available at http://www.mobilizing-against-inequality.info.

14. Full case study researched and written by Mirvat El Abd el ghani and Lowell Turner, available http://www.mobilizing-against-inequality.info.

15. For the British cases, see chapter 4 in this volume. For Dutch and Italian cases that include separate union structures for immigrant workers, see Marino (2012).

16. Most contemporary literature on French unions is quite pessimistic with regard to the influence and prospects for the labor movement. For an alternative grassroots perspective that points toward possibilities for revitalization, see Connolly (2010, 2012).

CHAPTER 6

The authors are greatly indebted to Otto Jacobi, Petra Wlecklik, and Wolf Jürgen Röder for their advice and support in completing this project. We also express our gratitude to several coresearchers and union activists, especially Chiara Benassi, Oliver Trede, Emilija Mitrovic, Ian Greer, Zyama Ciupijus, Nathan Lillie, Barbara Winkler, Sonja Marko, Agnes Schreieder, and Peter Bremme.

1. The DGB is by far the largest and dominant federation of unions in the private sector. This chapter deals with the policies of the DGB and its affiliates only.

2. Considerable fluctuation occurred however, especially during the recession of 1966–1967. See Kühne (2000: 45).

3. By 1987, over 7,000 migrant workers were elected members of works councils; in 1990 the number reached 8,381. See Kühne (2000: 56).

4. These were Turkey, Morocco, Tunisia, and Yugoslavia.

5. The rules on dual citizenship in Germany are highly prohibitive, especially regarding foreigners wishing to attain German citizenship while retaining their own. Stiff opposition comes mostly from conservatives and nationalists. Trade union support for this right for migrant workers has never been a high priority.

6. Statistical research by the union in this area revealed that fewer than 50,000 German domestic workers are paid consistent with workplace laws, including social security, and that there are several million other domestic workers who are part of this "informal" or illegal economy.

7. IG BCE was formed in 1997 through a merger of IG Chemie with Industriegewerkschaft Chemie-Papier-Keramik (Chemicals, Paper and Ceramics Union), Gewerkschaft Leder (Leather Workers' Union), and Industriegewerkschaft Bergbau und Energie (Mining and Energy Union). President of the 680,000-member union is Michael Vassiliadis, the highest ranking trade union leader of migrant descent in Germany.

8. In addition to the detailed case study provided at http://www.mobilizing-against-inequality.info by researchers Ian Greer, Zyama Ciupijus, and Nathan Lillie, they have collaborated on two other publications that provide considerable detail describing how difficult was the situation that IG Bau faced, as well as documenting the union's mistakes. See Lillie and Greer (2007) and Greer, Ciupijus, and Lillie (2013).

9. It is helpful to remember that much of this effort occurred during the time period that it was difficult for non-Germans to gain work permits.

10. The 2012 scandal around the failure of police and security forces to stop a series of murders committed by an underground right-wing terror group has raised fundamental questions about the political willingness of the authorities (especially the security forces) to take right extremism and antiforeigner attacks seriously.

CHAPTER 7

1. To repeat a point made earlier, for consistency we use the generic term "immigrant" here to designate the foreign-born. Increasingly, however, the term "migrant" is being used in the literature in the context of today's global economy. Bash, Blanc-Szanton, and Schiller (1992), for example, suggest that "migrant" better describes the circulatory nature of contemporary migration, not reducible to a linear movement from A to B, but rather characterized by the relatively short-term and multidirectional nature of workers' mobility and the continuing social, economic, political, and personal ties between the

societies of origin and immigration. Our intent is not to quibble about terminology so we leave this question unresolved, and at various points we use "immigrant" and "migrant" interchangeably.

2. The analysis presented in this chapter draws on case studies presented in chapters 3–6 of this volume. See case summaries in these chapters for more details, as well as full case study reports posted at http://www.mobilizing-against-inequality.info.

3. Another complication for terminology: in a context of open EU labor markets, it is increasingly common to refer to "migrants" rather than "immigrants" because of the gained free mobility across the EU internal borders.

4. The UMF is a grant scheme, launched by the previous Labour government, providing financial assistance to independent trade unions and their federations for a limited period. It was designed to support innovative modernization projects that contribute to a transformational change in the organizational effectiveness of a trade union (see chapter 4).

5. The main activity of the "holding branch" was to deliver services to the mostly Polish members (helping with work documents, language, etc.). The intended transfer to other union branches, however, did not occur, leaving the migrant branch isolated and unsustainable.

CHAPTER 8

1. For example, the Finnish Viking Line Case (C 438/05) and the Swedish Laval Case (C 341/05) in the European Court of Justice dealt with the interpretations of the PWD. In both cases, the court ruled in the company's favor, meaning that because there are no legal minimum wages in Sweden and Finland, the company needs to comply only with the home country's laws.

CHAPTER 9

I am gratefully indebted to the book editors for their contagious enthusiasm, vast knowledge base, and keen insights; to my fellow book contributors who continue to enrich my understanding of labor movements; to the many participants in the Transatlantic Social Dialogues in Ithaca and Europe with whom I have had the pleasure of eating, drinking, and merrily discussing labor and democracy. I thank Otto Jacobi, Wolf Jürgen Röder, and Nik Simon for helping me to further immerse myself in my family history; Hedy Weinberg and Hannah Cornfield for their constant inspiration; and Lowell Turner and Lee Adler for inviting me to participate as a coinvestigator and providing me with financial support from their research project on labor and immigrant integration in the Global North. I am also grateful to David Brady, Tom DiPrete, and Arne Kalleberg, sociologists extraordinaire who generously guided me to sources of international comparative data on labor and immigration.

1. The International Labour Organization (2012) defines "services" as "wholesale and retail trade, restaurants and hotels, transport, storage and communications, finance, insurance, real estate and business services, and community, social and personal services" and "industry" as "mining and quarrying, manufacturing, construction and public utilities (electricity, gas and water)."

2. Although employment has decreased in Germany's industry sector, German manufacturing is still regarded as the "motor for its economy, both during and after the global recession" (http://www.germany.info/Vertretung/usa/en/__pr/P__Wash/2012/05/24-manu facturing.html).

References

Adler, Lee, and Michael Fichter. 2012. "German Case Studies." Case studies prepared for this research project, available at http://www.mobilizing-against-inequality.info.

Alberti, Gabriella. 2010. "The Hotel Workers Campaign in London: 'Community Unionism' and the Challenges of Organizing Transient Labor." Working paper prepared for this research project, available at http://www.mobilizing-against-inequality.info.

——. 2011. "Cases of Immigrant Labor Organizing in the UK." Case studies prepared for this research project, available at http://www.mobilizing-against-inequality.info.

Alternet. 2011. "As London Explodes in Riots, There Is a Context That Can't Be Ignored: Brutal Cuts and Enforced Austerity Measures." August 9. http://www.alternet.org/newsandviews/article/647514/as_london_riots_enter_fourth_day%2C_there_is_a_context_that_can%27t_be_ignored/#paragraph2.

Always Wear a Smile: An Undocumented Domestic Worker Goes to Labour Court. 2008. Dir. Anne Frisius. http://www.kiezfilme.de/smile/index.htm.

Alzaga, Valery. 2011. "Justice for Janitors Campaign: Open-Sourcing Labour Conflicts against Global Neo-Liberalism." Open Democracy. http://www.opendemocracy.net/valery-alzaga/justice-for-janitors-campaign-open-sourcing-labour-conflicts-against-global-neo-libera.

Ancelovici, Marcos. 2010. "Globalization and the Formation of Trade Union Preferences in France." Paper presented at the Seventeenth International Conference of the Council for European Studies, Montreal, April 15–17.

Anderson, Bridget. 2010. "Migration, Immigration Controls and the Fashioning of Precarious Workers Work." *Work, Employment and Society* 24 (2): 300–317.

Anderson, Bridget, Martin Ruhs, Ben Rogaly, and Sarah Spencer. 2006. "Fair Enough? Central and East European Migrants in Low-Wage Employment in the UK." COMPAS (Centre on Migration, Policy and Society). http://www.compas.ox.ac.uk/fileadmin/files/Publications/Research_projects/Labour_markets/Changing_status/Fair%20enough%20paper%20-%201%20May%202006.pdf.

Anderson, Jeremy, Paula Hamilton, and Jane Wills. 2010. "The Multi-Scalarity of Trade Union Practice." In *Handbook of Employment and Society*, edited by S. McGrath Champ, A. Herod, and A. Rainnie, 383–397. Cheltenham, UK: Edward Elgar.

Andriessen, Iris, Eline Nievers, Jaco Dagevos, and Laila Faulk. 2012. "Ethnic Discrimination in the Dutch Labor Market: Its Relationship with Job Characteristics and Multiple Group Membership." *Work and Occupations* 39 (August): 237–269.

Appelbaum, Stuart. 2008. "An Injury to Eid Is an Injury to All." *In These Times*, December 9. http://www.inthesetimes.com/article/4047/.

Asset Skills. 2007. "The Role and Importance of Migrant Workers in the Cleaning Industry." http://www.assetskills.org/nmsruntime/saveasdialog.aspx?lID=322&sID=194.

Avci, Gamze, and Christopher McDonald. 2000. "Chipping Away at the Fortress: Unions, Immigration and the Transnational Labour Market." *International Migration* 38 (2): 191–213.

Baccaro, Lucio, Robert Boyer, Colin Crouch, Marino Regini, Paul Marginson, Richard Hyman, Rebecca Gumbrell-McCormick, and Ruth Milkman. 2010. "Discussion Forum I: Labour and the Global Financial Crisis." *Socio-Economic Review* 8: 341–376.

Baldassare, Mark, ed. 1994. *The Los Angeles Riots: Lessons for the Urban Future.* Boulder, CO: Westview Press.

Bamber, Greg J., Russell D. Lansbury, and Nick Wailes, eds. 2011. *International and Comparative Employment Relations: Globalisation and Change,* 5th ed. Los Angeles: Sage.

Barnier, Louis-Marie, and Evelyne Perrin. 2009. "La greve des sans-papiers d'avril 2008 et la CGT." In *Quand le travail se précarise, quelles résistances collectives?* Edited by Paul Bouffartigue and Sophie Béroud, 289–306. Paris: La Dispute.

Barron, Pierre, Anne Bory, Sebastien Chauvin, Nicolas Jounin, and Lucie Tourette. 2011. *On bosse ici, on reste ici! La grève des sans-papiers: une aventure inédite.* Paris: Editions La Découverte.

Bennhold, Katrin. 2005. "Suburban Officers Criticized as Insensitive to Racism." *New York Times,* November 8. http://www.nytimes.com/2005/11/08/international/europe/08police.html?pagewanted=all.

Benoit, Isabelle, Paul Gendrot, Anthony Jahn, Dominique Perez, Annick Vignes, and Brigitte Wieser. 2011. "Réseau Éducation Sans Frontières: Une vigilance citoyenne au service des sans papiers." *Recherche Socialiste* 54–55 (January–June): 21–34.

Bernhardt, Annette, Ruth Milkman, and Nik Theodore. 2009. "Broken Laws, Unprotected Workers: Violations of Employment and Labor Laws in America's Cities." Center for Urban Economic Development, National Employment Law Project, and UCLA Institute for Research on Labor and Employment, Los Angeles.

Béroud, Sophie, and Paul Bouffartigue. 2009a. "Précarisations salariales et resistances sociales: Vers un renouvellement du regard sociologique?" Paper presented at the 9èmes Journées Internationales de Sociologie du Travail, Nancy, June 25–26.

——, eds. 2009b. *Quand le travail se précarise, quelles resistances collectives?* Paris: La Dispute/SNEDIT.

Bertossi, Christophe. 2010. "What If National Models of Integration Did Not Exist?" *Perspectives on Europe* 40 (2): 50–56.

Biewen, Martin, and Andos Juhasz. 2010. "Understanding Rising Income Inequality in Germany." Discussion paper 5062, Institute for the Study of Labor, Bonn.

BIS (Department for Business, Innovation, and Skills). 2011. Trade Union Membership by Nikki Brownlie. http://www.bis.gov.uk/analysis/statistics/trade-union/union-membership-2011.

Borsos, John. 2012. "Wisconsin: Protest, Insurgency, Electoral Politics, and Labor's Future." *Working USA: Journal of Labor and Society* 15 (3): 441–446.

Bouchareb, Rachid, and Sylvie Contrepois. 2009. "The Impact of the Racial Quality Directive: A Survey of Trade Unions and Employers in Member States of the European Union—France." Fundamental Rights Agency. http://fra.europa.eu/fraWebsite/attachments/RED_France.pdf.

Brady, David. 2007. "Institutional, Economic, or Solidaristic? Assessing Explanations for Unionization Across Affluent Democracies." *Work and Occupations* 34 (February): 67–101.

——. 2009. *Rich Democracies, Poor People: How Politics Explain Poverty.* Oxford: Oxford University Press.

Briggs, Vernon. 2001. *Immigration and American Unionism.* Ithaca: Cornell University Press.

Broder, John. 2005a. "A Black-Latino Coalition Emerges in Los Angeles." *New York Times,* April 24. http://www.nytimes.com/2005/04/24/national/24mayor.html?ref=antoniovillaraigosa.

——. 2005b. "Latino Victor in Los Angeles Overcomes Division." *New York Times,* May 19. http://www.nytimes.com/2005/05/19/national/19angeles.html?ref= antoniovillaraigosa.

Bronfenbrenner, Kate, Sheldon Friedman, Richard W. Hurd, Rudolph A. Oswald, and Ronald L. Seeber, eds. 1998. *Organizing to Win: New Research on Union Strategies.* Ithaca: Cornell University Press.

Brown, Colin. 1984. "Black and White Britain: The Third PSI Survey." London: Heinemann Educational Books.

Burawoy, Michael. 2010. "From Polanyi to Pollyanna: The False Optimism of Global Labour Studies." *Global Labour Journal* 1 (2): 301–313.

——. 2011. "On Uncompromising Pessimism: Response to My Critics." *Global Labour Journal* 2 (1): 73–77.

Butterwegge, Carolin. 2012. *Von der "Gastarbeiter"—Anwerbung zum Zuwanderungsgesetz.* Bonn: Bundeszentrale für politische Bildung. http://www.bpb.de/ gesellschaft/migration/dossier-migration/56377/migration-in-der-brd.

California State Assembly. 1992. *To Rebuild Is Not Enough: Final Report and Recommendations of the Assembly Special Committee on the Los Angeles Crisis.* September 28. Sacramento: Assembly Publications Office.

Caroli, Eve, and Jérôme Gautié. 2008. *Low-Wage Work in France.* New York: Russell Sage Foundation.

Carré, Françoise, Marianne Ferber, Lonnie Golden, and Stephen Herzenberg. eds. 2000. *Nonstandard Work: The Nature and Challenges of Changing Employment Arrangements.* Champaign, IL: Industrial Relations Research Association.

Caspersz, Donella. 2010. "From Pollyanna to the Pollyanna Principle. A Response to Michael Burawoy's 'From Polanyi to Pollyanna: The False Optimism of Global Labour Studies.'" *Global Labour Journal:* 1 (3): 393–397.

Chin, Rita. 2007. *The Guest Workers Question in Postwar Germany.* Cambridge: Cambridge University Press.

Chun, Jennifer Jihye. 2009. *Organizing at the Margins: The Symbolic Politics of Labor in South Korea and the United States.* Ithaca: Cornell University Press.

Clawson, Dan. 2010. "'False' Optimism: The Key to Historic Breakthrough? A Response to Michael Burawoy's 'From Polanyi to Pollyanna: The False Optimism of Global Labour Studies.'" *Global Labour Journal* 1 (3): 398–400.

Colling, Trevor, and Mike Terry, eds. 2010. *Industrial Relations: Theory and Practice.* West Sussex: John Wiley & Sons.

Commons, John, David Saposs, Helen Sumner, E. Mittelman, H. Hoagland, John Andrews, and Selig Perlman. 1918. *History of Labour in the United States.* Vol. I. New York: Macmillan.

Connolly, Heather. 2010. "Organizing and Mobilizing Precarious Workers in France: The Case of Cleaners in the Railways." In *Globalisation and Precarious Forms of Production and Employment: Challenges for Workers and Unions,* edited by Carole Thornley, Steve Jeffreys, and Beatrice Appay, 182–198. Cheltenham: Edward Elgar.

——. 2010. *Renewal in the French Trade Union Movement: A Grassroots Perspective.* Oxford: Peter Lang.

——. 2012. "Radical Political Unionism in France and Britain: A Comparative Study of SUD-Rail and the RMT." *European Journal of Industrial Relations* 18 (3): 235–250.

Cornfield, Daniel. 2006. "Immigration, Economic Restructuring, and Labor Ruptures: From the Amalgamated to Change to Win." 2006. *WorkingUSA: The Journal of Labor and Society* 9 (June): 215–223.

——. 2007. "Seeking Solidarity . . . Why and With Whom?" In *Labor in the New Urban Battlegrounds: Local Solidarity in a Global Economy,* edited by Lowell Turner and Daniel B. Cornfield, 235–251. Ithaca: Cornell University Press.

Cornfield, Daniel. 2008. "Crackdown Shakes Up a Whole Community." *Tennessean,* March 5. http://tennessean.com/apps/pbcs.dll/article?AID=/20080305/OPIN ION01/803050411/1007/OPINION.

——. 2009a. "Immigrant Labor Organizing in a 'New Destination City': Approaches to the Unionization of African, Asian, Latino, and Middle Eastern Workers in Nashville." In *Global Connections & Local Receptions: Latino Migration to the Southeastern United States,* edited by Fran Ansley and Jon Shefner, 279–297. Knoxville: University of Tennessee Press.

——. 2009b. "Union Roles in Muslim Immigrant Worker Incorporation: The Case of Somalian Workers in Middle Tennessee." Case study prepared for this research project, available at http://www.mobilizing-against-inequality.info.

——. 2011. "Nashville Taxi Cab Drivers and Rural Tennessee Poultry Factory Workers." Case study prepared for this research project, available at http://www. mobilizing-against-inequality.info.

Cornfield, Daniel, and Angela Arzubiaga. 2004. "Immigrants and Education in the U.S. Interior: Integrating and Segmenting Tendencies in Nashville, Tennessee." *Peabody Journal of Education* 79 (2): 157–179.

Cornfield, Daniel, Angela Arzubiaga, Rhonda BeLue, Susan Brooks, Tony Brown, Oscar Miller, Douglas Perkins, Peggy Thoits, and Lynn Walker. "Final Report of the Immigrant Community Assessment of Nashville." 2003. Report prepared under contract #14830 for Metropolitan Government of Nashville and Davidson County, Tennessee. http://www.vanderbilt.edu/sociology/PDF/Nashville-Immigrant-Community-Assessment.pdf.

Cornfield, Daniel, and Bill Fletcher. 2001. "The U.S. Labor Movement: Toward a Sociology of Labor Revitalization." In *Sourcebook of Labor Markets: Evolving Structures and Processes,* edited by Ivar Berg and Arne Kalleberg, 61–82. New York: Kluwer Academic/Plenum.

Cornfield, Daniel, and Holly McCammon, eds. 2003. *Labor Revitalization: Global Perspectives and New Initiatives.* Amsterdam: Elsevier.

CoVe. 2008. "Hard Work, Hidden Lives." TUC report of the Commission on Vulnerable Employment, London.

CWOC. 2008. "Cleaning up the Carwash Industry. Empowering Workers and Protecting Communities." Report by the Carwash Workers Organizing Committee of the United Steelworkers. March 27.

Dagne, Ted. 2010. "Somalia: Current Conditions and Prospects for a Lasting Peace." CRS Report for Congress, Congressional Research Service, 7-5700, RL33911, February 4. http://fpc.state.gov/documents/organization/139249.pdf.

Datta, Kavita, Cathy McIlwaine, Yara Evans, Joanne Herbert, John May, and Jane Wills. 2007. "From Coping Strategies to Tactics: London's Low-Pay Economy and Migrant Labour." *British Journal of Industrial Relations* 45 (2): 404–432.

Dechaufour, Laetitia. 2009. "The Role of French Unions in the Civic Integration of Immigrant Workers." Case study prepared for this research project, available at http://www.mobilizing-against-inequality.info.

——. 2010. "The Griallete Case: I Don't Thank the CGT, Because We Are the CGT." Case study prepared for this research project, available at http://www.mobilizing-against-inequality.info.

Deeg, Richard. 2010. "Editor's Note." *Perspectives on Europe* 40 (2): 2–3.

Deutsche Welle. 2010. "Thousands Rally to Thwart Far-Right March on Duisburg Mosque." March 29. http://www.dw.de/thousands-rally-to-thwart-far-right-march-on-duisburg-mosque/a-5406493.

DGB (Deutscher Gewerkschaftsbund). 2008. *Nationaler Integrationsplan—DGB zieht Zwischenbilanz*. Pressemitteilung 133. Berlin: Author. http://www.dgb.de/presse/++co++dafcc92c-155f-11df-4ca9-00093d10fae2.

Didry, Claude, and Annette Jobert. 2008. "De la negotiation collective au dialogue social? Hypothèses sur l'évolution des relations professionelles en Europe." Paper presented at CAPRIGHT seminar I, Göttingen, September 25.

Donato, Katharine, Chizuko Wakabayashi, Shirin Hakimzadeh, and Amada Armenta. 2008. "Shifts in the Employment Conditions of Mexican Migrant Men and Women: The Effect of U.S. Immigration Policy." *Work and Occupations* 35 (November): 462–495.

Ebbinghaus, Bernhard. 2002. "Trade Unions' Changing Role: Membership Erosion, Organisational Reform and Social Partnership in Europe." *Industrial Relations Journal* 33 (5): 465–483.

EIRO. 2007. "Unions Fear ECJ Ruling in Laval Case Could Lead to Social Dumping." http://www.eurofound.europa.eu/eiro/2008/01/articles/eu0801019i.htm.

Eldring, Line, Ian Fitzgerald, and Jens Arnholtz. 2012. "Post-Accession Migration in Construction and Trade Union Responses in Denmark, Norway and the UK." *European Journal of Industrial Relations* 18 (1): 21–36.

Elger, Katrin. 2009. "Survey Shows Alarming Lack of Integration in Germany." *Spiegel Online International*, January 26. http://www.spiegel.de/international/germany/immigration-survey-shows-alarming-lack-of-integration-in-germany-a-603588.html.

Ellem, Bradon. 2003. "New Unionism in the Old Economy: Community and Collectivism in the Pilbara's Mining Towns." *Journal of Industrial Relations* 45 (4): 423–441.

Ellguth, Peter, and Susanne Kohaut. 2012. "Tarifbindung und betriebliche Interessenvertretung. Aktuelle Ergebnisse aus dem IAB-Betriebspanel 2011." *WSI-Mitteilungen* 65 (4): 297–305.

Erne, Roland. 2008. *European Unions: Labor's Quest for a Transnational Democracy*. Ithaca: Cornell University Press.

Ersanilli, Evelyn, and Sawitri Saharso. 2011. "The Settlement Country and Ethnic Identification of Children of Turkish Immigrants in Germany, France, and the Netherlands: What Role Do National Integration Policies Play?" *International Migration Review* 45 (Winter): 907–937.

Eurofound. 2010. "Country Profile France." http://www.eurofound.europa.eu/eiro/country/france.pdf.

Evans, Peter. 2000. "Fighting Marginalization with Transnational Networks: Counter-Hegemonic Globalization" *Contemporary Sociology* 29 (1): 230–241.

——. 2010. "Is It Labor's Turn to Globalize? Twenty-First Century Opportunities and Strategic Responses." *Global Labour Journal* 1 (3): 352–379.

Eyck, Tiffany Ten. 2009. "Muslim Workers Demand Time for Prayer at Meatpacking Plants." *Labor Notes*, October 19. from: http://labornotes.org/node/1946.

Fairbrother, Peter, and Charlotte Yates. 2003. *Trade Unions in Renewal*. London: Continuum.

Fantasia, Rick, and Kim Voss. 2004. *Hard Work: Remaking the American Labor Movement*. Berkeley: University of California Press.

Fernandez-Macías, Enrique. 2012. "Job Polarization in Europe? Changes in the Employment Structure and Job Quality, 1995–2007." *Work and Occupations* 39 (May): 157–182.

Fichter, Michael. 2008. "German Trade Unions and Right Extremism: Understanding Membership Attitudes." *European Journal of Industrial Relations* 14 (1): 65–84.

Findlay, Patricia, and Chris Warhurst. 2011. "Union Learning Funds and Trade Union Revitalization: A New Tool in the Toolkit?" *British Journal of Industrial Relations* 49 (S1): 115–134.

Fine, Janice. 2006. *Worker Centers: Organizing Communities at the Edge of the Dream.* Ithaca: Cornell University Press.

——. 2011a. "Laborers International Union of North America (LIUNA)." Working paper prepared for this research project, available at http://www.mobilizing-against-inequality.info.

——. 2011b. "New Forms to Settle Old Scores: Updating the Worker Centre Story in the United States." *Industrial Relations/Relations Industrielles* 66 (4): 604–627.

Fine, Janice, and Daniel Tichenor. 2009. "A Movement Wrestling: American Labor's Enduring Struggle with Immigration, 1866–2007." *Studies in American Political Development* 23 (1): 218–248.

——. 2012a. "Solidarities and Restrictions: Labor and Immigration Policy in the United States. *The Forum* 10 (1). http://www.degruyter.com/view/j/for.2012.10. issue-1/1540-8884.1495/1540-8884.1495.xml?format=INT.

——. 2012b. "An Enduring Dilemma: Immigration and Organized Labor in Western Europe and the United States." In *Oxford Handbook of the Politics of International Migration,* edited by Rosenblum and Tichenor, 532–572. Oxford: Oxford University Press.

Fiorito, Jack. 2004. "Union Renewal and the Organizing Model in the United Kingdom." *Labor Studies Journal* 29 (2): 21–53.

Fitzgerald, Ian. 2009. "Polish Migrant Workers in the North: New Communities, New Opportunities?" In *Community Unionism: A Comparative Analysis of Concepts and Contexts,* edited by J. McBride and I. Greenwood, 93–118. London: Palgrave Macmillan.

Fitzgerald, Ian, and Jane Hardy. 2010. "'Thinking Outside the Box'? Trade Union Organizing Strategies and Polish Migrant Workers in the United Kingdom." *British Journal of Industrial Relations* 48 (1): 131–150.

Flanders, Allan. 1972. "What Are Trade Unions For?" In *Trade Unions,* edited by W. McCarthy, 26–34. London: Pelican.

Fletcher, Bill, and Fernando Gapasin. 2008. *Solidarity Divided: The Crisis in Organized Labor and a New Path toward Social Justice.* Berkeley: University of California Press.

Fletcher, Bill, and Richard Hurd. 1998. "Beyond the Organizing Model: The Transformation Process in Local Unions." In *Organizing to Win: New Research on Union Strategies,* edited by S. Friedman, K. Bronfenbrenner, R. Hurd, R. Oswald, and R. Seeber, 37–53. Ithaca: Cornell University Press.

Fonow, Mary Margaret. 2003. *Union Women: Forging Feminism in the United Steelworkers of America.* Minneapolis: University of Minnesota Press.

Franklin, Sekou. n.d. "Driving Toward Poverty: Taxi Drivers in the *Athens* of the South." Preliminary report to Nashville-Davidson County's Transportation and Licensing Commission. http://www.thenashvillemovement.org/storage/reports/Driving%20Towards%20PovertyNEW.pdf.

Fraser, Alan. 2006. "Organizing Migrant Workers." Workers' Liberty. http://www.workersliberty.org/node/7196.

Freeman, Gary P. 1997. "Immigration as a Source of Political Discontent and Frustration in Western Democracies." *Studies in Comparative International Development* 32 (3): 42–65.

Frege, Carola, and John Kelly. 2003. "Union Revitalization Strategies." *Comparative Perspective European Journal of Industrial Relations* 9 (1): 7–24.

——. 2004. *Varieties of Unionism: Strategies for Union Revitalization in a Globalizing Economy*. Oxford: Oxford University Press.

Friedrich Ebert Stiftung. 2009. "Factors of Integration for Second and Third Generation Muslims: Perspectives from Germany and the United States." Transatlantic Academy Workshop Report, March. http://library.fes.de/pdf-files/bueros/usa/06213.pdf.

Frisius, Anne. 2008. *Always Wear a Smile: An Undocumented Domestic Worker Goes to Labour Court*. http://www.kiezfilme.de/smile/index.htm.

Fukuda-Parr, Sakiko. 2008. "The Human Impact of the Financial Crisis on Poor and Disempowered People and Countries." UN General Assembly: Interactive Panel on the Global Financial Crisis, New York.

Gall, Gregory, ed. 2003. *Union Organising*. London: Routledge.

Gall, Gregory, Adrian Wilkinson, and Richard Hurd, eds. 2011. *International Handbook on Labour Unions: Responses to Neo-Liberalism*. Northampton, MA: Edward Elgar.

Gammage, Sarah. 2008. "Working on the Margins: Migration and Employment in the United States." In *The Gloves-off Economy: Workplace Standards at the Bottom of America's Labor Market*, edited by Annette Bernhardt, Heather Boushey, Laura Dresser, and Chris Tilly, 137–162. Urbana-Champaign: Labor and Employment Relations Association.

Gangl, Markus. 2005. "Income Inequality, Permanent Incomes, and Income Dynamics: Comparing Europe to the United States." *Work and Occupations* 32 (May): 140–162.

Garea, Susan, and Sasha Alexandra Stern. 2010. "From Legal Advocacy to Organizing: Progressive Lawyering and the Los Angeles Car Wash Campaign." In *Working for Justice: The L.A. Model of Organizing and Advocacy*, edited by Ruth Milkman, Joshua Bloom, and Victor Narro, 125–140. Ithaca: Cornell University Press.

Gauci, Jean-Pierre. 2011. "Racism in Europe. ENAR Shadow Report 2010–2011." Brussels: European Network Against Racism.

Gautié, Jérôme, and John Schmitt. 2010. *Low-Wage Work in the Wealthy World*. New York: Russell Sage Foundation.

Geddes, Andrew. 2003. *The Politics of Migration and Immigration in Europe*. London: Sage.

Gentleman, Amelia, and Héléne Mulholland. 2010. "Unequal Britain: Richest 10% Are Now 100 Times Better Off Than the Poorest." *Guardian,* January 27. http://www.guardian.co.uk/society/2010/jan/27/unequal-britain-report.

Getman, Julius. 2010. *Restoring the Power of Unions: It Takes a Movement*. New Haven: Yale University Press.

Gordon, Jennifer. 2005. *Suburban Sweatshops: The Fight for Immigrant Rights*. Cambridge, MA: Belknap Press of Harvard University Press.

Graham, Sharon. 2007. "Organising out of Decline: The Rebuilding of the UK and Ireland Shop Stewards' Movement." http://www.employees.org.uk/annual-report-TGW.html.

Greene, Anne-Marie, Gill Kirton, and John Wrench. 2005. "Trade Union Perspectives on Diversity Management: A Comparison of the UK and Denmark." *European Journal of Industrial Relations* 11 (2): 141–149.

Greenhouse, Steven. 2001. "Los Angeles Warms to Labor Unions as Immigrants Look to Escape Poverty." *New York Times,* April 9. http://www.nytimes.com/2001/04/09/us/los-angeles-warms-to-labor-unions-as-immigrants-look-to-escape-poverty.html?ref=antoniovillaraigosa.

——. 2008a. "After 15 Years, North Carolina Plant Unionizes." *New York Times*, December 12. http://www.nytimes.com/2008/12/13/us/13smithfield.html.

——. 2008b. *The Big Squeeze: Tough Times for the American Worker*. New York: Alfred A. Knopf.

——. 2008c. "Muslim Holiday at Tyson Plant Creates Furor." *New York Times*, August 5. http://www.nytimes.com/2008/08/06/us/06muslim.html.

——. 2008d. "Tyson Reinstates Labor Day." *New York Times*, August 8. http://www.nytimes.com/2008/08/06/us/06muslim.html.

——. 2010. "Muslims Report Rising Discrimination at Work." *New York Times*, September 24. http://www.nytimes.com/2010/09/24/business/24muslim.html?sq=greenhousemuslims 2010&st=cse&adxnnl=1&scp=1&adxnnlx=1313169855-cFzRPTST+xYuJWVVCUpnGQ.

Greer, Ian. 2008. "Social Movement Unionism and Social Partnership in Germany: The Case of Hamburg's Hospitals." *Industrial Relations* 47 (4): 602–634.

Greer, Ian, Zinovijus Ciupijus, and Nathan Lillie. 2013. "The European Migrant Workers Union and the barriers to transnational industrial citizenship." *European Journal of Industrial Relations* 19 (1): 5–20.

Grieco, Elizabeth, and Edward Trevelyan. 2010. "Place of Birth of the Foreign-Born Population: 2009." U.S. Census Bureau American Community Survey Briefs, ACSBR/09-15. http://www.census.gov/prod/2010pubs/acsbr09-15.pdf.

Guardian and London School of Economics. 2011. *Reading the Riots: Investigating England's Summer of Disorder—Full Report*. http://www.guardian.co.uk/uk/interactive/2011/dec/14/reading-the-riots-investigating-england-s-summer-of-disorder-full-report.

Gumbrell-McCormick, Rebecca. 2011. "European Trade Unions and 'Atypical' Workers." *Industrial Relations Journal* 42 (3): 293–310.

Hall, Peter, and David Soskice, eds. 2001. *Varieties of Capitalism: The Institutional Foundations of Comparative Advantage*. New York: Oxford University Press.

——. 2001. "An Introduction to Varieties of Capitalism." In *Varieties of Capitalism: The Institutional Foundations of Comparative Advantage*, edited by Peter Hall and David Soskice, 1–70. New York: Oxford University Press.

Hagan, Jacqueline. 1998. "Social Networks, Gender, and Immigrant Incorporation: Resources and Constraints." *American Sociological Review* 63 (1): 55–67.

Hardt, Michael, and Antonio Negri. 2011. "The Fight for 'Real Democracy' at the Heart of Occupy Wall Street." *Foreign Affairs*, October 11. http://www.foreignaffairs.com/articles/136399/michael-hardt-and-antonio-negri/the-fight-for-real-democracy-at-the-heart-of-occupy-wall-street.

Hauptmeier, Marco, and Lowell Turner. 2007. "Political Insiders and Social Activists: Coalition Building in New York and Los Angeles." In *Labor in the New Urban Battlegrounds: Local Solidarity in a Global Economy*, edited by Lowell Turner and Daniel B. Cornfield, 129–143. Ithaca: Cornell University Press.

Haus, Leah. 1995. "Openings in the Wall: Transnational Migrants, Labor Unions and U.S. Immigration Policy." *International Organization* 49 (2): 299–304.

Hearn, Julie, and Monica Bergos. 2011. "Latin American Cleaners Fight for Survival: Lessons for Migrant Activism." *Race & Class* 53 (1): 65–82.

Heery, Edmund, John Kelly, and Jeremy Waddington. 2003. "Union Revitalization in Britain." *European Journal of Industrial Relations* 9 (1): 79–97.

Herod, Andy. 1998. *Organizing the Landscape: Geographical Perspectives on Labor Unionism*. Minneapolis: University of Minnesota Press.

——. 2001. *Labour Geographies: Workers and the Landscapes of Capitalism*. New York: Guilford Press.

Heyes, Jason. 2009. "Recruiting and Organising Migrant Workers through Education and Training: A Comparison of Community and the GMB." *Industrial Relations Journal* 40 (3): 182–197.

Hinton, William. 2005. "Pens Before Swords." *Nashville Scene*, December 8. http://www.nashvillescene.com/2005-12-08/news/pens-before-swords/.

Hirst, Paul, Grahame Thompson, and Simon Bromley. 2009. *Globalization in Question.* 3rd ed. Cambridge: Polity Press.

Hobsbawm, Eric. 1987. "Labour in the Great City." *New Left Review* 166: 37–51.

Holgate, Jane. 2005. "Organising Migrant Workers: A Case Study of Working Conditions and Unionisation at a Sandwich Factory in London." *Work, Employment & Society* 19 (3): 463–480.

——. 2009a. "Unionising the Low-Paid in London: The Justice for Cleaners Campaign." Case study prepared for this research project, available at http://www.mobilizing-against-inequality.info.

——. 2009b. "The Role of UK Unions in the Civic Integration of Immigrant Workers." Literature review prepared for this research project, available at http://www.mobilizing-against-inequality.info.

——. 2009c. "Contested Terrain: London's Living Wage Campaign and the Tensions between Community and Union Organising." In *Community Unionism: A Comparative Analysis of Concepts and Contexts,* edited by J. McBride and I. Greenwood, 49–74. London: Palgrave Macmillan.

——. 2011. "Temporary Migrant Workers and Labor Organization." *Working USA* 14 (2): 191–199.

——. 2012. "Temporary Migrant Workers and Labor Organization." In *Encyclopedia of Global Human Migration,* edited by I. Ness, vol. 5, 2925–2932. Hoboken, NJ: Wiley-Blackwell.

——. 2013. "Faith in Unions: From Safe Spaces to Organised Labour?" *Capital and Class* 37 (2): 239–262.

Holgate, Jane, and Jane Wills. 2007. "Organizing Labor in London: Lessons from the Living Wage Campaign." In *Labor in the New Urban Battlefields: Local Solidarity in a Global Economy,* edited by L. Turner and D. Cornfield, 211–223. Ithaca: Cornell University Press.

Holgate, Jane, Janroj Keles, Leena Kumarappan, and Anna Pollert. 2012. "Kurdish Migrant Workers in London: Experiences from an 'Invisible' Community." *Journal of Migration and Ethnic Studies* 38 (4): 595–612.

Hourwich, Isaac. 1912. *Immigration and Labor: The Economic Aspects of European Immigration to the United States.* New York: G.P. Putnam's Sons.

Hyman, Richard. 2007. "How Can Trade Unions Act Strategically?" *Transfer: European Review of Labour and Research* 13 (2): 193–210.

Hyman, Richard, and Anthony Ferner. 1994. *New Frontiers in European Industrial Relations.* Oxford: Basil Blackwell.

IAB (Institut für Arbeitsmarkt und Berufsforschung). 2009. *Handbuch Arbeitsmarkt 2009: Analysen, Daten Fakten Teil II.* Bielefeld: Bertelsmann.

IG Metall. 1966. *Die Ausländerwelle und die Gewerkschaften. Materialien und kritische Feststellungen zu den Versuchen, die deutschen und ausländischen Arbeitnehmer gegeneinander auszuspielen; Dokumentation.* Frankfurt am Main: IG Metall.

——. 2011a. "50 Jahre Anwerbeabkommen mit der Türkei." *IGMigration*, December 20. http://www.igmetall.de/cps/rde/xbcr/internet/igmigra20_final_0182111.pdf.

——. 2011b. *Mehr Chancen für Migranten.* Frankfurt am Main: IG Metall. http://www.igmetall.de/konsequente-gleichstellungspolitik-als-beitrag-zur-integration-9095.htm

International Labor Organization. 2012. *Key Indicators of the Labour Market.* 7th ed. http://kilm.ilo.org/manuscript/kilm04.asp.

International Labor Organization. 2012. *From Precarious Work to Decent Work.* http://www.ilo.org/wcmsp5/groups/public/---ed_dialogue/---actrav/documents/meetingdocument/wcms_179787.pdf

IOM. 2011. "World Migration Report: Communicating Effectively About Migration." International Organization for Migration, Geneva.

Iskander, Natasha. 2007. "Informal Work and Protest: Undocumented Immigrant Activism in France, 1996–2000." *British Journal of Industrial Relations* 45 (2): 309–334.

James, Phil, and Karmowska, Joanne. 2012. "Unions and Migrant Workers: Strategic Challenges in Britain." *Transfer: European Review of Labour and Research* 18 (2): 201–212.

Jamieson, Dave. 2013. "Car Wash Workers Ratify First Union Contract in New York City." *Huffington Post,* May 28. http://www.huffingtonpost.com/2013/05/28/car-wash-new-york-contract_n_3348685.html.

Jeffreys, Steve, and Beatrice Appay, eds. 2010. *Globalization and Precarious Forms of Production and Employment: Challenges for Workers and Unions.* Cheltenham: Edward Elgar Publishing.

Jenckner, Carolin. 2008. "Why No One Protested against Germany's Biggest Mosque." *Spiegel Online International,* October 27. http://www.spiegel.de/international/germany/muslim-integration-why-no-one-protested-against-germany-s-biggest-mosque-a-586759.html.

Jenkins, Roy. 1967. *Essays and Speeches.* Edited by Anthony Lester. London: Collins.

Jordan, Miriam. 2009. "Job Fight: Immigrants vs. Locals, Tennessee Residents Compete for Work They Once Scorned; An All-Night Wait for Slaughterhouse Shifts." *Wall Street Journal,* May 26. http://online.wsj.com/article/SB124303310871748603.html#.

Kalecki, Michal. 1943. "Political Aspects of Full Employment." *Political Quarterly* 14 (4): 322–331.

Kalleberg, Arne. 2011. *Good Jobs, Bad Jobs: The Rise of Polarized and Precarious Employment Systems in the United States, 1970s to 2000s.* New York: Russell Sage Foundation.

Kanas, Agnieszka, Barry Chiswick, Frank van Tubergen, and Tanja van der Lippe. 2012. "Social Contacts and the Economic Performance of Immigrants: A Panel Study of Immigrants in Germany." *International Migration Review* 46 (Fall): 680–709.

Kanas, Agnieszka, Frank van Tubergen, and Tanja van der Lippe. 2009. "Immigrant Self-Employment: Testing Hypotheses about the Role of Origin- and Host-Country Human Capital and Bonding and Bridging Social Capital." *Work and Occupations* 36 (August): 181–208.

Karahasan, Yilmaz. 2011. *50 Jahre Migration. Ohne Emanzipation—Wie geht es weiter? Vortrag zum "50 Jahre Anwerbeabkommen mit der Türkei."* http://www.migration-online.de/data/rbeabkommenmitdertrkeireferatiiiin12.punkteschrift2011.pdf.

Karmowska, Joanne, and James Phil. 2012. "Organizing Migrant Workers through Local Community: A Case Study of a Migrant Workers Union Branch." Twenty-Fourth SASE Annual Meeting, June 28–30, Cambridge.

Katz, Harry, and Owen Darbishire. 2000. *Converging Divergences: Worldwide Changes in Employment Systems.* Ithaca: Cornell University Press.

Katz, Harry, Thomas Kochan, and Alexander Colvin. 2008. *An Introduction to Collective Bargaining and Industrial Relations.* New York: McGraw-Hill.

Kelly, John, and Carola Frege. 2004. *Varieties of Unionism: Struggles for Union Revitalization in a Globalizing Economy.* Oxford: Oxford University Press.

Klein, N. 2008. "Banking Crisis: Expert Views: After a Week of Turmoil, Has the World Changed?" Guardian, September 20.

Koopmans, Ruud, Paul Statham, Marco Giugni, and Florence Passy. 2005. *Contested Citizenship: Immigration and Cultural Diversity in Europe.* Minneapolis: University of Minnesota Press.

Kromm, Chris. 2008. "Victory at Smithfield: Union Scores Big Win in North Carolina." *Facing South.* http://www.southernstudies.org/2008/12/victory-at-smithfield-union-scores-big-win-in-north-carolina.html

Kühn, Heinz. 1979. *Stand und Weiterentwicklung der Integration der ausländischen Arbeitnehmer und ihrer Familien in der Bundesrepublik Deutschland. Memorandum des Beauftragten der Bundesregierung.* Bonn: Bundesregierung. http://www.migration-online.de/data/khnmemorandum_1.pdf.

Kühne, Peter. 2000. "The Federal Republic of Germany: Ambivalent Promotion of Immigrants' Interests." In *Trade Unions, Immigration, and Immigrants in Europe, 1960–1993: A Comparative Study of the Attitudes and Actions of Trade Unions in Seven West European Countries,* edited by Rinus Penninx and Judith Roosblad, 39–64. New York: Berghahn Books.

Lambert, Rob. 2010. "Unionism in One Country is no Longer an Option: A Response to Michael Burawoy's; From Polanyi to Polyanna: The False Optimism of Global Labour Studies.'" *Global Labour Journal* 1 (3): 388–392.

Laybourn, Keith. 2009. "Trade Unionism in Britain since 1945." In *Trade Unionism since 1945: Towards a Global History. Volume 1: Western Europe, Eastern Europe, Africa and the Middle East,* edited by C. Phelan, 199–230. Oxford: Peter Lang.

Lee, Ching Kwan, and Yelizavetta Kofman. 2012. "The Politics of Precarity: Views beyond the United States." *Work and Occupations* 39 (November): 388–408.

Lehmer, Florian, and Johannes Ludsteck. 2011. "The Immigrant Wage Gap in Germany: Are East Europeans Worse Off?" *International Migration Review* 45 (Winter): 872–906.

Lena, Jennifer, and Daniel B. Cornfield. 2008. "Immigrant Arts Participation: A Pilot Study of Nashville Artists." In *Engaging Art: The Next Great Transformation of America's Cultural Life,* edited by Steven J. Tepper and Bill Ivey, 147–169. New York: Routledge.

Le Queux, Stéphane, and Ivan Sainsaulieu. 2010. "Social Movement and Unionism in France: A Case for Revitalization?" *Labor Studies Journal* 35 (4): 503–519.

Lillie, Nathan, and Ian Greer. 2007. "Industrial Relations, Migration, and Neoliberal Politics: The Case of the European Construction Sector." *Politics & Society* 35 (4): 551–581.

Lloyd, Caroline, Geoff Mason, and Ken Mayhew. 2008. *Low-Wage Work in the United Kingdom.* New York: Russell Sage Foundation.

Manhire, Toby. 2012. *The Arab Spring: Rebellion, Revolution, and a New World Order.* London: Guardian Books.

Marino, Stefania. 2012. "Trade Union Inclusion of Migrant and Ethnic Minority Workers: Comparing Italy and the Netherlands." *European Journal of Industrial Relations* 128 (1): 5–20.

Martínez Lucio, Miguel, and Robert Perrett. 2009a. "The Diversity and Politics of Trade Unions' Responses to Minority Ethnic and Migrant Workers: The Context of the UK." *Economic and Industrial Democracy* 30 (3): 324–347.

——. 2009b. "Meanings and Dilemmas in Community Unionism: Trade Union Community Initiatives and Black and Minority Ethnic Groups in the UK." *Work, Employment and Society* 23 (4): 693–710.

Marx, Jonathan. 2005. "Grazing in the Grass, Goats Are on the Rise in Tennessee." *Nashville Scene*, February 17. http://www.nashvillescene.com/2005-02-17/news/grazing-in-the-grass/.

Mathew, Biju. 2008. *Taxi: Cabs and Capitalism in New York City*. Ithaca: Cornell University Press.

McAlevey, Jane. 2013. "Make the Road New York: Success through 'Love' and 'Agitation.'" *The Nation*, June 10–17. http://www.thenation.com/article/174474/make-road-new-york-success-through-love-and-agitation?page=0,1.

McCluskey, Len. 2010. "Unions, Get Set for Battle: We Must Join Students in a Broad Strike Movement to Combat Attempts to Strangle the Welfare State." *Guardian*, December 19. http://www.guardian.co.uk/commentisfree/2010/dec/19/unions-students-strike-fight-cuts/print.

McGovern, Patrick. 2007. "Immigration, Labour Markets and Employment Relations: Problems and Prospects." *British Journal of Industrial Relations* 45 (2): 217–235.

McIlroy, J. 2008. "Ten Years of New Labour: Workplace Learning, Social Partnership and Union Revitalization in Britain." *British Journal of Industrial Relations* 46 (2): 283–313.

Menz, Georg. 2008. *The Political Economy of Managed Migration: Non-State Actors, Europeanization and the Politics of Designing Migration Policies*. Oxford: Oxford University Press.

"Metro Should Intervene for Cabbies." 2008. *Nashville City Paper*, August 4. http://www.nashvillecitypaper.com/content/city-voices/metro-should-intervene-cabbies.

Meurs, Dominique, Ariane Pailhé, and Patrick Simon. 2005. "Mobilité intergénérationnelle et persistence des inégalités." Documents de Travail 130. Paris: INED.

Miami Police Department. 1980. "Miami Riots, May 1980—After Action Report." NCJ 075626. https://www.ncjrs.gov/App/publications/Abstract.aspx?id=75626.

Milkman, Ruth, ed. 2000. *Organizing Immigrants: The Challenge for Unions in Contemporary California*. Ithaca: Cornell University Press.

——. 2006. *L.A. Story: Immigrant Workers and the Future of the U.S. Labor Movement*. New York: Russell Sage Foundation.

Milkman, Ruth, Joshua Bloom, and Victor Narro, eds. 2010. *Working for Justice: The L.A. Model of Organizing and Advocacy*. Ithaca: Cornell University Press.

Mishel, Lawrence, Jared Bernstein, and Heidi Shierholz, eds. 2009. *The State of Working America, 2008/2009*. Ithaca: Cornell University Press.

Mishel, Lawrence, Josh Bivens, Elise Gould, and Heidi Shierholz, eds. 2012. *The State of Working America*. 12th ed. Ithaca: Cornell University Press.

Mitrovic, Emilija. 2011. "Papierlos aber nicht rechtlos: der Fall Ana S." Case study prepared for this research project, available at http://www.mobilizing-against-inequality.info

Moore, Sian. 2009a. "Unison Migrant Workers Participation Project: Evaluation Report." http://www.unison.org.uk/acrobat/B4847.pdf.

——. 2009b. "Integrating Union Learning and Organising Strategies." UnionLearn Research Paper 8. London: TUC.

Mosley, Brian. 2007a. "Mosque Is Focus for Somali Worship." *Shelbyville Times-Gazette*, December 26. http://www.t-g.com/story/1299779.html.

——. 2007b. "Tyson Jobs Led Somalis to Shelbyville." *Shelbyville Times-Gazette*, December 27. http://www.t-g.com/story/1300124.html.

——. 2008a. "Refugee Program Stayed after Feds Confirm Fraud." *Shelbyville Times-Gazette*, November 16. http://www.t-g.com/story/1478471.html.

———. 2008b. "Tyson 'Regrets' Public Reaction." *Shelbyville Times-Gazette*, August 6. http://www.t-g.com/story/1450615.html.

———. 2008c. "Tyson Workers Revote; Labor Day Brought Back." *Shelbyville Times-Gazette*, August 8. http://www.t-g.com/story/1451367.html.

Munck, Ronaldo. P. 2010. "Globalization and the Labour Movement: Challenges and Responses." *Global Labour Journal* 1 (2): 218–232.

Mustchin, Stephen. 2012. "Unions, Learning, Migrant Workers and Union Revitalisation in Britain." *Work, Employment & Society* 26 (6): 951–967.

Narro, Victor. 2008. "Finding Synergy between Law and Organizing: Experiences from the Streets of Los Angeles." *Fordham Urban Law Journal* 35 (February): 339–372.

Narro, Victor, Kent Wong, and Janna Shadduck-Hernandez. 2007. "The 2006 Immigrant Uprising: Origins and Future." *New Labor Forum* 16 (1): 49–56.

Ness, Immanuel. 2005. *Immigrants, Unions, and the New U.S. Labor Market*. Philadelphia: Temple University Press.

New York Times. 2005. "Violence in France [map]." *New York Times*, November 8, p. A14.

Next Door Neighbors, Somali-Soomaali. 2009. Documentary. http://wnpt.org/productions/nextdoorneighbors/somali/index.html.

Nicot, Anne-Marie. 2007. "Employment and Working Conditions of Migrant Workers: France." Eurofound. http://www.eurofound.europa.eu/ewco/studies/tn0701038s/fr0701039q.htm.

Nissen, Bruce, and Monica Russo. 2007. "Strategies for Labor Revitalization: The Case of Miami." In *Labor in the New Urban Battlegrounds: Local Solidarity in a Global Economy,* edited by Lowell Turner and Daniel B. Cornfield, 147–162. Ithaca: Cornell University Press.

Nizzoli, Cristina. 2009. "De 'l'immigré clandestin' au 'travailleur sans papiers': L'Emergence d'une nouvelle figure sociale au travers du mouvement 2008–2009. Le role de la CGT." Memoire de master deuxième année de sociologie, Université de Provence.

Noiriel, Gérard. 1988. *Le Creuset Francais: Histoire de l'Immigration XIX–XX siècles*. Paris: Editions du Seuil.

Noiseux, Yanick. 2012. "Travail précaire et syndicalisme." *Les Nouveaux Cahiers du Socialisme* no. 7 (April). http://www.cerium.ca/Travail-precaire-et-syndicalisme.

OECD (Organization for Economic Cooperation and Development). 2008. "Growing Unequal? Income Distribution and Poverty in OECD Countries." http://www.oecd.org/dataoecd/45/24/41525323.pdf.

———. 2010. "Going for Growth." http://www.oecd.org/document/51/0,3343,en_2649_34117_44566259_1_1_1_1,00.html.

———. 2012. "Data on Inequality." www.oecd.org/els/social/inequality.

ONS (Office for National Statistics). 2010a. "Achur, James. Trade Union Membership 2010." http://stats.bis.gov.uk/UKSA/tu/TUM2010.pdf.

———. 2010b. "Estimated Population Resident in the UK by Foreign Country of Birth." http://www.ons.gov.uk/ons/rel/migration1/migration-statistics-quarterly-report/august-2011/population-by-country-of-birth-and-nationality-jan10-dec10.xls.

———. 2012. "Unemployment Statistics, UK." http://www.ons.gov.uk/ons/key-figures/index.html.

O'Reilly, Jacqueline, John Macinnes, Tizana Nazio, and Jose M. Roche. 2008. "The United Kingdom: From Flexible Employment to Vulnerable Workers." In *Gender and the Contours of Precarious Employment*, edited by Leah Vosko, Martha Macdonald, and Iain Campbell, 108–126. New York: Routledge.

Osmer, Chloe. 2009. "CLEAN Carwash Campaign Leadership Brigade." Internal Campaign Document.

Pai, Hsiao-Hung. 2004. "The Invisibles: Migrant Cleaners at Canary Wharf." *Feminist Review* 78 (1): 164–174.

Parks, James. 2003. "Immigrant Workers Freedom Ride." http://www.aflcio.org/about us/thisistheaflcio/publications/magazine/0903_iwfr.cfm.

Penninx, Rinus, and Judith Roosblad, eds. 2000. *Trade Unions, Immigration, and Immigrants in Europe, 1960–1993.* Amsterdam: Berghahn Books.

Perrett, Robert, and Miguel Martínez Lucio. 2008. "The Challenge of Connecting and Co-ordinating the Learning Agenda: A Case Study of a Trade Union Learning Centre in the UK." *Employee Relations* 30 (6): 623–639.

Perrett, Robert, Miguel Martínez Lucio, Jo McBride, and Steve Craig. 2012. "Trade Union Learning Strategies and Migrant Workers: Policies and Practice in a New-Liberal Environment." *Urban Studies* 49 (3): 649–667.

Pezet, Eric. 2012. "CFTC/CFDT Attitudes towards Immigration in the Paris Region: Making Immigrant Workers' Conditions a Cause." *Urban Studies* 49 (30): 685–701.

Pichler, Florian. 2011. "Success on European Labor Markets: A Cross-National Comparison of Attainment between Immigrant and Majority Populations." *International Migration Review* 45 (Winter): 938–978.

Piotet, Francoise. 2009. "La CGT, une anarchie (plus ou moins) organisée?" *Politix* 85 (1): 9–30.

Plotke, David. 1999. "Immigration and Political Incorporation in the Contemporary United States." In *The Handbook of International Migration: The American Experience,* edited by Charles Hirschman, Philip Kasinitz, and Josh DeWind, 294–318. New York: Russell Sage.

Polanyi, Karl. 1944. *The Great Transformation: The Political and Economic Origins of Our Time.* Boston: Beacon.

——. 1957. "The Economy as Instituted Process." In *The Sociology of Economic Life,* edited by Mark Granovetter and Richard Swedberg, 22–32. Boulder, CO: Westview Press.

Popp, Maximilian, Özlem Gezer, and Christoph Scheuermann. 2011. "German Turks Struggle to Find Their Identity." *Spiegel Online International,* November 2. http://www.spiegel.de/international/germany/at-home-in-a-foreign-country-german-turks-struggle-to-find-their-identity-a-795299.html.

Porter, Bruce, and Marvin Dunn. 1984. *The Miami Riot of 1980.* Lexington, MA: Lexington Books.

Portes, Alejandro. 2009. "The New Latin Nation: Immigration and the Hispanic Population of the United States." In *Global Connections and Local Receptions: Latino Migration to the Southeastern United States,* edited by Fran Ansley and Jon Shefner, 3–34. Knoxville: University of Tennessee Press.

Portes, Alejandro, and Rubén Rumbaut. 2006. *Immigrant America: A Portrait.* 3rd ed. Berkeley: University of California Press.

Prasad, Monica. 2005. "Why Is France so French? Culture, Institutions, and Neoliberalism, 1974–1981." *American Journal of Sociology* 111: 357–407.

Pries, Ludger. 2003. "Labour Migration, Social Incorporation and Transmigration in the Old and New Europe: The Case of Germany in a Comparative Perspective." *Transfer* 9 (3): 432–451.

Quintin, Marion. 2009 and 2010. "The CGT Campaign Supporting the 'Sans Papiers'—Acts I and II." Case studies prepared for this research project, available at http://www.mobilizing-against-inequality.info.

Rainbird, Helen, and Mark Stuart. 2011. "The State and the Union Learning Agenda in Britain." *Work, Employment & Society* 25 (2): 202–217.

Rainnie, Al, Andy Herod, and Susan McGrath Champ. 2007. "Spatialising Industrial Relations." *Industrial Relations Journal* 38 (2): 102–118.

Ram, Monder, Paul Edwards, and Trevor Jones. 2007. "Staying Underground: Informal Work, Small Firms, and Employment Regulation in the United Kingdom." *Work and Occupations* 34 (August): 318–344.

Reich, Robert. 2010. *Aftershock: The Next Economy and America's Future.* New York: Alfred A. Knopf.

Reynolds, David. 2007. "Building Coalitions for Regional Power." In *Labor in the New Urban Battlegrounds: Local Solidarity in a Global Economy,* edited by Lowell Turner and Daniel B. Cornfield, 73–94. Ithaca: Cornell University Press.

Rienzo, Cinzia. 2011. "Migrants in the UK Labour Market: An Overview." Oxford: Migration Observatory.

Roca-Servat, Denisse. 2010. "Justice for Roofers: Toward a Comprehensive Union Organizing Campaign Involving Latino Construction Workers in Arizona." *Labor Studies Journal* 35 (3): 343–363.

——. 2011. "The Struggle for Rights and Labor-Community Coalitions: The Los Angeles CLEAN Carwash Campaign." Case study prepared for this research project, available at http://www.mobilizing-against-inequality.info.

Rogers, Ali, Bridgit Anderson, and Nick Clark. 2009. "Recession, Vulnerable Workers and Immigration. Background Report." Centre on Migration, Policy and Society (COMPAS). http://www.compas.ox.ac.uk/research/labourmarkets/labour marketproject/.

Ross, Janell. 2008. "Cultures Clash in Shelbyville." *Tennessean*, August 24.

Rustenbach, Elisa. 2010. "Sources of Negative Attitudes toward Immigrants in Europe: A Multi-Level Analysis." *International Migration Review* 44 (Spring): 53–77.

RWDSU. 2008. "Executive Board Focuses on Organizing Strategies, Economy's Impact on Workers." November 25. http://www.rwdsu.ca/news_view.php?id=28&rwdsu session=ca40ac1408a60c8a9b1dce0ec74683e0.

Ryan, Louise, Rosemary Sales, Mary Tilki, and Bernadetta Siara. 2008. "Social Networks, Social Support and Social Capital: The Experiences of Recent Polish Migrants in London." *Sociology* 42 (4): 672–690.

Sassen, Saskia. 2001. *The Global City: New York, London, Tokyo.* Princeton: Princeton University Press.

Schain, Martin A. 1994. "Ordinary Poliltics: Immigrants, Direct Action, and the Political Process in France." *French Politics and Society* 12 (2–3): 65–84.

——. 2008. *The Politics of Immigration in France, Britain, and the United States: A Comparative Study.* New York: Palgrave Macmillan.

Schmidt, Werner, and Andrea Müller. 2012. *German Co-determination and Migrant Integration at Industrial Workplaces.* Paper presented at the Sixteenth ILERA World Congress, Philadelphia, PA, July 2–5. http://ilera2012.wharton.upenn. edu/RefereedPapers/MullerAndrea%20WernerSchmidt.pdf.

Schmitter, Philippe, and Gerhard Lehmbruch, eds. 1979. *Trends in Corporatist Intermediation.* Beverly Hills: Sage.

Seifert, Wolfgang. 2012. *Geschichte der Zuwanderung nach Deutschland nach 1950.* Berlin: Bundeszentrale für politische Bildung. http://www.bpb.de/politik/ grundfragen/deutsche-verhaeltnisse-eine-sozialkunde/138012/geschichte-der-zuwanderung-nach-deutschland-nach-1950.

Semple, Kirk. 2008. "Somali Immigrant Workers Test a Nebraska Town." *New York Times*, October 16. http://www.nytimes.com/2008/10/16/world/americas/16iht-letter.1.17008659.html.

Siebenhüter, Sandra. 2011. "Integrationshemmnis Leiharbeit: Auswirkungen von Lei-harbeit auf Menschen mit Migrationshintergrund." OBS-Arbeitsheft 69, Otto Brenner Stiftung.

Simms, Melanie, Jane Holgate, and Edmund Heery. 2012. *Union Voices. Tactics and Tensions in UK Organizing.* Ithaca: Cornell University Press.

Smith, Craig. 2005. "Immigrant Rioting Flares in France for Ninth Night," *New York Times,* November 5. http://www.nytimes.com/2005/11/05/international/europe/05france.html?pagewanted=all&_r=0.

Smith, Helena. 2012. "Greek Crackdown on Illegal Immigrants Leads to Mass Arrests." *Guardian,* August 7. http://www.theguardian.com/world/2012/aug/07/greece-crackdown-illegal-immigrants-arrest.

Solomos, John, and John Wrench. 1993. *Racism and Migration in Western Europe.* London: Berg.

Sonenshein, Raphael. 1993. *Politics in Black and White: Race and Power in Los Angeles.* Princeton: Princeton University Press.

The staff of the *Los Angeles Times.* 1992. *Understanding the Riots: Los Angeles before and after the Rodney King Case.* Los Angeles: Los Angeles Times.

Stan, Adele. 2011. "National Taxi Workers Alliance Gets AFL-CIO Charter at Future of Work Event." AFL-CIO Now, October 20. http://www.aflcio.org/Blog/Organizing-Bargaining/National-Taxi-Workers-Alliance-Gets-AFL-CIO-Charter-at-Future-of-Work-Event.

Standing, Guy. 2011. *The Precariat: The Dangerous New Class.* London: Bloomsbury Academic.

Statistisches Bundesamt. 2013. *Migration.* https://www.destatis.de/EN/FactsFigures/SocietyState/Population/Migration/Tables/MigrationTotal.html

Steinmo, Sven, Kathleen Thelen, and Frank Longstreth, eds. 1992. *Structuring Politics: Historical Institutionalism in Comparative Analysis.* Cambridge: Cambridge University Press.

Stiglitz, Joseph. 2006. *Making Globalization Work.* New York: W.W. Norton.

Streeck, Wolfgang. 2009. *Re-Forming Capitalism: Institutional Change in the German Political Economy.* Oxford: Oxford University Press.

——. 2011. "The Crises of Democratic Capitalism." *New Left Review* 71 (September/October): 5–29.

——. 2011. "Taking Capitalism Seriously: Towards an Institutionalist Approach to Contemporary Political Economy." *Socio-Economic Review* 9 (1): 137–167.

Stuart, Mark, Hugh Cook, Jo Cutter, and Jonathan Winterton. 2010. "Evaluation of the Union Learning Fund and UnionLearn." A report of the 2009 survey of union learning representatives and their managers. Centre for Employment Relations Innovation and Change at Leeds University Business School.

Suleyman, Remziya. 2012. "Tennessee Muslims Instrumental in Getting the Vote Out." *Huffington Post,* November 7. http://www.huffingtonpost.com/common-ground-news-service/tennessee-muslims-instrumental-in-getting-the-vote-out_b_2088299.html.

Summers, Deborah. 2009. "Brown Stands by British Jobs for British Workers Remark." *Guardian,* January 30. http://www.theguardian.com/politics/2009/jan/30/brown-british-jobs-workers.

Tapia, Maite. 2012. "Marching to Different Tunes: Commitment and Culture as Mobilizing Mechanisms of Trade Unions and Community Organizations." *British Journal of Industrial Relations* 51 (4): 666–688.

Tattersall, Amanda. 2010. *Power in Coalition: Strategies for Strong Unions and Social Change.* Ithaca: Cornell University Press.

Taylor, Charles. 1992. *Multiculturalism and "The Politics of Recognition."* Ed. Amy Gutmann. Princeton: Princeton University Press.

Tennessee Immigrant and Refugee Rights Coalition. 2008. "Taxi Cab Association." April 30. http://www.tnimmigrant.org/news.php?viewStory=136.

The Telegraph. 2011. "Nicolas Sarkozy Declares Multiculturalism Had Failed." February 11. http://www.telegraph.co.uk/news/worldnews/europe/france/8317497/Nicolas-Sarkozy-declares-multiculturalism-had-failed.html.

Terray, Emmanuel. 1999. "Le Travail des Etrangers en Situation Irrégulière ou la Délocalisation sur Place." In *Sans-Papiers: l'Archaïsme Fatal,* edited by Etienne Balibar, Jacqueline Costa-Lascoux, Chemillier-Gendreau, and Emmanuel Terray, 9–34. Paris: La Découverte.

Thomas, Jo. 1981. "Study Finds Miami Riot Was Unlike Those of 60's." *New York Times,* May 17. http://www.nytimes.com/1981/05/17/us/study-finds-miami-riot-was-unlike-those-of-60-s.html.

Thornley, Carole, Steve Jeffreys, and Beatrice Appay, eds. 2010. *Globalisation and Precarious Forms of Production and Employment: Challenges for Workers and Unions.* Cheltenham: Edward Elgar.

Tobia, P.J. 2006. "The Nativists Are Restless: The Backlash against Immigrants Is at Full Boil in Tennessee." *Nashville Scene,* November 30. http://www.nashvillescene.com/Stories/Cover_Story/2006/11/30/The_Nativists_Are_Restless/index.shtml.

Townsend, Mark. 2010. "Black People Are 26 Times More Likely Than Whites to Face Stop and Search." *Guardian,* October 17. http://www.guardian.co.uk/uk/2010/oct/17/stop-and-search-race-figures.

Trede, Oliver. 2011. "The IG Metall and the Integration of Immigrant Workers in Kiel." Case study prepared for this research project, posted at http://www.mobilizing-against-inequality.info.

TUC. 2009. "Report of the TUC Black Workers' Conference." http://www.tuc.org.uk/equality/tuc-16413-f0.cfm.

Turner, Lowell. 2003. "Reviving the Labor Movement: A Comparative Perspective." In *Labor Revitalization: Global Perspectives and New Initiatives,* edited by Daniel Cornfield and Holly McCammon, 23–58. Amsterdam: Elsevier.

——. 2005. "From Transformation to Revitalization: A New Research Agenda for a Contested Global Economy." *Work and Occupations* 32 (4): 383–399.

——. 2007a. "The Advantages of Backwardness: Lessons for Social Europe from the American Labour Movement." *Social Europe* 2 (4): 147–153.

——. 2007b. "An Urban Resurgence of Social Unionism." In *Labor in the New Urban Battlegrounds: Local Solidarity in a Global Economy,* edited by Lowell Turner and Daniel B. Cornfield, 1–18. Ithaca: Cornell University Press.

——. 2009. "Institutions and Activism: Crisis and Opportunity for a German Labor Movement in Decline." *Industrial and Labor Relations Review* 62 (3): 294–312.

——. 2011. "A Future for the Labor Movement?" In *International Handbook on Labour Unions: Responses to Neo-Liberalism,* edited by Gregory Gall, Adrian Wilkinson, and Richard Hurd, 311–328. Northampton, MA: Edward Elgar.

Turner, Lowell, and Daniel B. Cornfield, eds. 2007. *Labor in the New Urban Battlegrounds: Local Solidarity in a Global Economy.* Ithaca: Cornell University Press.

Turner, Lowell, Harry Katz, and Richard Hurd, eds. 2001. *Rekindling the Movement: Labor's Quest for Relevance in the Twenty-First Century.* Ithaca: Cornell University Press.

Tyson Foods. 2008a. "Labor Day Reinstated as Paid Holiday at Shelbyville, TN, Plant; Tyson Foods Requested Change from Union." Press release, August 8. http://www.tyson.com/Corporate/PressRoom/ViewArticle.aspx?id=3021.

Tyson Foods. 2008b. "Labor Day Still Recognized at Tyson Foods; Union Contract Provision only at Shelbyville, TN Plant." Press release, August 4. http://www.tyson.com/Corporate/PressRoom/ViewArticle.aspx?id=3012.

UFCW. 2008. "Workers at the World's Largest Meatpacking Plant Choose Union Representation." Press release, December 12. http://www.ufcw.org/press_room/index.cfm?pressReleaseID=415.

——. 2009. "Workers at World's Largest Pork Plant Ratify First-Ever Union Contract." Press release, July 1. http://www.ufcw.org/press_room/index.cfm?pressReleaseID=446.

UnionLearn. 2007. *Migrant Workers in the Labour Market: The Role of Unions in the Recognition of Skills and Qualifications.* Lucio, Miguel Martínez, Robert Perrett, Jo McBride, and Steve Craig. Research Paper 7. http://www.unionlearn.org.uk/sites/default/files/7.pdf.

Unite. 2011. "Community Membership Pledge to Organise the Marginalised—and Revolutionise British Trade Unionism." http://www.unitetheunion.org/news__events/latest_news/community_membershippledge_to.aspx.

U.S. Bureau of African Affairs. 2010. "Background Note: Somalia." http://www.state.gov/r/pa/ei/bgn/2863.htm.

U.S. Bureau of Labor Statistics. 1994. "Union Members in 1993." News release USDL: 94-58, February 9. http://www.bls.gov/news.release/history/union2_020994.txt.

——. 2011. "Union Members—2010." News release USDL: 11-0063, January 21. http://www.bls.gov/news.release/union2.t01.htm.

——. 2012a. "Labor Force Statistics from the Current Population Survey." http://www.bls.gov/cps/cpsaat01.htm.

——. 2012b. "Labor Force Statistics from the Current Population Survey." http://data.bls.gov/pdq/SurveyOutputServlet.

U.S. Bureau of the Census. 2008. "2008 American Community Survey." http://factfinder.census.gov/servlet/DTTable?_bm=y&s_name=ACS_2008_1YR_G00_&-CONTEXT=dt&-mt_name=ACS_2008_1YR_G2000_B04001&-redoLog=true&-geo_id=01000US&-format=&-_lang=en&-SubjectID=17477948.

——. 2010. "2010 Statistical Abstract of the United States." http://www.census.gov/prod/2009pubs/10statab/pop.pdf.

USW. 2010. "USW Taxi Drivers Union Offers Free Rides to Flood Victims in Nashville." http://www.usw.org/media_center/news_articles?id=0560.

Van Dyke, Nella, and Holly McCammon, eds. 2010. *Strategic Alliances: Coalition Building and Social Movements. Volume 34: Social Movements, Protest and Contention.* Minneapolis: University of Minnesota Press.

ver.di. 2009. "Der Fall Ana S.—Eine Haushälterin ohne Papiere zieht vors Arbeitsgericht." August 17. http://besondere-dienste.hamburg.verdi.de/themen/migrar/ana.

Virdee, Satnam, and Keith Grint. 1994. "Black Self-Organization in Trade Unions." *Sociological Review* 42 (2): 202–226.

Vosko, Leah, Martha Macdonald, and Iain Campell, eds. 2008. *Gender and the Contours of Precarious Employment.* New York: Routledge.

Voss, Kim, and Irene Bloemraad, eds. 2011. *Rallying for Immigrant Rights: The Fight for Inclusion in 21st Century America.* Berkeley: University of California Press.

Wahlbeck, Östen. 1998. "Community Work and Exile Politics: Kurdish Refugee Associations in London." *Journal of Refugee Studies* 11 (3): 215–230.

Waldinger, Roger, and Michael Lichter. 2003. *How the Other Half Works: Immigration and the Social Organization of Labor.* Berkeley: University of California Press.

WASH (Workers Aligned for a Sustainable and Healthy New York). 2012. "The Dirty Business of Cleaning NYC's Cars: Carwash Workers Face Low Pay. Offensive Conditions, and Poor Treatment." http://www.washnewyork.org/files/car-wash-report.pdf.

Waterman, Peter. 1993. "Social-Movement Unionism: A New Union Model for a New World Order?" *Review (Fernand Braudel Center)* 16 (3): 245–278.

——. 2011. "Beyond Polanyi and Pollyanna—Oscar Wilde?" *Global Labour Journal* 2 (1): 78–83.

Watt, Andrew. 2009. "Six Things That Didn't Cause the Crisis—But Really Ought to Have." *Social Europe Journal* (September 24). http://www.social-europe.eu/2009/09/six-things-that-didnt-cause-the-crisis-but-really-ought-to-have/.

Watt, Andrew, and Andreas Botsch, eds. 2010. *After the Crisis: Towards a Sustainable Growth Model.* Brussels: European Trade Union Institute.

Watts, Julie R. 2002. *Immigration Policy and the Challenge of Globalization: Unions and Employers in Unlikely Alliance.* Ithaca: Cornell University Press.

Weaver, Matthew. 2010. "Angela Merkel: German Multiculturalism Has 'Utterly Failed.'" *Guardian,* October 17. http://www.guardian.co.uk/world/2010/oct/17/angela-merkel-german-multiculturalism-failed.

Webster, Edward, Rob Lambert, and Andreis Bezuidenhout. 2008. *Grounding Globalization: Labour in the Age of Insecurity.* Oxford: Blackwell.

Weil, David. 2010. "Improving Workplace Conditions through Strategic Enforcement." Report to the Wage and Hour Division of the Department of Labor, Washington, DC.

——. 2011. "Enforcing Labour Standards in Fissured Workplaces: The US Experience." *Economic and Labour Relations Review* 22 (2): 33–54.

Wilkinson, Richard, and Kate Pickett. 2009. *The Spirit Level: Why Greater Equality Makes Societies Stronger.* New York: Bloomsbury Press.

Willon, Phil. 2009. "Villaraigosa's Tightrope: Cut City Spending without Angering Labor," *Los Angeles Times,* April 14. http://articles.latimes.com/2009/apr/14/local/me-mayor-unions14.

Wills, Jane. 2001. "Community Unionism and Trade Union Renewal in the UK: Moving Beyond the Fragments at Last?" *Transactions of the Institute of British Geographers* 26 (4): 465–483.

——. 2004. "Organising the Low Paid: East London's Living Wage Campaign as a Vehicle for Change." In *The Future of Worker Representation,* edited by G. Healy, E. Heery, P. Taylor, and W. Brown, 264–282. Basingstoke: Palgrave Macmillan.

——. 2008. "Making Class Politics Possible: Organizing Contract Cleaners in London." *International Journal of Urban and Regional Research* 32 (2): 305–323.

——. 2012. "The Geography of Community and Political Organisation in London Today." *Political Geography* 3 (2): 114–126.

Wills, Jane, and Melanie Simms. 2004. "Building Reciprocal Community Unionism in the UK." *Capital and Class* 82 (Spring): 59–84.

Winchester, David. 2007. "Employment and Working Conditions of Migrant Workers: United Kingdom." Eurofound. http://www.eurofound.europa.eu/ewco/studies/tn0701038s/uk0701039q.htm.

Winder, Robert. 2004. *Bloody Foreigners: The Story of Immigration to Britain.* London: Little, Brown.

Wrench, John. 1997. *Trade Unions, Migrants and Ethnic Minorities in the European Union: National Differences and Common Dilemmas.* Esbjerg, Denmark: South Jutland University Press.

——. 2000. "British Unions and Racism: Organisational Dilemmas in an Unsympathetic Climate." In *Trade Unions, Immigration and Immigrants, 1960–1993: A Comparative Study of the Actions of Trade Unions in Seven West European Countries,* edited by R. Penninx and J. Roosblad, 133–155. New York: Berghahn Books.

——. 2004. "Trade Union Responses to Immigrants and Ethnic Inequality in Denmark and the UK: the Context of Consensus and Conflict." *European Journal of Industrial Relations* 10 (1): 7–30.

——. 2007. *Diversity Management and Discrimination: Immigrants and Ethnic Minorities in the EU.* Aldershot: Ashgate.

Zatz, Noah. 2008. "Working Beyond the Reach or Grasp of Employment Law." In *The Gloves-Off Economy: Workplace Standards at the Bottom of America's Labor Market,* edited by Annette Bernhardt, Heather Boushey, Laura Dresser, and Chris Tilly, 31–64. Champaign, IL: Labor and Employment Relations Association.

Contributors

Lee H. Adler teaches public sector collective bargaining and public education law at the ILR School at Cornell University, and represents public sector unions throughout New York state.

Gabriella Alberti is lecturer in Work and Employment Relations at Leeds University Business School.

Daniel B. Cornfield is professor of sociology at Vanderbilt University and editor of the journal *Work and Occupations*.

Michael Fichter teaches international political economy at the Global Labour University in Berlin.

Janice Fine is associate professor of Labor Studies and Employment Relations at the School of Management and Labor Relations, Rutgers University. Prior to entering academia, Fine worked as an organizer for many years.

Jane Holgate is professor of work and employment relations at Leeds University Business School and coordinator of the London Unions Research Network and the Critical Labour Studies Network.

Denisse Roca-Servat is assistant professor and researcher of the Territory Group (Grupo Territorio) at the School of Social Sciences at the Universidad Pontificia Bolivariana in Medellin, Colombia.

Maite Tapia is assistant professor at the School of Human Resources and Labor Relations at Michigan State University.

Lowell Turner is professor of international and comparative labor at the ILR School at Cornell University, and director of the Worker Institute at Cornell.

Index

ACORN, 173n.16

AFL-CIO
immigrant worker policy shift (2000), viii, 9, 35, 37, 38, 39, 46, 50, 170n.13, 172nn.1,6,7
Immigrant Workers Freedom Ride, viii, 10, 38, 158–159, 172n.8
and labor-community coalitions, 40
legal strategies, 149
and national immigration policies, 144, 172n.6
and 1980s employer sanction policy, 172n.2
Organizing Institute, 44
Sweeney election, 39
taxi workers inclusion, ix, 37, 174n.32
undocumented workers policy, 138
See also CLEAN Carwash Campaign

AFSCME (American Federation of State, County and Municipal Employees), 41, 172n.10, 173nn.15,16

AFT (American Federation of Teachers), 172n.10, 173nn.15,16

Agee, Lynn, 48

American Federation of State, County and Municipal Employees (AFSCME), 41, 172n.10, 173nn.15,16

American Federation of Teachers (AFT), 172n.10, 173nn.15,16

Amicus (United Kingdom), 175n.4

anti-immigrant attitudes. *See* nativism

APEX strike (United Kingdom), 54

Arab Spring (2012), 139

Arizona Justice for Roofers (1999–2006) (United States), 44–45, 159, 173n.24, 174n.27

Association of Professional, Executive, Clerical and Computer Staff (APEX) (United Kingdom), 54

austerity measures, 5, 56–57

Autre Monde (France), 23, 77

Avendaño, Ana, vii–x, 172n.6

Aznar, Jose Maria, 175n.1

Bamber, Greg, 169n.1

Beck, Lewis, 48

biculturalism, 45, 46, 159

Billon, Maud, 77

blaming and shaming tactics, 21, 117, 125–126

Blanche, Francine, 76, 176n.11

BNP (British National Party), 62, 146, 161–162

Brandworkers (United States), 42, 173n.20

British immigrant organizing, 52–68
challenges, 64–65, 66–68
and civil unrest, 160–161
current context, 55–57
and economic crisis, 55–57
and economic inequality, 18, 57
educational initiatives, 58, 59, 60–61, 64, 66, 67, 145–146
Filipino care workers campaign, 62–63, 161
GMB migrant workers' branch, 60–61, 63–64, 120, 161
historical context, 53–55
hotel workers campaign (2007–2009), 63, 67, 117–118, 121, 161
and immigrant identities, 67, 120–121, 137
and immigrant integration models, 52, 161, 175n.1
immigrant worker terminology, 170n.12
and labor-community coalitions, 10, 58–59, 62–63, 66, 67–68, 123–124, 141
and labor movement revitalization, 65–66, 143
and national immigration policies, 53, 54, 135, 144, 145, 175n.2
and nativism, 56, 136
and race issues, 53–55, 56, 57, 160–161, 175n.3
and Right extremism, 54, 62, 146, 161–162
and social movement unionism, 126
strategies overview, 57–61
temporal patterns, 160–162
and union policies towards immigrant workers, 9, 21, 52–55, 175n.2
and unions as countermovements, 17–18
See also Justice for Cleaners campaign

British Nationality Act (1948), 53

British National Party (BNP), 62, 146, 161–162

Brown, Gordon, 56, 136

business cycle. *See* macroeconomic cycles